**WITHDRAWN
NDSU**

NEW TECHNOLOGY AND WESTERN SECURITY POLICY

*International Institute for Strategic Studies conference papers
published by Archon Books in association with the IISS*

Christoph Bertram (*editor*):
    PROSPECTS OF SOVIET POWER IN THE 1980s
    THE FUTURE OF STRATEGIC DETERRENCE
    THIRD-WORLD CONFLICT AND INTERNATIONAL
      SECURITY
Robert O'Neill (*editor*):
    THE CONDUCT OF EAST–WEST RELATIONS IN THE 1980s
    NEW TECHNOLOGY AND WESTERN SECURITY POLICY

NEW TECHNOLOGY AND WESTERN SECURITY POLICY

Edited by

ROBERT O'NEILL

ARCHON BOOKS

© International Institute for Strategic Studies 1985

All rights reserved. No reproduction, copy or transmission of this publication may be made without written permission.

No paragraph of this publication may be reproduced, copied or transmitted save with written permission or in accordance with the provisions of the Copyright Act 1956 (as amended).

Any person who does any unauthorised act in relation to this publication may be liable to criminal prosecution and civil claims for damages.

First published in 1985 in the United Kingdom by
THE MACMILLAN PRESS LTD
Houndmills, Basingstoke, Hampshire RG21 2XS
and London
and in the United States by
ARCHON BOOKS, an imprint of
The Shoe String Press, Inc.
925 Sherman Avenue
Hamden, CT 06514

Printed in Great Britain by
Anchor Brendon Ltd.
Tiptree, Essex

Library of Congress Cataloging-in-Publication Data
Main entry under title:

New technology and Western security policy.

Includes index.
1. Munitions—Addresses, essays, lectures.
2. North Atlantic Treaty Organization—Armed Forces—Addresses, essays, lectures. I. O'Neill, Robert John.
UF530.N49 1986   355'.03301821   85-21417
ISBN 0-208-02123-X

CONTENTS

STRATEGIC SYSTEM DEVELOPMENT AND NEW TECHNOLOGY:
WHERE SHOULD WE BE GOING? 1

 LT-GEN. BRENT SCOWCROFT
  *Formerly of the USAF and National Security Advisor to
  President Ford. Currently a Consultant on Foreign and
  National Security Policy, Washington DC*

THE FUTURE OF LAND-BASED STRATEGIC WEAPONS: PART I . 12

 DR PETER J. SHARFMAN
  *Programme Manager, International Security and
  Commerce, Congressional Office of Technology
  Assessment (OTA), Washington DC*

THE FUTURE OF LAND-BASED STRATEGIC WEAPONS: PART II . 24

 LOUIS C. FINCH
  *Assistant Chief, Foreign Affairs and National Defense
  Division, Congressional Research Service (CRS),
  Washington DC*

TECHNOLOGICAL DEVELOPMENT AND FORCE STRUCTURE WITHIN THE
WESTERN ALLIANCE: PROSPECTS FOR RATIONALIZATION AND THE
DIVISION OF LABOUR: PART I. 38

 DR INGEMAR DÖRFER
  National Defence Research Institute, Stockholm, Sweden

TECHNOLOGICAL DEVELOPMENT AND FORCE STRUCTURE WITHIN THE
WESTERN ALLIANCE: PROSPECTS FOR RATIONALIZATION AND THE
DIVISION OF LABOUR: PART II 46

 JOHN ROPER
  Editor, International Affairs, *Royal Institute of
  International Affairs (RIIA), London*

NEW TECHNOLOGY, STABILITY AND THE ARMS-CONTROL DEADLOCK:
PART I 53

 PROF. WOLF GRAF VON BAUDISSIN
  *Formerly Director, Institute for Peace Research and
  International Security Affairs, University of Hamburg,
  West Germany*

CONVENTIONAL FORCE DEVELOPMENT AND NEW TECHNOLOGY:
HOW REAL ARE THE GAINS IN PROSPECT? 60

    HENRI CONZE
        *Deputy Director, International Division, Armaments
        Directorate, Ministry of Defence, Paris*

NEW CONVENTIONAL FORCE TECHNOLOGY AND THE NATO–WARSAW
PACT BALANCE: PART I 66

    DR STEVEN L. CANBY
        *Fellow, The Wilson Center for International Scholars,
        Washington DC*

NEW CONVENTIONAL FORCE TECHNOLOGY AND THE NATO–WARSAW
PACT BALANCE: PART II 84

    DONALD R. COTTER
        *Director, Center for Strategic Concepts, McLean,
        Virginia, USA*

TECHNOLOGY AND THE FUTURE OF ARMS CONTROL . . . 98

    WALTER B. SLOCOMBE
        *Lawyer, Member of the firm of Caplin and Drysdale,
        Washington DC, and formerly Deputy Under-
        Secretary for Policy in the US Department of Defense,
        1981–84*

NEW TECHNOLOGY, STABILITY AND THE ARMS-CONTROL DEADLOCK:
PART II 107

    DR BARRY M. BLECHMAN
        Institute for Defense Analyses, Alexandria, Virginia, USA

NEW TECHNOLOGY AND INTRA-ALLIANCE RELATIONSHIPS: NEW
STRENGTHS, NEW STRAINS   116
   HON. DAVID M. ABSHIRE
      US Permanent Representative to the North Atlantic
      Council, Brussels

DEFENCE RESEARCH AND DEVELOPMENT AND WESTERN INDUSTRIAL
POLICY: PART I   130
   PROF. SIR RONALD MASON
      Professor of Chemistry, University of Sussex, and formerly
      Chief Scientific Adviser to Ministry of Defence, London

DEFENCE RESEARCH AND DEVELOPMENT AND WESTERN INDUSTRIAL
POLICY: PART II   134
   HENRI MARTRE
      President and Director General, SNIAS, Paris

THE 'STAR WARS' DEBATE: THE WESTERN ALLIANCE AND STRATEGIC
DEFENCE: PART I   140
   FRED S. HOFFMAN
      Director, Pan Heuristics, Marina-del-Rey, California

THE 'STAR WARS' DEBATE: THE WESTERN ALLIANCE AND STRATEGIC
DEFENCE: PART II   149
   PROF. LAWRENCE FREEDMAN
      Professor of War Studies, Kings's College, University of
      London

CONCLUSIONS   166
   ROBERT O'NEILL
      Director, International Institute for Strategic Studies,
      London

Index   173

Strategic System Development and New Technology: Where Should We be Going?

LT-GEN. BRENT SCOWCROFT

Any discussion of strategic system development and technology, focused on the question of where we should be going, must be anchored in something more than abstractions, theoretical constructs or pursuit of technology for its own sake. Consideration must be given to the strategic concepts, political imperatives and constraints, economic limitations, 'mirror-imaging' and other factors which have heavily influenced the course of strategic system development. Nor does the present state and process of strategic force development occur in a historical vacuum – though we frequently tend, especially in the United States, to behave otherwise. Some historical sense of the route we have travelled in order to reach our present condition may therefore help to put our choices for the future into somewhat better perspective.

Weapons and Warfare
The history of efforts to analyse and predict the impact of major weapon developments on the nature and conduct of warfare and the inter-relationship with strategy are not such that we should undertake to analyse such major future developments as strategic defence with any great sense of confidence. Indeed, our estimates of the future character of conflict based on major weapon developments have frequently infact been very wide of the mark.

For example, the use of the railroad in the American Civil War, and especially in the Franco-Prussian War, led strategists to the conclusion that future wars would be based on mobility and that decisive advantage could be expected to go to the side which utilized the railroad to mobilize rapidly and attack, thus getting in a decisive blow before the opponent was prepared. This assumption was integral to military force development prior to World War I. Any conflict which occurred would obviously be brief, with a clear edge going to the side which was able to strike first. Those assumptions, as we know, were a factor in the precipitating events of World War I, but they turned out to be very wrong. One of the major reasons the expectations were so far from the mark and the war such a bloody stalemate was the underestimation of the impact of a new weapon – the machine gun. The machine gun, properly employed, offered an important advantage to the defence.

Conventional wisdom during the interwar period (outside Germany at least) was that the defence had obtained a decisive advantage in warfare and that the next war, if one occurred, was likely to be a repetition of World War I. Once again this assumption had an impact on force development and planning, and again the prognosticators were wrong. They were wrong in part because of the development late in World War I of a weapon system designed to counter the machine gun – the tank. The crude early versions of the tank masked the full potential of this new development. There were strategists who recognized the implications of the tank but, except in Germany, they tended to be ignored.

Likewise, we have made, and continue to make, assumptions about the impact of nuclear weapons on the nature of conflict. Those assumptions, in some aspects, began shortly after World War I, with a strategic assessment made by an Italian general, Guilio Douhet. Douhet concluded that World War I had demonstrated the permanent ascendancy of the defence over the offence in land warfare. A new weapon had come along, however, which could overcome that situation and revolutionize warfare. That weapon was the airplane. Douhet hypothesized that the airplane offered an alternative to the traditional necessity to defeat the enemy's forces in the field in order to obtain victory. The airplane could take the conflict directly to the enemy population and, in a brutal but brief assault, break the enemy's morale and thus his will to resist. Paradoxically, attacking population centres would actually be humane, because that would be the quickest way to break national morale and terminate the conflict. It would all be over with great rapidity, avoiding a repetition of the awful carnage of trench warfare. Quick, even pre-emptive attack would destroy enemy airfields and air forces on the ground, leaving the population naked to aerial bombardment which would quickly lead to surrender.

The logic was impressive, once the basic assumptions were accepted. After a brief but all-out aerial assault, victory would go to the side which had struck first with the greatest force.

Douhet's writings struck a responsive chord in many of the young airmen in Europe and the United States. Only in the Soviet Union did his views appear to make little impression. In both Great Britain and the United States, Douhet's principles had a profound impact on the strategy for the air war against Germany in World War II.

In practice, Douhet's assumptions proved wrong in two critical, closely inter-related aspects. He vastly underestimated both the weight of effort which would be required and the resilience of civilian morale, at least in the case of World War II. The tonnage of bombs dropped in that war exceeded Douhet's estimates many times, without the decisive results he predicted.

Strategic bombing was an important element in the Allied victory, especially in the impact on industrial installations playing a critical role in the German war effort. That effect, however, was produced only over an extended period and in conjunction with a massive military ground campaign which consumed resources at a prodigious rate. There has been considerable debate about the extent to which strategic bombing contributed to the German defeat, but, in Douhet's own terms, it had been a failure.

The development which rescued Douhet's strategy from probable oblivion and, indeed, saw it triumph, was the advent of the nuclear weapon. The damage which could be done by only a few nuclear weapons was so horrendous that Douhet's hypotheses seemed finally to be fulfilled many times over.

Massive Retaliation
Thus it was that the first US strategy of the missile age vindicated Douhet. That strategy was massive retaliation, and it was based on the notion that the United States would respond to any Soviet aggression anywhere, not at that point and in kind, but with a 'massive' attack on the Soviet heartland employing nuclear weapons.

Whatever the influence of Douhet within the US Air Force, however, it seems clear that massive retaliation was adopted for reasons more economic than strategic in nature. Faced with the troop requirements for the defence of NATO and the costly experience of the Korean War, massive retaliation seemed a 'cheap' way to defend the West against any Soviet expansionist designs. It was doubly attractive because the Soviet Union had no reciprocal military capability.

While massive retaliation made considerable military sense under the circumstances of the time, it seemed to lack adequate political credibility. It was never implemented in the case of third-world conflicts and much of the military history of NATO involves attempts to bolster its credibility. Whatever its military legacy, however, massive retaliation had a fateful impact on attitudes within the Atlantic Community towards nuclear weapons and warfare.

The period of Western nuclear monopoly was short-lived, and soon there began a debate about how to respond to the growing Soviet nuclear arsenal. There were two alternative approaches which received serious consideration. The first was to continue the philosophy of massive retaliation by promising to 'punish' Soviet aggression by direct and massive attack on the USSR herself. The other alternative was to revert to a more traditional military approach, that is, to focus US strategic forces on the destruction of Soviet military, especially strategic, forces.

Assured Destruction
The decision, once again, was based primarily on economic considerations. The strategic force required to defeat Soviet military forces (counter-force) would depend on the size of those forces and would therefore expand as Soviet forces expanded. Conversely, punishing the Soviet Union by imposing 'unacceptable' destruction on the Soviet homeland (assured destruction) would require fewer and relatively fixed forces, expanded only to the extent necessary to ensure that sufficient forces would remain after a Soviet attack to deliver the required punishment.

Following the adoption of the doctrine of assured destruction, there ensued a debate over the extent of the destruction of Soviet population and industrial floor space required reliably to deter a Soviet attack. This was an internal US debate, in which the economic impact of the size of the strategic forces required apparently played a larger role than did attempts at assessment of Soviet views about deterrence.

Assured destruction was in certain respects the Douhet strategy turned on its head. Rather than a strategy for winning a war by attacks aimed at destroying the enemy's will to resist, the new doctrine was designed to prevent a war by threatening punishment to an enemy *after* he had already attacked. It turned an offensive strategy into a defensive policy devoid of military objective and placed even more weight on Douhet's assumption about the decisive nature of morale by assuming it to have equal deterrent value, i.e., in advance, as well. This philosophical position reinforced attitudes engendered by massive retaliation and is perhaps the principal ingredient in most contemporary US attitudes towards nuclear war.

The growth of Soviet strategic forces, among other factors, also led to both offensive and defensive development in US strategic forces. The US strategic bombing force was the early backbone of US strategic forces. However, growing concern about Soviet air defences and the vulnerability of bombers to attack on the ground provided impetus for a search for alternative means of nuclear delivery. There were other incentives as well. The psychological impact of the German V-1 and V-2 missiles, together with the influx of German missile scientists in 1945, steered the United States in the direction of missile technology. In addition, the massive retaliation strategy ensured that the big military budgets would go to weapons with a 'strategic' label on them. Interservice rivalry, then, played a role in the development of naval strategic systems and in the Army's taking up the cause of strategic defence, about which more below.

The multiplicity of US strategic offensive forces (the Triad), therefore, was not purely the outgrowth of far-sighted military logic, but however dubious some aspects of its origin, it has proved to be of great military value. The differing combinations of strengths and weaknesses of the Triad elements have had a synergistic effect on US strategic force capability. The development and refinement of the elements of the Triad seem to have gone on over the years in some isolation from the intellectual currents about nuclear war as described above.

It is true that improvements in the quality of strategic forces would be mandated under either an assured destruction or a counter-force policy for force employment. The force must under either policy or strategy appear to be able to survive attack and be able to reach the target in sufficient numbers to be able to accomplish its objective. The force must also be perceived to be able to destroy the targets attacked and have command and control adequate to direct the force through the execution of its mission.[1] The greatest difference in qualitative requirements is that for accuracy. In an assured destruction force, demands on accuracy are minimal, to the point that they become lesser-included qualities of the other requirements of the force. The requirements for command and control are also substantially different. For assured destruction, command and control must be able to pass a single attack order. For a counter-force strategy, management of the force over perhaps an extended period of time under repeated attack is essential.

Other than these, the principal differences are the numbers required to pass the challenges of survivability and penetration attrition, and to achieve the objective, all of which tend to be much higher for counterforce. One additional variable for assured destruction is the extent of devastation required for deterrence. That question was actively debated in the United States in the 1960s, with decisions of the Administration apparently based more on the economics of the defence budget than an analysis of the attitudes and values of Soviet leaders. Given these similarities and differences in force requirements for different nuclear policies, it is not surprising that the most heated debates in the United States have been over accuracy and force size.

The issue of strategic defence also arose from the growth of Soviet strategic nuclear forces, both offensive and defensive, and the fact that emphasis in the US defence budget was being placed on strategic forces. Extensive and expensive bomber warning systems and interceptors were developed and deployed. With the serious deployment of Soviet ICBMs, attention turned as well to the possibility of ballistic missile defence (BMD).

Ballistic Missile Defence
The first US anti-ballistic missile (ABM) proposal was for full-scale defence of American cities, a system called *Sentinel*. Considerations of cost and technology, in addition to those of principle, led to a more limited version – *Safeguard* – designed against a more limited threat such as that which could be posed by the People's Republic of China. Further modifications focused the proposed system on defence of US ICBM fields, the ABM Treaty further restricted the numbers of interceptors, and the system was abandoned upon completion.

The ABM debate was a heated one, and the *Safeguard* system proposed passed the Senate by a single vote. Arms-control advocates argued that ABM was destabilizing. It would tend to encourage a first strike, based on the calculation that such an attack would so reduce the offensive forces of the opponent that an ABM system could adequately cope with those remaining. In a somewhat similar vein, proponents of assured destruction claimed that an ABM system would weaken deterrence. Others maintained that ABM deployment would stimulate increased offensive weapon deployment, as the other side sought to maintain its ability to penetrate. Some opposed it on grounds of high and escalating costs and of rather crude technology, which would render it of little or at least of dubious effectiveness.

In the end, the Administration won Congressional funding with the argument that it was essential to proceed if there was to be any hope of interrupting Soviet ABM deployment, which was proceeding apace. In the SALT I negotiations, the Administration gave up a potentially superior system in order to restrict Soviet ABM deployment to very low levels. Whatever the strategic merits of that decision, the mood of the Congress probably made it mandatory.

There was one other strategic weapon development heavily influenced by the nascent appearance of the ABM – the 'MIRVing' of strategic missiles. The decision to deploy MIRV has been widely criticized as both accelerating and destabilizing the arms race. Yet hindsight is clearly superior to foresight in this instance and the motivation to proceed with MIRVing was understandable under the circumstances.

MIRV were considered critical as a counter to an ABM system. Even when negotiations were under way on an ABM Treaty, continuation of the MIRV programme was deemed essential to demonstrate to the Soviet Union that her ABM system would not be effective against US missiles and also to provide a hedge against failure of the ABM negotiations or Soviet non-observance of an ABM Treaty.

MIRV also played a role in securing ratification of the SALT I Agreements. Conservatives, concerned that the Interim Agreement on Offensive Weapons permitted the Soviet Union more ICBM and more SLBM, were mollified by the knowledge that the US had a large and, for some time, growing superiority in warheads, thanks to the MIRV programme.

In light of all these factors favouring the MIRV programme, it is hardly surprising – perhaps not wise but hardly surprising – that the Administration took a short-rather than a long-term approach to the MIRV issue. The possibility cannot be dismissed that cancellation of the programme could have made continuation of the ABM programme more attractive to the Soviet Union and thus changed the negotiating balance on the SALT I Agreements.

Limited Strategic Options
The debate over strategic nuclear policy became active once again early in the 1970s. The issue this time was reliance on assured destruction to cover all contingencies of crisis or war initiation. Arguments were raised that the President should have more options available to him than simply to order wholesale destruction of the Soviet Union. That option might not only be inappropriate to the provocation but was so apocalyptic a response that the President might hesitate to order it; at least the Soviet leadership might *think* that the President would not order it. In either case, deterrence would be weakened. Conversely, deterrence would be strengthened if the Soviet leaders thought that the President had nuclear options which would make response to any nuclear aggression more likely.

Supporters of assured destruction made very contrary arguments. The best deterrence was the threat of total societal destruction. A limited nuclear response would inevitably escalate to full-scale conflict in any event and having limited options might make nuclear conflict seem fightable. That, in turn, would make a nuclear conflict more likely.

The terms of that argument continue to this day, but official US policy has moved significantly in the direction of providing more limited attack options to the President. Whether that begins to sanction the idea of limited nuclear war and whether or not that is useful or dangerous depends heavily on one's view of deterrence.

Deterrence is the objective of the strategic nuclear forces procured by the West. That fact and this outline of the development of strategic forces roughly to the present, make clear the central role which attitudes towards deterrence play in decisions about force modernization, size, diversification and weapon types.

Despite the key role which concepts of deterrence play in the design of our strategic forces, Americans have frequently approached the subject from an unusual perspective. We have had endless debates about what constitutes deterrence but they have frequently tended to be focused on the circumstances which would deter Americans or those which should in logic constitute deterrence, rather than on how the Soviet Union may view various situations or circumstances.

Concepts of Deterrence
Deterrence is not a new phenomenon. George Washington, for example, observed (with others) that the best way to preserve peace was to prepare for war. The nuclear weapon, and the overwhelming advantage it has given to the offence, however, has given a new and critical character to deterrence. It is now possible for a weaker or losing power to strike a devastating nuclear blow at the opponent.

But deterrence is an ambiguous phenomenon. Its adequacy can be tested only in failure. What appears to be the logic or the fact of deterrence may be irrelevant. For the West, on the defensive, deterrence is nothing more or less than what the Soviet leaders believe that it is. Therefore, we must try to calculate what the Soviet Union believes deterrence to be, not what we believe it to be.

That is a much more difficult task. But from what can be gleaned from Soviet literature, strategic force posture, force deployments and concepts of force employment, there is little evidence that the Soviet Union subscribes to the concept of assured destruction. Soviet leaders seem instead to have a much more traditional view of strategic warfare, one in which nuclear weapons may play a decisive, but not revolutionary, role. A country which, for example, practices the lengthy process of reloading missile silos in military exercises can hardly be expected to be sympathetic to the notion of assured destruction or, as it is sometimes described, deterrence through pain. A country which seems to view military conflict in traditional terms with traditional objectives is unlikely to subscribe to a policy which, if it had to be executed, has neither military or political objective. Instead, the Soviet Union is likely to be deterred under extreme circumstances only by the belief that she cannot achieve her objectives; that is, by deterrence through denial. If this analysis is correct, or if there is some significant possibility that it may be correct, it is essential that alternatives for force modernization and new developments be analysed and pursued in such manner that the Soviet Union can never, under any circumstances, calculate, by whatever criteria her leaders may utilize, that resort to strategic nuclear weapons is a feasible course of action.

As this outline thus far has tried to describe, we are where we are partly as a result of accident, partly as a result of conflict and compromises between different concepts, and partly because of decisions sometimes made for reasons far removed from the fundamental strategic realities of our position. Our objectives have been, and should continue to be, the protection of the vital interests of the West against a threat which, thus far, has been dedicated to its destruction without, in the process, destroying ourselves or our civilization. As we have already seen, differing views as to how best to do this are at the heart of our strategic debate.

Part of the reason for the emotionalism of the current debate is the tendency to weight differentially the twin objectives to which we should be dedicated. Many appear to treat the threat of nuclear destruction as secondary, focusing instead on the threat to our values posed by an aggressive Soviet Union. Others seem to see primarily the threat of nuclear conflict and tend to equate the United States and the Soviet Union and the values each is seeking to protect or extend, in some cases even to the extent of considering the United States to be the principal problem. Focusing on either objective while ignoring or denigrating the other makes the task relatively simple. It is the attainment of both which is the test of our wisdom, patience and determination.

Strategic Choices for the Future
In light of all this, let us examine where we should be going, considering emerging technology and the appearance again of strategic defence as a serious option. In doing this, let us look first at the current scene and what technological development is doing to the current strategic balance and the Triad and then project these developments into the future.

ICBM Survivability
The development which has been causing the greatest current strategic concern is the increase in missile accuracy. It has made feasible the attack of targets such as hardened silos at a cost in weapons which in most cases (depending on hardness) is not incommensurate with the value of the target. The result has been a decrease in ICBM survivability and a perceived increase in instability, by providing an incentive for a first strike. This change has occurred differentially between the United States and the Soviet Union. The greater number of ICBM warheads and the larger throw-weight on the Soviet side has meant that the USSR can threaten US point or hardened targets to a degree the United States cannot begin to reciprocate. That, in turn, has an impact on crisis stability which, depending on one's view of deterrence, is troubling.

Deployment of the MX missile is designed to rectify, in part, the latter disparity and, in the next decade, improvements in SLBM accuracy with deployment of the *Trident* II missile should eliminate it, assuming no change in the current arms-control rules regarding MIRV. In the future, accuracies will improve even further. Improved inertial guidance, mid-course star or satellite update, and terminal guidance will make accuracies virtually operationally perfect. This will mean that large warhead yield will no longer be required to compensate for errors in accuracy, and that even non-nuclear warheads might be used for some missions now requiring nuclear weapons.

As accuracy improves, problems of survivability for ICBM forces are increased. The response in the past to improvements in accuracy has been to increase silo hardness, but that is a competition which hardness must eventually lose, as warhead inaccuracies become less than the radius of the fireball.

Other devices for enhancing ICBM survivability are mobility, concealment or deception, and defence. After serious consideration of a scheme combining deception and mobility (the MPS plan of the Carter Administration), the United States has turned to mobility and a small single-warhead missile (thus reducing the value of the target) as the means of improving survivability. Since the mode of attack against mobile targets is a barrage attack creating excessive overpressure, survivability becomes a function of the area of deployment and the hardness of the mobile vehicles. In view of probable potential political constraints on the area of deployment, it will be important to develop a transporter with sufficient hardness to prevent a barrage attack at an exchange ratio which might appear reasonable to the USSR.

A small missile mobile deployment will be very costly, especially as compared with deployment of MIRVed missiles in silos. Therefore, an offensive arms-control agreement which substantially constrains Soviet warheads would make an important contribution to reducing the costs of the small missile deployment.

Another method for improving ICBM survivability is to turn to a ballistic missile defence system. As discussed earlier, BMD in any truly significant form was ruled out by the 1972 ABM Treaty. On technical grounds, however, the idea deserves consideration. There have been in the past two principal hurdles for ICBM defence which have appeared daunting. The first of these has been saturation of the defence by the offence, either through warheads cheaper than the interceptors or through various penetration aids or decoys. The other problem has been the vulnerability of the battle-management radar to attack. A concentrated attack on the radar could blind the system and render it useless.

While systems based on different principles (e.g. lasers) would have different hardware, the problems of saturation and a secure pointing and tracking mechanism would remain. The future of offence or defence interaction in this area is cloudy at this juncture, but even current technology could be effective in raising costs to the attacker if the ICBM deployment is such (e.g. using concealment/deception) as to provide leverage to the defence.

Submarines and Bombers
Current SLBM developments are focused sharply on minimizing or eliminating the weaknesses in the system. One of the most significant of these improvements is to give the SLBM force the accuracy of ICBM force, thus making the systems interchangeable in that respect and adding greatly to force flexibility. Steps are also being taken to improve reliability of communications with the submarine force under all conditions. While confidence in SLBM communications, by their nature, will perhaps remain lower than that in the ICBM force, significant improvement can be projected.

The bomber force has two major operational weaknesses apart from its relatively long time-to-target, which is a more or less fixed characteristic. The first of these is its vulnerability to attack on the ground or just after take-off. The bulk of the bomber force must rely on warning of attack for survival. The first essential measure for enhanced bomber survivability, therefore, is to improve reliability and timeliness of attack warning. Steps towards this are currently being taken.

The next step is to ensure sufficient time after warning to permit safe escape of the bomber force from its bases. That is being done by basing more of the force at interior bases and by deploying new bombers with more rapid escape capability.

The only practical way for the bomber to avoid the need to rely on tactical warning is to keep a portion of the force on airborne alert. While that was done for a considerable time with the US strategic bomber force, it remains very costly in both material and personnel.

The other major problem for the bomber force is to ensure that it can penetrate the very substantial Soviet air defences. That problem is being dealt with in two ways. The first is to equip the current force with air-launched cruise missiles (ALCM). The cruise missile multiplies the number of targets with which the Soviet defence must try to cope, while reducing greatly the value of each one. It also permits attack at a low level with an individual target size which makes interception very difficult. For the future force, the bomber itself is being made very difficult to detect, through a variety of passive and active measures which make timely interception by air defence forces extremely difficult. Some of those same measures can be adapted to the cruise missile, making even less likely the prospect of interception.

The Future of the US Triad
What is the future of the Triad? Can it be maintained? Need it be maintained? If so, at what cost? To take the third of these questions first, the value of the Triad remains. The United States is a defensive power. Anything which complicates the calculations of the aggressive power adds to deterrence. A robust Triad is best calculated to deal with the ambiguities in deterrence and to reduce to a minimum the chances that an aggressor's analysis, whatever the value system on which it may be based, would result in a decision to attack, even under great stress.

The SLBM force, with ICBM accuracy, should probably be the mainstay of US strategic forces. But the submarine, if detected, is very vulnerable to attack. Given increased reliance on the submarine force, a missile and bomber hedge against possible developments in anti-submarine warfare (ASW), however remote they may appear at the present time, is important if not vital. Communications with the submarine force, especially the two-way communications essential for battle management if the SLBM becomes the primary rather than a fall-back force, will remain of concern. There is also some virtue in having a significant portion of the strategic forces on sovereign territory, in order that it cannot be attacked without clear recognition of the solemn consequences. Also, the bomber force is uniquely suited to attack targets whose location is not precisely known, or which are mobile, such as major units of the Soviet army on the march.

If the major future uncertainties regarding the SLBM force are the robustness of communications and prospects for ASW, those for the bomber force will remain survivability and penetration and, for the ICBM force, survivability. If neither the ICBM nor the bomber force can with reasonable confidence be improved so as to deal with its projected weaknesses, they do not serve well as a hedge against possible increased vulnerability of the now secure SLBM force.

The principal problem for the bomber force will remain the time required to get off the ground and a safe distance from its bases. So far as penetration is concerned, a combination of stealth technology and cruise missiles appears adequate to cope with projected air defences, at least into the medium term. But weapons such as depressed-trajectory SLBM and sea-launched cruise missiles (SLCM) could seriously jeopardize bomber survivability. Moving bombers as far inland as possible and developing adequate detection of cruise and depressed trajectory missiles is feasible but costly.

The problem of ICBM survivability, a vexing issue for more than a decade, has yet to be solved. Current efforts to improve survivability have already been described. Given projected developments in accuracy, mobility or active defence or both appear the most feasible ways to go. In addition to the land-mobile ICBM presently being developed, air-mobile and sea-mobile deployments are also possible. In these cases, however, care would have to be taken to ensure that their vulnerabilities were different from those of the bomber and the ballistic missile submarine (SSBN), or the benefits of the ICBM leg of the Triad would be greatly vitiated. For the air-mobile ICBM, this would perhaps require an aircraft which would permit continuous airborne patrol at acceptable costs. For a sea-mobile system, it would require a vehicle not susceptible to the open-ocean ASW techniques which would be used against the SSBN.

For all these forms of mobility, costs could be so high as to be considered prohibitive. In the case of land mobility, costs could perhaps be reduced and survivability increased by combining limited mobility with a point BMD. Failing that, the possibility cannot be excluded that a political decision would be made to abandon survivability for the ICBM. The cost to deterrence, if the analysis in this Paper is valid, could be considerable. Under these circumstances, there would also be the instability inherent in a dangerous, vulnerable force. For all strategic force elements, it is also necessary to consider the possibility of the deployment of satellites (radar, electronic intelligence and perhaps others) which could provide real-time intelligence and fire direction to Soviet forces. This could cut the intelligence cycle time to minutes and pose a new order of threat to US forces.

C³

There are three other issues which should not be overlooked: command, control and communications (C³), SLCM and strategic defence, primarily (in its current manifestation) the Strategic Defence Initiative (SDI) of the United States. The requirements of C³ for warning, evaluation, decision (including preserving a decision-maker) and execution, not to mention battle management during the unimaginable conditions of nuclear war, are awesome and insatiable. As is the case with the ICBM, fixed C³ modes are increasingly vulnerable.

The approaches to dealing with this vulnerability thus far have included mobility, proliferation and redundancy, and moving into space. All of these are expensive and there is a potential threat to C³ satellites by Soviet anti-satellite (ASAT) systems. The problem of attacking satellites in high earth orbit, especially from the ground, is not trivial but neither can it be ignored. Whether arms control could or should be employed to deal with this threat is beyond the scope of this Paper.

Paradoxically, the threat to C³ could become more severe in the event of the development of highly survivable strategic offensive forces. If cost-effective attack against those forces (excepting, of course, non-alert bombers and submarines in port) does not appear feasible, attacks on C³, in attempts to decapitate or to separate the decision-makers from control of the forces, may appear more remunerative.

SLCM

The SLCM has been developed to exploit the US advantage in cruise missile technology, the maritime strength of the United States, and the fact that thus far the SLCM is unconstrained by any arms-control agreement. The flexibility and versatility of the SLCM are obvious. Yet one must wonder whether the SLCM may not turn out to be another example of the MIRV syndrome, where we exploited short-term advantage at considerable long-term cost. It is not at all clear that the long-term advantage, in a situation where both sides have modern SLCM, does not lie with the USSR. Many of the major cities and industrial areas of the United States are located near very open and accessible coasts. In the Soviet case, important centres tend to be situated much farther inland and the coasts themselves are not nearly as accessible. In addition, the USSR has a very extensive air defence network, whereas the United States not only has no serious air defence system, but has extremely limited capability even to detect low-flying objects. In other words, unrestricted deployment of nuclear-armed SLCM may not be in the long-term interest of the United States.

Strategic Defence

The subject of strategic defence has once again become a prominent issue, primarily as a result of President Reagan's speech of 23 March, 1983, popularly known as the 'Star Wars' speech. Something of this nature is perhaps almost an inevitable eventual outgrowth of the strategic situation as it has developed since the advent of nuclear weapons. During this entire period, strategic offence has been dominant. The result has been the current perilous situation where each side can visit unbelievable damage upon the other at a moment's notice. Furthermore, it is not clear, looking forward, that any future pattern of development of offensive weapons can offer a way out of this grim condition.

The current defencelessness contributes to a sense at least of uneasiness, and a conscious policy of defencelessness is bound to be something less than satisfying. What seems to be emerging in the United States is a reaction at both ends of the political spectrum against deterrence and the despair which in the current situation it tends to promote. The reaction of the Left is to seek a political solution – somehow to rid the world of nuclear weapons. The particular approaches to that objective are numerous. The Right seeks the same sort of solution, but through technology – to render nuclear weapons impotent by erecting a defensive shield which will protect against them.

This brings us to the issue of strategic defence. Strategic defence can present itself in several manifestations or varieties, among which four will be discussed briefly: a shield which would, in effect, render nuclear missiles obsolete; a comprehensive but not leak-proof defence; a comprehensive but thin defence; and a point defence designed to protect offensive systems.

With respect to the technology for a comprehensive defence, the kill mechanisms currently considered potentially most effective are non-nuclear. They are generally of two types: directed energy, either laser or particle beam; and high kinetic energy projectiles. The most daunting technological problem may be pointing and tracking, which must be done with sufficient accuracy and over a long enough period to achieve the destruction of hundreds or perhaps thousands of objects nearly simultaneously. The defensive systems would also have to defeat various defensive measures designed to protect the offensive missiles and warheads. In order to have any serious hope of defeating a heavy offensive attack with systems now foreseeable, it would be essential to attack the missiles initially while they were in the boost phase of their flight and therefore most vulnerable. This, in turn, would require that the defensive systems be space-based, or have at least some components in space, thus leaving them open to attack away from the protective cloak of sovereign territory.

To be successful, given the destructiveness of nuclear weapons, a shield defence would have to function both technologically and operationally in a way far superior to that of any military system to this point in history. In addition, no attempt to shield the United States from ballistic nuclear attack would ignore weapon delivery by aircraft, cruise missile, or even clandestine means. Despite our long experience with the airplane, a foolproof air defence is still a dream.

What can be said of a heavy but not absolute defence? Such a defence can at least be grasped intellectually and its consequences analysed dispassionately. A heavy defence, probably of unknowable effectiveness, would clearly increase the uncertainties for a potential attacker. Increasing uncertainty adds to the effectiveness of deterrence and a heavy defence would be an advantage in that respect. Those uncertainties would, however, create other effects as well. The most basic strategic military requirement in present and foreseeable circumstances, both for the Soviet Union and the United States, is to maintain the ability to penetrate. A strategic nuclear force which lost that ability would be impotent. Creation of a heavy defence, therefore, would almost certainly call forth offensive counter-measures, either in numbers, quality, decoys and aids to penetration, or all of these. Historically, this has invariably been the reaction. For example, the US response to the possibility of a Soviet ABM system was the development of MIRV. The response to the improvement and enhancement of Soviet air defences has been the development of cruise missiles and stealth technology. It seems clear that the least likely response to the deployment of a heavy defence would be to reduce reliance on offensive nuclear weapons.

Arriving at the merits of attempting a heavy strategic defence involves a comparison of the advantage of additional deterrence against the offence/defence interaction which almost certainly would ensue, with its expenses and possible instabilities. Little work has been done thus far which would permit a confident prediction about the results of such analysis. In addition, consideration must be given to the possibility of enhanced crisis instability, stemming from the calculation that the effectiveness of a heavy defence could be greatly increased by an offensive first strike which would reduce the number of attackers with which the defence would have to cope.

A light but comprehensive strategic defence would avoid concern about maintaining the capability to penetrate. By the same token, however, it would add little to uncertainty and therefore to deterrence. Why, then, should it be considered at all? One of the concerns frequently voiced about the present situation is the 'hair-trigger' nature of the balance, with the constant possibility of some inadvertency triggering a conflict. A light defence, able to deal with perhaps up to one hundred warheads, would provide substantial insurance against accidental launch, the 'mad colonel' syndrome, however unlikely, or a provocation attack by a third power.

This type of strategic defence is almost certainly a technologically feasible enterprise. The principal uncertainties or problems would be the costs and how to bound it in capability, in order that it does not appear to have capability which would provoke an offensive counter deployment, as in the case of a heavy defence.

Point defence as a means of providing survivability to the ICBM force has been discussed. Point defence could be solely endo-atmospheric or a combination of 'exo-' and 'endo-' systems. The latter would provide greater potential for intercept, but could raise questions about the nature and intent of the system, possibly provoking an untoward response by the offence. Combined with certain types of ICBM deployments, a useful terminal defence system might be possible even under the current constraints of the ABM Treaty.

Conclusion

What can we conclude from this brief survey of technology and strategic nuclear forces? Accuracy is clearly obviating the need for nuclear warheads of massive yield, though the need for weapons with a barrage capability could be an exception to that tendency. As noted earlier, accuracy could permit the substitution of conventional for nuclear warheads for many purposes. That does not mean, however, that we are in the twilight of the nuclear age. Some possible targets, such as silos and C^3 facilities, would seem to require the force of a nuclear detonation in order to generate adequate damage. In addition, in the current and foreseeable atmosphere of US–Soviet relations, any attack is likely to be presumed to be with nuclear warheads and a response made accordingly.

Technology is likely in the future to contribute, in the case of offensive weapons, to greater stability. Both sides, in their own interest and even in the absence of arms-control agreements, are likely to attempt to improve survivability and reduce the value of individual targets as they modernize their forces. These protective impulses should improve the stability of the strategic balance.

The impact of technology on strategic defence is much more problematical. Technology in defence could be a force for good or for ill, and arms control could be especially important in determining which outcome will eventuate.

On the whole, however, we have no reason to fear technology. Guided by intelligence and prudence, technology could definitely be a force for good, especially for the West. There seems to be little reason to fear that it will be a monster out of control, unless we refuse to learn from the past. Certainly we should not take refuge in nostrums such as nuclear freezes which would serve to prevent us from making improvements in the present unsatisfactory state of strategic stability.

NOTE

[1] William J. Perry describes the chief characteristics of strategic forces as lethality, survivability, penetrativity and connectivity. For further information see his 'Technological Prospects' in Barry M. Blechman (ed.), *Rethinking the US Strategic Posture* (Cambridge, Mass: Ballinger, 1982).

The Future of Land-based Strategic Weapons: Part I

DR PETER J. SHARFMAN

Introduction

The world has now lived with strategic nuclear missiles for a generation. From one point of view, this fact bears testimony to the short-sightedness, lack of imagination and reckless optimism of the political leadership of the major powers. These missiles should be viewed as a success precisely because not one of them has ever been fired in anger. But whether one believes in the balance of terror or finds it horrifying (or, as in the case of the author of this Paper, both), there is general agreement that nuclear strategic missiles are likely to remain with us for some time. Moreover, many observers suspect that in some future international crisis, the decisions as to whether these missiles would or would not be used might hinge upon the details of their capabilities and deployments. For this reason, controversies over the nature and shape of strategic missile deployments continue to engage the attention of a far wider audience than those who must design the missiles, find ways of basing them, and find ways of paying for them.

Over the years, there has been a succession of controversies over what kinds of missiles were appropriate, how many were needed, and how they should be based. The terms of these controversies have evolved over time, but they remain issues. The issue of 'what kind of missiles?' has given rise to questions of big missiles or small missiles, ballistic missiles or cruise missiles, and how accurate our missiles ought to be if strategic stability is to be maximized. Of course these questions are interwoven with the large questions of strategy: what is the relationship between successful deterrence on the one hand and thinking and planning for nuclear war ('if deterrence fails') on the other? What is the relationship between our formal military doctrines and the capabilities we actually deploy in shaping a prospective enemy's image of our actual intentions? If a nuclear war did take place, what would it be like?

The issue of *how many missiles?* has become deeply intertwined with arms-control negotiations regarding both intermediate-range nuclear forces and strategic nuclear forces, but even apart from arms-control considerations, Britain and France are moving towards a great increase in the number of SLBM warheads and the US Congress has engaged in heated debates followed by very close votes over the question of how many MX (or *Peacekeeper*) missiles are needed. At the core of these debates is a tension between two alternative criteria for answering the question of 'how much is enough?' One can design a force able to destroy the highest priority targets, or one can design a force which appears to balance adequately the forces of the other side.

The issue of *how should the missiles be based?* has become increasingly complex as technology has removed one major option of the past – the invulnerable missile silo – but opened up a variety of possible new basing modes. Controversies over missile basing hinge on a variety of technical factors. These include: survivability against various kinds of postulated attacks; flexibility and responsiveness to changes in plans occasioned by unforeseen developments in a crisis, limited war, or major war; and cost. They seem to hinge even more on political factors, including both the effects on the enemy's perceptions (i.e., deterrence) and the effects on our public opinion.

Over the years, the missile forces of the five nuclear powers have grown and evolved. To some extent the changes in their postures have been responses to the perceived actions of the other nuclear powers. To some extent they have been adaptations to arms-control treaties and negotiations. However, the primary considerations in procuring and deploying nuclear missiles have been *history*, in the sense that previous decisions, existing deployments, and existing institutional arrangements have played major roles in shaping each new decision, and *changes in the available technologies* which are perceived to bring new opportunities and risks.

This Paper addresses only a limited subset of today's issues regarding nuclear missiles, namely *issues regarding nuclear missile basing which arise primarily out of technological change*. No effort is made to address the questions of how many missiles or what kinds of missiles, except insofar as decisions about basing modes may limit the ranges of choices of kinds of missiles and numbers, and hence strong views about kinds and numbers may drive one to particular positions regarding basing. As we shall see, positions on missile basing are often derived, more or less logically, from the momentum of past decisions (i.e., history), from arms-control considerations, from the pressures of existing institutional structures, and from considerations of the overall strategic balance. In short, any serious consideration of missile basing involves giving at least passing attention to the whole range of issues involved in strategic nuclear policy. Nevertheless, for the purposes of this Paper, no effort is made here to provide a fair survey, much less an analysis, of these related subjects.

Thus, this Paper addresses a particular cluster of issues, abstracted from a larger context as if this larger context were not itself problematical and controversial. The reader should assume, in the absence of warnings to the contrary, that the unstated background against which missile basing is debated is the conventional wisdom of deterrence theory, and the familiar axioms of NATO and US strategic deterrence. In such a context, arguments about missile basing can be viewed as revolving around five issues:

- Survivability: how much vulnerability can we tolerate?
- Is there deterrent value in basing missiles close to populations?
- Responsiveness: a necessity or a slogan?
- Flush on strategic warning: is it prudent?
- Is diversity the answer?

Survivability

An issue which arises in connection with every possible basing mode is the question of survivability. For a given basing arrangement, how survivable will our missiles be against an enemy attack – either with today's capabilities or with the greater capabilities which we believe the enemy will have in the future? What degree of confidence can we have in our answer to this question? What additional degree of survivability might be obtained by making changes, either in existing deployments or in the plans for future deployments? And, most important and most difficult question of them all, what difference does it make? It is this latter question which I propose to address here.

There are obvious reasons why survivability – to the extent that it is achievable – is desirable. In general, these reasons fall into two categories. If these missiles were ever attacked, the more of them that survived, the greater our military capability would be. If this were the main reason for survivability, then it would be a straightforward matter of estimating whether the cost per surviving missile would be lower for a few highly survivable missiles or for a larger force that could be expected to suffer significant attrition. But survivability contributes to deterrence of an attack. Since we know of no way to quantify the value of stability, but we are sure that this value is very great, arguments about missile survivability often bear a greater resemblance to theology than to cost accounting.

This theology is founded upon two analytical distinctions, which are as clear in the artificial world of the analyst as they would be cloudy in the real world which national leaders would face during a severe crisis. The first distinction is between 'deterrence by threat of retaliation' and 'deterrence by denial'. The former conveys to the enemy the idea that we cannot prevent him from destroying what he wishes to destroy, but we can make him wish that he had never done so. The latter conveys the idea to the enemy that, despite his best efforts, he would fail to achieve his objective. As one thinks about the implications of this distinction, it becomes clear that the best deterrent threat would combine the two – the enemy would see that there was no point in doing whatever it is we wish to deter, and also that to make the attempt would result in his being much worse off than before. It should also be clear that deterrent threats deal with probabilities rather than certainties – the enemy can always hope that we *might* not carry out the threatened retaliation, or that his forces *might* achieve their objective by overcoming a military disadvantage. (It is sobering to recall that the US military posture in December 1941 should have been adequate to deter the Japanese attack on Pearl Harbor.) Finally, it is noteworthy that deterrence by denial is consistent with the historic function and purpose of military forces – protection of whatever it is that one is defending – whereas deterrence by threat of retaliation seems more characteristic of the terrorist than of the warrior. We should never forget, however, that retaliation in a nuclear war is not merely 'punishment' or 'inflicting pain', but at least possibly the destruction of the enemy's entire society.

The second analytical distinction is between three possible motivations for being the first to use nuclear weapons, or the first to use them on a large scale, or the first to use them against targets far from the battle-field. One possible motivation is military advantage – the idea that the use of nuclear weapons will make it possible, or easier, to achieve one's military objectives. The second possible motivation is 'pre-emption for damage limiting' – the idea that the enemy is about to use nuclear weapons himself, and that by going first one can blunt the effectiveness of the enemy's attack. The third possible motivation is desperation – one faces an intolerable situation, and hopes that the use of nuclear weapons will somehow transform that situation.

Now the requirements of deterrence vary depending upon the motivation that one is trying to overcome. If the enemy is considering the use of nuclear weapons in order to achieve a military advantage, it is clear that deterrence by denial ('even if you attack and make no mistakes, you will still not obtain the military advantage you seek') is better than deterrence by retaliation ('you may gain an advantage, but you will find the costs of this victory unacceptably high'). Of course the combination ('you will be defeated, and pay a heavy price as well') is the best deterrent. In contrast, if the enemy is contemplating an attack out of desperation, deterrence by threat of retaliation ('if you attack, you will make your bad situation much worse') is more effective than deterrence by denial ('if you attack, you probably will not accomplish anything'), while the combination is of course better still. Finally, it appears that either denial or threat can deter pre-emption: the purpose of pre-emption (by definition) is to limit damage to oneself, and this fails either if the pre-emptive attack is ineffectual or if it leads to a devastating retaliatory strike.

Applying this rather abstract reasoning to the question of missile survivability, we see that the survivability of all (or perhaps most) of a missile force allows for deterrence by denial and deterrence by threat of retaliation, whereas the survivability of part of the missile force allows for deterrence by threat of retaliation but not for denial. How then does survivability affect deterrence?

In the extreme cases, the reasoning is clear, easy, and scarcely disputed. If a missile force is completely invulnerable to any attack using the means which a putative enemy has available to him, then the enemy will not be tempted at all to attack this missile force. On the other hand, if a missile force is completely vulnerable to an attack, then an enemy which believes that war is inevitable – and perhaps even an enemy who believes that war is highly probable – has every incentive to attack first. This incentive, it is feared, would change a situation of probable war into one of actual war. There is one intermediate case which is also fairly straightforward, although it actually involves some hidden assumptions about targeting policies that may not be as clearly correct as they appear: if attacking our missiles would require an enemy to expend both a greater *number* of his own missiles than the number of ours he expects to destroy, and also a greater proportion of his missiles than the *proportion* of ours which he expects to destroy, then this situation is virtually as stable as the case of complete survivability.

There remains, however, the difficult case in which an enemy is believed to be able to destroy a significant fraction of one's missile force in a first strike, using either a smaller number or a smaller percentage of his own missiles. This case is of more than theoretical interest, because it is the situation today of silo-based ICBM in the United States, and will become the case for Soviet silo-based ICBM once the United States has deployed a force of MX (*Peacekeeper*) and D-5 (*Trident II*) missiles. In theory, this situation should tempt both sides to pre-empt (that is, to launch a first strike) once they are convinced that war is inevitable. The reason is simply that the side striking first would inflict more damage and suffer less damage than the side striking second. However, in reality no sane military commander or political leader will ever be convinced that strategic nuclear warfare is *inevitable* until nuclear strikes have actually taken place; the most that is conceivable is that there would be a conviction that nuclear war has become *probable*. In such a circumstance, it would be imprudent (to say the least) to give the orders that would change nuclear war from a probability to a reality simply to obtain a marginal reduction in the damage which the other side could inflict. We cannot say that such a decision is impossible, but so long as the damage to be expected from a second strike is substantial, a pre-emptive first strike with the primary object of taking advantage of a favourable exchange ratio of ICBM in order to limit damage from a retaliation does not seem to be much of a risk. (Perhaps it would be more precise to assert doubts about the possibility of deterrence in the first place against a leadership prepared to pre-empt as a damage-limiting – rather than damage-denying – measure).

We may apply comparable reasoning to the often-cited scenario in which an enemy is tempted to attack our vulnerable strategic forces by the idea that once our (vulnerable) ICBM had been destroyed, we would be capable of retaliating only against urban-industrial targets, and would be deterred from doing so by the threat of a counter-retaliation (a 'third strike') against our own cities. A leadership which would order a first strike on the basis of such calculations would be gambling the physical survival of its country on the belief that the victim would not find something to do other than destroy cities or surrender, nor react with such grief and rage as to destroy the hostage enemy cities whatever the cost. Considering that the larger the pre-emptive attack the greater the grief and rage, and the smaller the pre-emptive attack the greater the surviving capability of the victim, the attacker must have a quite implausible degree of confidence in his ability to predict the responses of the victim's leadership to a totally unprecedented situation. Here again, we must ask whether a prospective enemy who would be tempted by a partially vulnerable force to seek military victory by means of a pre-emptive attack can be deterred at all.

Is it the case, then, that missile vulnerability does not jeopardize stability at all? One cannot push the reasoning so far. Note that a condition for vulnerability not leading to pre-emption is that very substantial capabilities for retaliation must still survive. One can afford a degree of vulnerability, therefore, only if one also has large and capable forces which are survivable, and it may even be the case that the larger one's survivable forces, the safer it is to have some vulnerable forces as well. (This is true to the extent that the enemy *perceives* the incremental survivable forces as being able to inflict incremental damage which is 'significant'). If that is the case, then we must say that, although the possession of some vulnerable strategic nuclear forces does not in itself seriously jeopardize stability, there comes a point at which the survivable forces become small enough for each increment of vulnerability marginally to reduce crisis stability.

In short, we can say that missile survivability is always desirable. A degree of survivability is essential, but the larger and more capable the survivable forces, the less dangerous it is to have some vulnerable forces as well. Having said this much, what are the arguments on the other side – what are the reasons for deploying or retaining stategic forces which are believed to be vulnerable?

15

In the same spirit as the arguments which hold that *any* vulnerability leads to instability, we can pose some theoretical arguments for the stabilizing effect of having some vulnerable ICBM forces. In the first place, a highly capable but vulnerable ICBM such as the MX (*Peacekeeper*) is a much better weapon for a first strike than for a second strike, and so deploying such missiles tends to convince prospective enemies that we are seriously contemplating a first strike if circumstances so require. It so happens that a willingness to use strategic nuclear weapons first if necessary is a critical aspect of agreed NATO strategy, and more generally it underlies the US posture of 'extended deterrence'. It is not that the United States actually *would* launch a first strike in any given circumstance – nobody, including the President of the United States, really knows for sure whether there is any circumstance other than nuclear attack on the United States which would lead the United States to use strategic nuclear weapons – but rather that it is US policy to have the option and the capability to escalate to the use of strategic nuclear weapons, and to rely upon this capability to deter enemies from acts of war short of nuclear attack on the United States. Deployment of vulnerable ICBM tends to strengthen the credibility of extended deterrence – and, as many observers have noted, extended deterrence needs all the help it can get. The problem with this argument is that the deployment of forces that make more sense as first-strike forces than as second-strike forces tends to frighten us as well as our enemies. If deployment of the MX in silos were to be justified publicly by the argument that a capable first-strike weapon is needed to enhance the credibility of extended deterrence, the impact on public opinion and on Alliance cohesion might well weaken our credibility more than the deployment would strengthen it.

A second theoretical argument for vulnerability suffers from the same flaw. It can be argued that the impact of a second-strike retaliation is inherently incredible against any but the largest enemy attack, *if* the leadership has time enough to think about what it is doing. The most credible retaliation is one that is reflexive, that is based upon previously-made plans that are carried out without time for sober second thoughts. (For the theoretical underpinning of this paradox, see Schelling's work a generation ago[1] on how it may be rational to make a threat which it would not be rational to carry out if the threat fails to deter). In this case, a threat to launch one's ICBM immediately upon receipt of confirmation that the enemy has launched his missiles ('launch under attack') is more credible than a threat to ride out an enemy attack, think it over, and then retaliate. Vulnerable missiles therefore strengthen deterrence by giving a prospective enemy a reason to believe one's threats to launch under attack. But again, the impact on public opinion and Alliance cohesion of elevating the launch-under-attack option from a disagreeable necessity to a sought-after posture would undo all the theoretical benefits.

There are, however, some real and serious reasons for allowing some of our missile forces to be vulnerable. They arise from the fact that Soviet missiles are becoming extremely accurate, and Soviet military intelligence is believed to be excellent and getting better. In consequence, strategic planners have come to assume that any missile whose location is known to the Soviet Union must be considered vulnerable. (The concept of 'deep underground basing' constitutes a sort of exception to this rule: a missile buried sufficiently deeply can survive even if the enemy knows where it is, but it cannot exit from its deep hole or tunnel if the enemy can locate, and therefore destroy, its door (or 'portal'). Hence, deep underground concepts generally include the idea that the portal will be created (by buried tunneling machinery, for example) after the enemy attack is over. This greatly limits the range of application of missiles based in this way). Therefore, survivability can be obtained only by measures which carry along with them their own disadvantages.

There are several generic ways of making missiles survivable against an attack by highly accurate enemy missiles. One approach is to hide the missiles. This is essentially what missile-carrying submarines do, but hiding on land (especially in an open society) is generally felt to be too difficult. Another approach is to keep the missiles moving over a wide area at a reasonable speed. A combination of moving and hiding was the Carter Administration's proposed 'shell game' for basing MX missiles. A third approach is to defend the missiles with an active ballistic missile defence. At the present state of technology, an active defence would not make missiles *survivable* in a strict sense, but rather would require an enemy to use unreasonably large forces to destroy the missiles by overcoming the defence. The same applies to concepts such as super-hardening, closely-spaced basing, or closely-spaced basing combined with a shell game ('multiple protective shelter' (MPS)) concept.

All of these concepts suffer from two kinds of drawbacks: excessive financial costs; and degradation of military capability compared to the capabilities of vulnerable silo-based missiles. Some of them – notably the various forms of airborne alert and the various forms of mobility over public roads – also suffer from the unwillingness of the public to accept the perceived (and real!) risks of accidents. Even apart from the problem of public attitudes, the significance of financial cost emerges clearly by examining the Carter Administration's policy. It clearly believed in missile survivability, as witness the dollar costs and political unpopularity it was willing to incur to put in place its proposed shell game basing for the MX missile. But the Carter Administration never seriously considered either rebasing the existing (vulnerable) *Minuteman* missiles – an OTA (Office of Technology Assessment) study not only showed that this would be technically feasible but also that it had received no serious study during the Carter Administration[2] – or increasing the MX deployment to the point where the *Minuteman* missiles could be phased out.

The assertions made that survivably-based missiles would have less military capability than silo-based missiles is a controversial one. Some aspects of this controversy are discussed more fully below. Others, such as the advantages and disadvantages of abandoning the 1972 ABM Treaty and undertaking a serious defence of missile silos, are outside the scope of this Paper. The arguments can be briefly summarized. Any form of effective hiding of the missiles (most notably but not exclusively submarine basing) makes it extremely difficult and perhaps impossible to arrange the command, control and communications (C^3) facilities and procedures to allow the missiles to be fired within a very short time after the order to do so is given. Any form of land mobility imposes practical limits on the size of the missiles, which in turn makes the cost per deliverable warhead quite high, and especially so if high accuracy is desired. Any form of free mobility (as distinct from moving among a finite number of pre-surveyed locations) will tend to reduce accuracy, although the mobile missiles of the future can, if desired, be made more accurate than the fixed missiles which are operational today. Finally, deployment of an active defence presumably means that the Soviet Union will also deploy active defences, and such Soviet defences would have the effect of degrading the military effectiveness of our own missiles.

All of these considerations have led the governments of the Western nuclear powers to a rather uncomfortable position. (There is some reason to suppose that the Soviet and Chinese governments are in the same position, but their military policies are less open to public inspection.) We say that missile survivability is extremely important, even essential, but we do not really seem to mean what we say. Instead, the United States, Britain and France have adopted a new sort of 'triad' posture: some of our missiles are highly survivable (such as those on submarines at sea); some are survivable on condition that enough warning is received (such as submarines in port, bombers, and possibly GLCM and *Pershing* II); and some are not really survivable at all (such as MX, and GLCM and *Pershing* II if Soviet intelligence is good enough). This is not, as the foregoing discussion has shown, an unreasonable policy. However, it is extremely uncomfortable, and in the long run probably impossible, for democracies to maintain a military posture which they dare not explain frankly to their publics.

Should Missiles be Close to Populations?
A second major issue revolves around the question of *where* missiles should be based. Should they be at sea (i.e. on submarines, since surface-ship basing is so vulnerable, even to non-nuclear attack, as to appear quite unattractive)? or should they be based on land? If on land, should a major effort be made to find a location which is not only sparsely populated and distant from dense populations, but also not upwind of large numbers of people?

One consideration which has occasionally proved decisive is the attitude of the prospective neighbours of a missile. In theory, one would suppose that anybody would use whatever political influence he had to avoid the placement of nuclear missiles anywhere near his home. After all, who would want to live near a target? In practice, the political reaction to missile placement has been less consistent than one would have suspected. It is reliably reported that the farmers of North Dakota and South Dakota are generally pleased to have *Minuteman* missiles located in their fields – apart from the rent which the Air Force pays, the Air Force keeps the roads open through the deepest winter snows in order to be able to get to the missiles, and the civilians in the region benefit.

When the issue arose of where to base the MX missile, one of the early candidate areas was central Kansas. Kansas was abruptly removed from the list after a senior Air Force General incautiously referred to the multiple protective shelter concept (i.e. the shell game) as a 'warhead sponge'. The General had in mind the idea that a Soviet attack on an MPS deployment would subject the Soviet Union to a highly unfavourable exchange ratio – each MX destroyed would cost the Soviet Union the payload of almost three SS-18 ICBM or their equivalent, so that a major attack on the MX would disarm the Soviet Union rather than disarm the United States. However, the Governor of Kansas saw this scenario more in terms of the total destruction of Kansas than of the partial disarmament of the Soviet Union, and announced that MX would never be welcome in Kansas. When the attention of the Air Force shifted from Kansas to Nevada and Utah, the reaction was quite different, though still largely hostile. The people (and politicians) of Nevada and Utah professed to believe in deterrence, and generally maintained that MX would on balance protect them from attack rather than make them targets. Their objection was more to the disruptive effects in peacetime of such a huge construction project. (One cannot help feeling some sympathy for the Air Force – moving away from populated areas to escape political problems necessarily meant going to an ecologically fragile region – because regions with robust ecological conditions attract intensive human use.) Eventually, the Air Force settled upon Warren Air Force Base in Wyoming as the site for MX. The Governor and most public opinion in Wyoming welcomed the deployment. However, the neighbouring state of Colorado has sued to halt it.

Looking into the future, there will doubtless be a severe political conflict over deployment of the new small ICBM (unofficially called the 'Midgetman') which Congress has decreed as the successor to the MX. Congress has required that this new missile be small enough (in both size and weight) to fit on a standard large tractor-trailer truck, which could roam the entire Interstate Highway System. (A missile of this size could also easily fit on standard railroad cars.) It is certainly true that a missile carrier disguised as a freight hauler, and moving freely over all the major highways of the United States, would be difficult, if not impossible, for the Soviet Union to target. But it is equally true that most civilian motorists would shrink from the thought that the vehicle growing ever larger in the rear-view mirror might contain a nuclear warhead and a large quantity of rocket fuel. Those civilians knowledgeable enough to know how unlikely it would be that a traffic accident could cause the nuclear materials to disperse – much less detonate – would also know that a severe crash might well set off the rocket fuel.

Apart from the political questions of what is euphemistically called 'public interface', there are some strategic issues as well. For one thing, since one cannot deny that a nuclear war is possible, and that it is more than possible that there would be a significant number of survivors, it seems responsible to deploy one's forces so as to minimize the likely casualties of one's own population. Put more concretely, it is possible that the Soviet Union would either prefer to avoid attacking Western populations (in order to preserve them as hostages) or would choose to concentrate on 'military targets', without much regard for whether the associated deaths of civilians would be many or few. In either case, we might save literally millions of lives by putting our prime military targets – our strategic missiles – at a safe distance from our population centres.

However, there are countervailing considerations. For one thing, missiles fired from submarines may be all too anonymous. No doubt in peacetime the Soviet Union possesses the means to distinguish between test launches of US, British and French SLBM since the missiles in flight have a variety of distinctive 'signatures' or observable characteristics. (The task of distinguishing a US missile assigned to the US SIOP from a US missile assigned to NATO might be somewhat more difficult). However, their ability to make such a distinction in wartime is problematical to say the least. Moreover, a submarine which fires a single missile in anger reveals its location and potentially renders itself vulnerable to a severe and immediate counter-attack, so that there is a strong incentive for a submarine which fires one missile to fire all its missiles as quickly as possible.

Therefore, there is a built-in contradiction in the idea of a limited strategic war fought between opposing missile forces with little or no damage to civilian populations. The submarine-based missiles, which are far from the populations they protect, are inherently unsuited to limited use with clear and precise boundaries to limit escalation.

Indeed, some have argued that basing missiles on the very soil that is to be protected (so-called 'sovereign basing') enhances stability in a crisis precisely because it ensures that any enemy attack on one's strategic forces will do so much damage to population and industry that retaliation becomes all the more credible. In other words, the greatest potential weakness in our deterrent is the possibility that the leaders of the Soviet Union would persuade themselves that we would have no sensible response if they struck first – and placing our missiles near populations would ensure that such a Soviet first strike would either fail to disarm us, or do so much damage that we would respond whether it was sensible to do so or not.

Just as in the issues of survivability, all arguments like this are double-edged. Our extended deterrent – the NATO 'flexible response' strategy that deters potential attacks of all sizes by a threat that could mean either retaliation in kind or escalation – relies upon the possibility that a limited nuclear war could be kept limited, and hence is a 'thinkable' NATO response to aggression. Basing missiles near populations tends to undercut the possibility of a limited strategic nuclear war, and hence undermines the NATO deterrent.

The answer to this argument, as formulated most notably in the US Defense Department during Harold Brown's tenure, runs as follows. The Soviet Union perceives that the NATO countries (mistakenly) believe that limited nuclear war is possible. Therefore NATO might well escalate to the use of nuclear weapons in response to massive conventional aggression. Because this belief in the limitation of nuclear war is mistaken, NATO escalation would lead to an all-out nuclear war that would destroy not only NATO but the Soviet Union as well. Hence, the Soviet Union will avoid her own destruction by refraining from aggression.[3]

Put differently, basing our missiles near our own populations will surely frighten the Soviet Union, and hence will enhance deterrence unless it incidentally frightens us even more.

What is the Real Value of 'Responsiveness'?
One of the advantages that is frequently cited for fixed land-based missiles is 'responsiveness', and other basing modes are often evaluated in terms of this criterion. 'Responsiveness' means the ability to respond very rapidly, with very great flexibility, to an order to fire, even from an ordinary peacetime posture. A perfectly

responsive force is ready to fire at all times can be retargeted almost instantly, and is controlled in such a tight yet flexible way that the National Command Authorities (NCA) could order the launch of any desired fraction of the force, from a single missile to the entire force.

One justification for such responsiveness is the possibility that in a nuclear war, especially a limited one, a national leader might wish to order a kind of attack that had not been foreseen, and was not in the breifing books which describe the alternative war plans or 'options'. A second justification is that a national leader wishing to bring a desperate situation under control might feel the need to regulate the timing of missile launches with great precision.

Both of these ideas draw some support from history. The outbreak of World War I provided several cases in which the leaders of great powers were limited by existing war plans – limited to such an extent that they were unable to issue the orders which they believed would have been most appropriate in the circumstances. It is not unreasonable to suppose that if the Tsar and Kaiser had been able the improvise limited mobilizations general war might have been averted. As for timing, the detailed histories of the Cuban Missile Crisis of 1962 show that President Kennedy's concerns for issuing 'signals' that would be clear to the Soviet leadership failed to override the US Navy's concerns for the security and effectiveness of its ships and men.

Nevertheless, it is hardly plausible to suppose that any national leadership could think through the retargeting of thousands of nuclear warheads during the minutes of an acute crisis or limited nuclear war. Indeed, an intelligent choice among a handful of carefully-worked-out options may be impossible in the time available. Precision in 'signalling' presupposes that the enemy leadership has both the time and the inclination to reflect on the significance of an unexpected event. It is plausible that the enemy can distinguish between an attack by ten missiles and an attack by one thousand; to rely upon finer distinctions might be foolhardy in the extreme.

Furthermore, the set routines and procedures which tend to limit responsiveness are also a defence against the accidental or unauthorized firing of a strategic nuclear missile. Whether in peacetime or in a state of severe crisis or limited war, it is perhaps more important for national leaders to prevent an unauthorized missile launch than to be able to order such a launch on the spur of the moment. Any arrangement which enhances responsiveness tends to degrade control – beyond a certain point the trade is surely unwise.

All of this suggests that there may be a case for a small responsive force – one that could carry out some improvized attack which was small enough both to be worked out in detail in a matter of minutes, and to be correctly observed and, perhaps, understood by the enemy. However, it is hard to see the benefits from attempting to make most or all of a super-power's total force 'responsive'. It is asking quite a lot that such a force be able to execute existing plans on short notice with high reliability.

'Flushing' on Strategic Warning

There is a class of basing modes in which there is a substantial difference between a fully-alert posture ('general alert' in the jargon of systems analysis) and the normal peacetime posture ('day-to-day alert'). For example, a road-mobile missile might be kept within a military base while on day-to-day alert, and sent out travelling over public roads when on generated alert. The reason for the difference is that the generated alert posture is much more survivable, while the day-to-day alert posture is much cheaper, and perhaps more acceptable to the public.

A special case of such basing is one in which the transition to generated alert can be accomplished in a few minutes. An example of such a transition today would be a bomber, normally located at the end of a runway, taking off on receipt of warning. At least one concept under study for basing the new small ICBM ('Midgetman') calls for the missile transporter to leave a military base at such a high speed that significant dispersal ('significant' dispersal becomes less in area as the missile and its transporter become 'harder' to nuclear blast) can be achieved within minutes. In this case the missile can remain on day-to-day alert until warning is received of an enemy missile launch. The missiles go on to generated alert ('flush') on receipt of tactical warning.

One can have considerably less confidence in such a system if the transition to a survivable state takes many minutes, or perhaps hours. In this case, if the order to 'flush' is delayed until the actual launch of enemy missiles is detected, it will be too late. Hence the system must be 'flushed' on the basis of *strategic* warning – that is, an assessment, based on whatever sources of intelligence are available, that an enemy attack may well be about to occur in the near future. Existing systems of this character include GLCM, the system of airborne command posts, and submarines in port.

Now strategic warning has historically proved highly unreliable. In retrospect it is always clear that the necessary indicators were there – the failure was one of assessment. Unfortunately, the indicators of an attack may be present many times when no attack occurs; *unambiguous* indicators are rare indeed, if they exist at all. And even when the intelligence analysis is accurate, it may not be properly communicated to those who should act on it, but who must cope with the 'noise' of many communications that are of varying significance. (See Roberta Wohlstetter's classic study of Pearl Harbor.[5])

Thus the debate over flush-on-strategic-warning systems runs as follows. The proponents argue that it is less than ideal, but nothing else provides so much survivability at an affordable cost. The opponents respond that the system is extremely vulnerable to a surprise attack, and hence is a dangerously destabilizing incentive to plan and carry out just such a surprise attack. The proponents respond that a 'bolt from the blue' attack is out of the question, because no national leadership would run the risks of nuclear war unless some vital interest was in immediate jeopardy. A nuclear war would only arise from a most severe crisis, and the crisis itself would provide strategic warning. The opponents counter by pointing to the risk that strategic warning would be ambiguous or misunderstood. The degree of the enemy's desperation may be misunderstood, or perhaps the attack would come just after generated forces are returned to their day-to-day posture in response to the beginning of negotiations.

No conclusive answer is possible. However, another consideration must be taken into account. For a national leadership which comes to realize that nuclear war is a possible outcome of a crisis, the shift from day-to-day alert to generated alert is only partly a question of military readiness. It is also – and more immediately – both a potentially helpful and potentially disastrous move of crisis management.

It is inconceivable that a major missile force could make the transition from (relatively) vulnerable to (relatively) survivable without the enemy's intelligence services observing it and reporting it to the highest levels. How will the enemy perceive it? As a signal of resolve? Or as an escalatory step that must be matched? As an indication that we have become stronger for the time being? Or as an indication that in an hour or so we *will* become stronger, and therefore that the time for attack is now? As an indication that we fear war? Or as an indication that we plan to start a war?

At the same time, it is very likely that our own people – and mass media – will notice the transition to generated alert. What will be the reaction – resolve or panic? Support for the government? Or hostility? Will the public response be so intense as to influence the enemy's thinking? If so, in what way?

The historical example that comes most readily to mind is not reassuring. In October 1973, US forces were placed on a higher state of alert ('Defcon 3') as a signal to the Soviet Union not to intervene in the Middle East. We do not know what effect, if any, this had on the plans or the judgments of the Soviet leadership. We do know that the decision was taken in order to send a signal, without regard for its impact on the actual readiness of US forces. We also know that within hours the UPI wire service was running the story – which did not in fact panic the US population, but which did enrage allies who had not yet been consulted.

In short, it seems likely that it will be the exigencies of crisis management, not a concern for the vulnerability of certain strategic missile forces, that will shape the decision as to whether to disperse the forces as the crisis becomes more severe. This must surely be a source of concern. But the other possibility – that the course of a crisis would be shaped not by deliberate leadership decisions but by the requirements to ensure the survivability of certain missile systems – appears even worse. Here are the echoes of the summer of 1914.

Diversity
At this moment, the fashionable answer to these difficult questions is 'diversity'. There is no such thing, the argument runs, as a perfect missile basing system; they all have their defects and their drawbacks. By investing in a mixed portfolio of basing approaches, we can ensure that each defect in each component is compensated by the remainder of the missile force. In this spirit, we have seen here that survivability may not be necessary for the entire force so long as the vulnerable fraction is not too large. We have seen that basing close to the population to be defended may enhance stability – but since it risks millions of lives, it should be done cautiously and as infrequently as appears safe. We have seen that responsiveness is probably useful primarily for a small fraction of the overall force. Finally, we have seen that we should not rely absolutely on any prediction that flush-on-strategic-warning forces would in fact receive timely orders to go on alert.

Hence there is a strong case for diversity. But two caveats are necessary. First, diversity is *not* the answer if one or more of the diverse basing modes require a large size in order to function. Multiple protective shelter-basing, for example, relies upon having more aimpoints than the enemy can conveniently target. A small MPS system offers no advantage over single shelters (such as traditional silos). Hence MPS, if it is sensible at all, is sensible only when as many of one's missiles as possible are MPS-based; to have a few missiles MPS-based while others are mobile or deep underground offers no advantage at all.

The second caveat is to avoid multiple basing modes which all suffer from the same defect or drawback – a sort of common failure mode. For example, diverse systems each of which tempted the enemy to pre-empt in a crisis would not 'really' diverse at all. Neither would diverse systems which all depended on strategic warning.

With this in mind, it may be useful to think of our strategic forces not in the traditional triad of land, sea and air, but in a new triad which focuses on their strengths and weaknesses:

1) Submarine forces, highly survivable, but of limited responsiveness, and lacking in the deterrent value of sovereign basing.
2) Fixed silo-based ICBM, quite vulnerable, but highly responsive and suitable for extended deterrence.
3) Bomber and land-mobile ICBM forces, whose survivability and effectiveness are conditioned upon receipt of, and action upon, timely warning.

Viewed in this way, there is a strong case that we need all three, but much less of a case for their traditional equality in size and importance. It is quite likely, in fact, that the submarine-based missile force will gradually grow in size and importance while the fixed-silo ICBM force gradually declines.

Conclusion
The question which confronts policy-makers, not only in the United States but elsewhere in NATO, is whether to spend large sums of money in the next few years on the procurement of missiles, and if so what missiles to buy and how to base them. In other words, what are the choices for the future?

There are two considerations which can be regarded as fundamental. The first is that nuclear missiles serve a function in our deterrent posture which is essential, and no changes are in sight which would render them less essential. It is possible that a technological revolution in ballistic missile defence will someday give the defence an inherent advantage over the offence comparable to the advantage which the offence now holds, but this will not happen in the next few years. It is possible too that sweeping arms-control agreements (such as a 'freeze') will rule out the acquisition of additional nuclear missiles, but such an agreement in the near future appears too improbable to form a sensible basis for planning. This being the case, to abandon the idea that nuclear missiles are of vital importance to our defence would amount to a revolution in US and NATO strategy. Despite the widespread dissatisfaction with US and NATO strategy as it now exists, no alternative proposal has garnered much support.

The second fundamental point is that there is now no such thing as a fully satisfactory basing mode for nuclear missiles. Given today's technologies, every possibility brings with it serious problems and risks, as well as significant financial costs. This means that every proposal for the procurement and basing of new missiles will carry with it obvious drawbacks, and therefore will be likely to arouse significant political opposition. It also suggests that the case for diversity in missile basing will remain persuasive.

The major technical uncertainty of the near future is the degree of survivability which would prove to be attainable for relatively small, land-based missiles. We simply do not know whether a hardened mobile missile carrier can be made to withstand 40 psi, or only 20 psi. We also do not know what such machines would cost, although we can make educated guesses that they are likely to be expensive. We also expect to learn more in the near future about the costs and technical risks of 'superhard' silos or deep underground basing. At the moment, debate about such questions is premature, but they are quite likely to be debated in the late 1980s.

What can be said is that the most prudent course available seems to be to diversify basing modes, but with a greater emphasis on those that are most survivable and a lesser emphasis on those that are most responsive. In the absence of a clean technical solution to the problem of survivable basing on land, this means that the weight of expenditures and of strategic significance will gradually shift from land-based missiles to submarine-based missiles. The case for deploying some MX missiles is much stronger than the case for deploying many MX missiles. The case for improvement of the submarine-launched forces (not only of the United States, but also of Britain and France) will be stronger than the case for increasing or improving the land-based forces.

The result is that the posture of the NATO countries by 1994 will be very different from their posture in 1974. Yet writing in 1984, midway through this transition, there is no basis to call for, or predict, drastic changes of policy. NATO leaders will simply continue to do the best they can to choose wisely among a set of costly and dangerous alternatives.

NOTES

[1] Thomas Schelling, *The Strategy of Conflict* (Cambridge, Mass: Harvard UP, 1960), Chapters 2 and 3.
[2] US Congress, Office of Technology Assessment (OTA), *MX Missile Basing* (Washington: USGPO, 1981), pp. 101–3.
[3] Former Secretary of Defense Harold Brown's testimony to Congress (US DOD Report, Washington DC, January 29, 1980), p. 67
[4] Graham Alison, *Essence of Decision* (Boston: Little, Brown, 1971), pp. 129–30.
[5] Roberta Wohlstetter, *Pearl Harbor; Warning and Decision* (Palo Alto, Ca: Stanford UP, 1962).

The Future of Land-based Strategic Weapons: Part II

LOUIS C. FINCH

All aspects of strategic forces have been scrutinized in public debate. None, however, has presented so vexing a problem over the last decade as finding a solution to the perceived problem of the vulnerability of silo-based ICBM. Valiant attempts have been made, first through finding technical solutions to ICBM basing – for example, multiple aim point basing, multiple protective shelters, and closely spaced 'dense pack' basing – and later through the recommendations of the Scowcroft Commission to proceed with a combination of interim silo-basing of MX, development of mobile ICBM basing options and arms-control measures. But problems still remain. (In the case of earlier ICBM basing schemes, all were rejected for a variety of technical, political and economic reasons. In the case of the Scowcroft recommendations, recent actions in the US Congress suggest that the political consensus on which they were based is eroding, and the arms-control proposals on which they rely heavily have thus far been rejected by the USSR.)

With this setting, the discussion which follows considers what future issues are raised by silo-based ICBM vulnerability. It does so not by reviewing the many options for basing ICBM or by considering in detail the many arms-control approaches that address this issue. These have been analysed exhaustively elsewhere. Rather, the analysis will examine the proposition that the West, whether by design or accident, has force plans that may solve the ICBM vulnerability problem – not directly, by improvements to that system, but indirectly through improvements to the rest of the West's strategic forces that may make the silo-based ICBM vulnerability problem less significant.

The views expressed in this Paper are those of the author and do not represent the views of the Congressional Research Service of the Library of Congress.

Western 'Strategic' Forces

The composition of Western strategic nuclear forces is often narrowly defined to include a specific subset of forces – namely the US strategic Triad of ICBM, SLBM and bombers. For reasons of budget debate strategy, arms-control negotiating postures and national control, there are often good rationales for this approach. For the purposes of deterrence – of considering which forces might affect Soviet behaviour in dissuading them from launching an attack against the US and her allies – a broader definition seems worth considering. In particular, consideration of *all* Western nuclear forces that are capable of striking targets in the Soviet homeland may be a good starting point.

The Data Annexe at the end of this Paper gives a graphic portrayal of the forces that meet this definition. The general categories and rough size of these forces in the early 1990s are shown in Table 1 on the next page.

In listing all these forces as 'strategic', one should begin with a note of caution. While at various times in arms-control negotiations the Soviet Union has proposed a similar categorization of forces, the purpose here is not to signify acceptance of her position. For example, one should be quick to point out that many of them – specifically NATO INF forces and British and French nuclear forces – are not deployed with the principal aim of deterring attacks on the United States, but to deter attacks on her allies and friends. As such, the United States would not be certain that these forces would be available to respond to attacks on her. Thus, the United States would never be likely to accept these forces as equivalent to Soviet forces aimed at the US.

In a more practical vein, it is important to realize that these forces do not represent an aggregate capability for simultaneous attack on the Soviet Union. It would be a tremen-

Table 1: Western 'Strategic' Forces

Force Category	Approx. No. deliverable warheads (early 1990s)
Silo-based US ICBM	1,700–2,000
US SLBM	3,100–8,200
Penetrating bombers	1,500–2,500
Mobile ICBM	700–1,000
Submarine-launched cruise missiles	300–500
Ship-launched cruise missiles	300–500
Air-launched cruise missiles	2,800–4,800
Ground-launched cruise missiles	500
Pershing II INF missiles	100
US land-based tactical INF aircraft*	1,300
Sea-based tactical aircraft	800
British and French ballistic missiles	1,300
British and French INF aircraft	300
Other NATO INF aircraft*	300

* Not all these aircraft may have the range to strike the USSR from peacetime bases. However, techniques such as air refuelling, forward staging and one-way missions could provide that range and would need to be considered by Soviet military planners.

SOURCES: Sources for data are given in the appendix. Range of values driven principally by assumptions on whether START agreement is in effect.

dous operational problem to co-ordinate a response to Soviet aggression using this conglomeration of forces – especially if they and their supporting command-and-control network were degraded in unpredictable ways by an initial Soviet attack.

Despite all these caveats, in the equation of deterrence the Soviet Union would need to take all of the forces in Table 1 into account. Even for forces that are not US intercontinental forces, if the Soviet Union were to contemplate attacks solely against the American homeland, she could not with great confidence assume that responses would not come from elsewhere.

The specific numbers of forces ultimately to be deployed may vary, depending, among other things, on outcomes in arms-control negotiations and on the priorities that Western countries place on strategic force spending. Whatever the specific deployments, however, one might observe from this table that the Soviet Union will in general face a force with a very large number of weapons and a very wide variety of delivery systems. This is the case with or without silo-based ICBM. This force will include systems – cruise missiles, 'stealth' bombers, *Pershing* missiles, French and British SLBM with multiple warheads, mobile ICBM, and SLBM with hard target capability – that are very different in character from the forces of the mid-1970s or even those of today. In broad terms, these weapons would seem to pose a highly diverse and proliferated force that would be extremely complex for the Soviet Union to deal with in military terms – a very different situation to that posed by the Western forces of the 1970s when the ICBM vulnerability debate began.

Implications for Deterrence

Despite this overall trend, one cannot assert that this 'strategic' force of the West would necessarily be sufficient for deterrence. It may be that there are weaknesses – silo-based ICBM vulnerability to pre-emptive attack being a case in point – that the Soviet Union could exploit to give herself an advantage sufficient to justify starting a conflict. The discussion that follows looks at a variety of views of what constitutes a sufficient basis for deterrence with an eye towards the role that silo-based ICBM, in conjunction with other forces, might play in preserving deterrence.

Integrity of the Strategic Triad

Since the early 1960s, the architecture of US strategic forces has been a 'Triad' of forces – manned bombers, SLBM and silo-based ICBM. Its rationale is that each category of force provides a unique combination of attributes (survivability mechanisms, means of penetrating enemy defences, command-and-control arrangements, target destructiveness and responsiveness to warning of an attack). Taken as a whole, the triad does two things:

- It provides a hedge such that, in the event that one or even two of the categories were to fail (through enemy actions or unforeseen technical problems), there would still be a substantial force capable of responding to a Soviet attack.

– It makes enemy attacks on these forces more complicated to plan and execute.

These 'hedging' and 'attack-complicating' concepts have underpinned, and will continue to underpin, deterrence theory. In the mid-1970s concern emerged over the growing possibility that one of the Triad's main elements – silo-based ICBM – would be vulnerable to Soviet attack. This of course threatened to undermine the triad concept of hedging, reducing the hedges available from three to two: bombers and SLBM.

While initially a source of great concern when the vulnerability problem for silo-based ICBM first emerged, Western strategic forces (as described above and in the Data Annexe) have evolved and will continue to evolve considerably, both in variety and capability. They will go well beyond the three force elements in the original Triad. US intercontinental forces alone, for example, will apparently evolve by the early 1990s from the Triad of the mid-1970s to a 'hexad'[1] with the addition of ALCM-carrying bombers, sea-launched cruise missiles and small, mobile ICBM. Developments in US and Western INF serve further to extend the hedging concept and to complicate Soviet attack planning – bolstering the underpinnings of the original concept.

Considering these force structure trends in the context of the vulnerability of silo-based ICBM, what might therefore have been a major problem in the earlier hedging structure of US strategic forces may have been substantially relieved as Western forces have expanded and diversified. Further, this diversification would also seem on the face of it to serve the second goal of that Triad – that of complicating Soviet attack planning.

To illustrate these points, Table 2 (on the next page) briefly compares several attributes of silo-based ICBM with other elements in Western strategic forces. The overall impression from this table is the great variety of similarities and differences between silo-based ICBM and other forces. This suggests a rather robust hedging/attack-complicating structure when Western strategic forces are taken as whole.

Considering the details of Table 2, those attributes that are strongly associated with hedging against the possible failure of silo-based ICBM to perform are pre-launch survivability, defence penetration, command-and-control means and political control. The many 'differences' in the table suggest that failure of a silo-based ICBM in one of these attributes would not necessarily result in a failure of the same attribute in other systems.

Another aspect of Table 2 relates to offensive capability to attack targets – counter-silo capability and time of flight to target. The counter-silo capability refers to combinations of weapon accuracy and warhead destructive power sufficient to destroy ICBM silos (or other 'hard' targets such as some command and control facilities). By the 1990s, almost all the systems on the list appear likely to have this capability, showing great overlap with silo-based ICBM. The other offensive attribute – time of flight – is differentiated by whether a system is a ballistic missile (with short time of flight) or flies through the atmosphere (with comparatively long time of flight). Table 2 indicates that at least some systems share silo-based ICBM capabilities in this area (the significance of this attribute is a subject of debate and will be considered in more detail later).

Deterrence and Assured Destruction
While there is widespread agreement with the principle of extracting a price from the Soviet Union through retaliation as a mechanism for deterrence, there are a variety of opinions as to how big and what kind of price she would find intolerable. In the past, some have argued that having the military capacity to ride out a Soviet attack and retaliate by destroying a large percentage of Soviet economic and industrial strength was sufficient for deterrence. Whether or not this is indeed the case is a debate beyond the scope of this Paper. Nevertheless, having this capacity – a so called assured destruction capacity – could affect Soviet behaviour.

For those who believe that the West should continue to have an assured destruction capability, it may in military terms be something relatively easy to come by. In particular, destruction of industrial/economic targets requires nothing special in the way of accuracy or short times of flight to targets.

Table 2: Comparison of Silo-based ICBM and other Strategic Force Attributes in the early 1990s

System	Pre-launch survival	Defence penetration	Flight time to target	Counter-silo capability	Command/ control	Political control
SLBM	D	S	S	S	D	S
Pentrating bombers	D	D	D	S	D	S
Mobile ICBM	D	S	S	S	D	S
Submarine SLCM	D	D	D	S	D	S
Ship SLCM	D	D	D	S	D	S
ALCM	D	D	D	S	D	S
GLCM	D	D	D	S	D	D[1]
Pershing II	D	S	S	S	D	D[1]
Land-based tactical air	D	D	D	S	D	D[1]
Sea-based tactical air	D	D	D	S	D	S
UK/French missiles	D[2]	S	S	S	D	D
UK/French aircraft	D	D	D	S	D	D
Other NATO INF aircraft	D	D	D	S	D	D[1]

[1] Assumes assigned to NATO command structure.
[2] French land-based missiles would have survival mechanisms similar.

KEY:
S = Same as silo-based ICBM.
D = Different to silo-based ICBM.

Virtually any of the forces listed in Table 1 could participate effectively in such attacks.

In terms of numbers of weapons that would need to survive a Soviet attack and carry out an assured destruction strike, this is a matter of some uncertainty. As one possible benchmark, Figure 1 displays some graphs based on data presented by Enthoven and Smith[2] showing percentages of Soviet industrial capacity and population destroyed as a function of equivalent megatons (EMT) of weapons delivered on target in an attack. The data used to develop this figure may be open to dispute (for example, alternative assumptions of the effectiveness of the Soviet civil defence programme could change the results), but if it is anywhere close to being correct the size of the force needed to survive a Soviet

Fig. 1: Soviet Population and Industry Destroyed

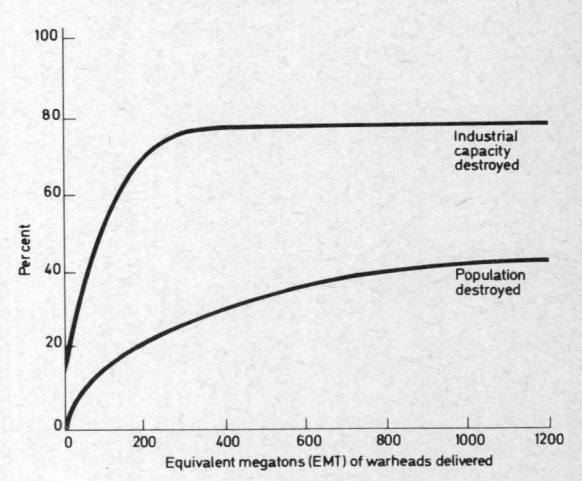

attack and achieve high levels of destruction of these types of targets (say 70% of Soviet industry) would be relatively small (some 200 EMT). Measured against this requirement, the current US SLBM force carries approximately 850 EMT, the current US bomber force carries approximately 1,100 EMT, and even French and British SLBM forces could in the 1990s have 280 EMT

Thus it would seem quite possible that enough of the Western forces listed in Table 1 would survive a Soviet attack (even if *none* of the silo-based ICBM survived) to deliver a retaliatory strike with enough destructive power to operate out on the flat part of the curves in Figure 1. Hence, if one accepts the notion of assured destruction of industrial/economic targets as an important element in deterring Soviet attacks, and if one accepts the data in Figure 1 as essentially correct, one would find this part of the deterrence equation satisfied, even if silo-based ICBM did not survive a Soviet attack.

Counter-attack of Military Targets
A prevalent theme in US security policy for some time has been that a surviving assured destruction capability against industrial/economic targets will not be sufficient to deter all kinds of Soviet attacks. This is based on the view that the Soviet Union might believe that she could launch a limited attack against our military forces, mostly sparing Western populations, and the US President (or other Western leaders) would not launch an attack against Soviet cities.

Relating this notion of deterrence to silo-based ICBM, the following scenario is often used to illustrate concern over their vulnerability:
– The Soviet Union begins by attacking US ICBM silos, and (assuming that they are vulnerable) destroys them. Believing that she has effectively disarmed the US in terms of capability to retaliate, she seeks concessions from the US and the West.
– With no ICBM left, the US President is unable to respond against appropriate military targets highly valued by the Soviet Union (the remaining Soviet ICBM in their silos and hardened command-and-control facilities).
– The US President refuses to respond with his surviving strategic forces (bombers and SLBM) against Soviet industrial/economic targets (and necessarily against the Soviet population) both because of the inhumanity of destroying the Soviet people, and because such a strike could provoke a Soviet response against the people of the United States and the rest of the West.
– The US President is in the end left with one choice, an unacceptable choice, of surrender to Soviet demands.

Other Weapons
If one accepted this scenario then, as US ICBM became vulnerable, deterrence would suffer significantly. And especially under the narrow view of the US strategic Triad corresponding to forces in the mid-1970s (see Figures A and B in the Data Annexe), the scenario above is easier to sustain. At that time, the only US weapon system under development that would be capable of retaliating against Soviet ICBM silos and hardened command-and-control facilities with short times of flight (providing little warning) was the MX ICBM.

Looking at the forces now planned for the foreseeable future, the consequences may not be as grim. Most significantly, the *Trident D-5* SLBM (to be deployed by both the US and Britain) is credited with having the capability to destroy Soviet ICBM silos and other hardened targets with short times of flight. (There is some dispute over whether SLBM could substitute for ICBM. The ability to communicate reliably with them in crisis or conflict may not be adequate. Declining numbers of submarines for launching SLBM may make them more vulnerable to enemy pre-emptive attacks. Launching only some missiles in a limited response may expose the submarine to Soviet anti-submarine warfare measures.)

In addition to new SLBM, there may also be other weapons systems capable of executing an appropriate response against appropriate Soviet targets. For instance, there is a common assumption that ballistic missiles, because of their short times of flight, are the only weapons suitable for retaliation against Soviet silos. While it is a fair argument that such short warning times are necessary for a first strike – to catch an enemy by surprise before he can decide to launch a counter-attack – this capability may not be needed for retaliation. To understand this, consider the following reasoning: once the Soviet Union had launched an initial strike, she would have to anticipate a Western response; knowing this, she would decide either to launch her remaining ICBM in silos upon warning of a US response, or she would decide to ride out an attack. If she adopted the first policy, the result would be a Soviet ICBM second-wave attack, whether the Western retaliation came from ballistic missiles (with minutes of warning time) or bombers and cruise missiles (with hours of warning time). If she adopted the second policy, the result would be no Soviet second-wave attack (and possible destruction of her remaining silos), independent of whether the Western response came from ballistic missiles or aircraft and cruise missiles.

Under this reasoning, Soviet responses and options would be the same with minutes or hours of warning. It follows, then, that aircraft and cruise missiles (with long times of flight and long warning times) would have equal deterrent weight to faster ballistic systems and would be appropriate to respond in a second strike against Soviet ICBM silos. In this case, virtually all the Western forces listed in Table 1 would be appropriate candidates to respond against Soviet silos and other hard targets, making the survivability of US silo-based ICBM much less crucial.

Other Targets

There is another line of argument that might open to question the scenario presented earlier. It concerns what types of targets are appropriate for US retaliation and would be effective in extracting such a high price from the Soviet Union as to discourage her from attacking in the first place. The scenario assumed that Soviet hard targets – ICBM silos and command-and-control facilities – were the targets to achieve this objective. In the case of ICBM silos, however, the price to the Soviet Union in destroying them is not entirely clear. In the first place, some of the silos will be empty, since their missiles would have been launched in the initial Soviet attack. (Empty silos might be used to fire reload ICBM, giving them some residual value, but reloads could also be fired from non-silo launchers, diminishing the value of destroying empty silos.) Also, those Soviet missiles that remain in their silos could easily be launched on warning of a Western retaliatory strike, something the USSR might well do if she attached high value to the military potential of these forces. Finally, the US may well decide not to have a first-strike capability to destroy all Soviet ICBM, so she certainly would not have a second-strike capability to do so.

As for hardened command-and-control facilities, one could reason that the Soviet Union would not logically put herself in a position of being completely dependent on them for the viability of her strategic forces. It seems likely that her hardened command-and-control facilities are backed by dispersed (and essentially invulnerable) facilities, perhaps including something like US airborne command posts. If this is the case, destroying non-essential hardened, fixed command and control would seem not to be very costly to the Soviet Union and thus not very effective for deterrence.

If hardened ICBM silos and command-and-control facilities are not important targets for deterrence, then a crucial question is which targets are? There are very large military complexes associated with Soviet conventional and other nuclear forces that might be subject to attack. In terms of the value the USSR would place on these targets (relative to ICBM silos and command-and-control facilities) one could argue that they are highly prized by the Soviet leadership – especially conventional forces and most particularly the Red Army.[3] The rationale here is that it is these forces (not strategic nuclear forces) that enable the Soviet leadership to dominate and suppress its own people and its allies.

If one believes that retaliating against Soviet hard targets (silos and command-and-control facilities) with short warning time *is* important for deterrence, and that SLBM are inadequate in numbers or capabilities to substitute for ICBM, then the vulnerability of silo-based ICBM may be important. But if one believes that the destruction of softer nuclear and conventional force targets is sufficient for deterrence (and perhaps that destruction of hard targets alone is not sufficient for deterrence), then silo-based ICBM would seem less significant. This is because the totality of Western strategic forces listed in Table 1 would have a capability at least equal to ICBM in destroying these softer targets.

A Problem for the Future: Barrage Attacks
The discussion above suggests that the rest of Western strategic forces could compensate for silo-based ICBM vulnerability and may well provide a retaliatory capability sufficient to preserve deterrence. This, of course, is based on the premise that a substantial portion of other Western 'strategic' forces could survive a Soviet first strike. It is not clear, however, that this premise is necessarily correct.

With the exception of US and French ballistic missiles in silos, all the weapons on the Western strategic forces list in Table 1 rely on some form of dispersal for survival. Mobile ICBM, GLCM and *Pershing* II disperse on land; SLBM and SLCM disperse at sea; and aircraft upon warning of an attack take off and disperse in the air. Thus, rather than hedging against failure to survive in distinctly different ways, they all have in common dispersal for survival.

One means of undermining dispersal would be a Soviet barrage attack, where large numbers of weapons are detonated nearly simultaneously throughout the areas in which Western forces might be dispersed. If successful, such an attack could then accomplish a disarming first strike on virtually the totality of Western strategic forces – thus giving the Soviet Union a strong military incentive to pursue such an approach, much to the detriment of deterrence.

Whether these barrage attacks are practical is quite another matter. Some arguments that these attacks are unrealistic include the assertions that:

- They would require Soviet technological developments to be able to give some rough idea of the simultaneous location of all Western missiles dispersed on land, of submarines at sea and of aircraft in the air. (It would seem impractical for the Soviet Union simply to barrage all the oceans and all the territories of the West.) There is no public evidence of the Soviet Union overcoming these technological hurdles in the near future.
- Such massive attacks would be likely to destroy the countries whose wealth and resources the Soviet Union would want to control in the post-war period.
- Barrage attacks would be likely to destroy a large portion of Western population. This would hardly be construed as a limited counter-military strike. If they were not successful in destroying virtually all of the West's nuclear forces, they would almost certainly provoke a Western strike directed at Soviet cities, the West then having little more to lose.
- Attacks of this magnitude could trigger major, long-term modifications to the environment to the detriment of the Soviet Union as well as the West. Results of studies by Dr Carl Sagan and others indicate that one type of exchange involving 5,000 megatons would have a major impact on the global climate lasting several years.[4]

Despite these reasons to discount the possibility of barrage attacks, they should not be dismissed entirely, because they affect almost all the West's forces. At what level of Soviet forces this becomes a problem is difficult to determine, but Moran and Wilson have estimated that approximately 17–20,000 larger-yield warheads might put US retaliatory forces at risk.[5] While this estimate does not cover the destruction of all the Western forces listed in Table 1, it gives a sense of the magnitude of the problem.

If barrage attacks were ever thought to be a serious threat to Western forces, there are at least two ways of providing some relief. The first is by arms control.[6] Ballistic missiles would almost certainly be the weapons of choice for a barrage attack as they are the only weapons with sufficiently short times of flight to allow a near simultaneous strike over widely-dispersed areas. This requirement is more cheaply met by silo-based ICBM than SLBM (where the added expense of buying and operating submarines drives costs up). Thus, any arms-control measures that put reasonably low ceilings on the size of ballistic missile forces – especially silo-based ICBM – would be particularly useful in avoiding the threat of barrage attacks.

A second mechanism to reduce incentives for barrage attacks might be deployment of ballistic missile defences. If these defences could destroy a significant number of Soviet ballistic missile warheads, this thinning-out process might be sufficient to discourage Soviet barrage attacks.

US First Use
Apart from retaliation, another role for Western nuclear forces – one in which silo-based ICBM have played an important part in the past – is for a nuclear first strike as a deterrent to Soviet aggression against US allies and friends. One specialized role for these ICBM would be to strike pre-emptively against some Soviet ICBM or other hard targets. With the deployment of the *Trident D-5* SLBM, also with a counter-silo capability, ICBM would not be unique in this role. Some of the second-strike difficulties, sometimes argued to be a problem for SLBM, might be less of a problem for D-5 SLBM in a first-strike role. Further, since this would be a strike occurring before Soviet nuclear attacks, vulnerability of silo-based ICBM would not be a problem in carrying out such an attack. Finally it is not clear how much deterrent effect the capability to take out part (but not all) of the Soviet ICBM force would have on persuading the Soviet Union not to launch a conventional attack. (By US no-disarming-first-strike policy, a significant portion of the Soviet ICBM force would still remain after a US attack.)

The Soviet Side to the Deterrence Equation
Having Western forces capable of retaliation is not a sufficient condition for deterrence. The vulnerability of Soviet ICBM in their silos may cause deterrence to fail. The Soviet Union might calculate that (contrary to US assurances) the West did indeed have the capability to destroy her ICBM force pre-emptively. (As Figures C and D in the Data Annexe show, ICBM form the bulk of Soviet current capability). In these circumstances, the Soviet Union might decide to initiate a nuclear conflict, not so much to gain military advantage as to avoid losing her ICBM force.

If one assumes that the West carries out force modernization plans (especially MX and D-5) without unilateral restraint, then the answer to this part of the deterrence puzzle has to lie with Soviet actions. In particular, the Soviet Union may need to follow a course similar to that of the West – namely one of force diversification and proliferation – as a hedge against silo-based vulnerability. Indeed it appears, based on information in the 1984 edition of the US Government publication, *Soviet Military Power*,[7] that the Soviet Union has active weapons systems development programmes that may modify what has hitherto been substantial reliance on silo-based ICBM. Specifically, these systems include:

– The new *Blackjack* bomber;
– A family of air-, sea- and ground-launched long-range cruise missiles;
– The SS-X-25 (apparently mobile) ICBM;
– The new SS-NX-23 SLBM that may be modified before 1990 with improved accuracy;
– A new variant of the *Bear* bomber (*Bear H*) probably designed to carry long-range cruise missiles.

The Strategic Force Balance
Another substantial role that ICBM play is in the *perceived* balance in the size of forces between the West and the Soviet Union – a role that at least has a marked political effect on the current security debate, and hence arguably an effect on deterrence as well.

In public discussions, the balance of forces between the US and the Soviet Union is almost always portrayed by some measure of peacetime force levels.[8] Some examples of these measures are balance in:

– Numbers of warheads;
– Numbers of delivery vehicles;
– Amount of EMT (destructive power);
– Amount of throw-weight (payload capacity).

Whether or not these balances are accurate reflections of the relative capabilities of opposing forces is a matter beyond the scope of this Paper. What is clear, however, is that, to the extent the US or USSR wants to alter the balance as measured by these means, silo-based ICBM can play an important role.

This role relates to ICBM costs and capabilities. On the cost side, silo-based ICBM are cheap relative to other strategic forces (silos are relatively inexpensive to build, and, once deployed, ICBM require little maintenance and manpower). SLBM, on the other hand, require expensive, manpower-intensive submarines for deployment. Aircraft are also expensive to procure and maintain and require high manning levels. Mobile ICBM require expensive mobile launchers and high manpower levels to keep continuously deployed. With regard to capabilities, silo-based ICBM have less restrictive weight or volume constraints than other systems. Thus, they are potentially able to carry substantial numbers of warheads and large throw-weights and EMT.

Given these attributes, if one wanted to maximize the traditional measures of force balance for a given budget, silo-based ICBM would be the system of choice (even though they might not be the best choice in terms of military capabilities). However, using this as a major criterion for structuring Western forces can create a dilemma.

As an illustration, a given amount of money spent on silo-based ICBM might result in great gains in numbers of warheads or throw-weight when compared to the same amount invested in small, mobile ICBM. (As an example of the magnitude of this cost differential, for a 1,000-warhead force, the US Department of Defense indicates that the approximate procurement and operating costs for ten years for a small mobile ICBM is $69 billion versus $17 billion for an MX in *Minuteman* silos.[9]) On the other hand, in terms of deterrence, silo-based ICBM might contribute less than an equal-cost force of mobile ICBM, even though they have several times the number of warheads. This is due to the silo-based ICBM's lack of survivability and substantially greater capability to threaten to disarm Soviet ICBM. As an alternative however, mobile ICBM would clearly result in lower numbers of warheads, throw-weight and equivalent megatonnage for the same money, leaving the impression that the United States was falling behind the Soviet Union in the strategic arms competition.

The cost leverage differential becomes particularly acute if the US were to try to match the already large and perhaps growing (see Figure D in the Data Annexe) Soviet silo-based force on a warhead-for-warhead basis with more survivable systems (such as mobile ICBM). In a competition of this nature, the US would be caught in the trap of having to spend many dollars for her force for every dollar the Soviet Union would spend on her (cheaper) silo-based ICBM.

To break out of this adverse cost/leverage dilemma that balancing Soviet ICBM force levels creates, the West might consider some combination of the following options:

– Arms-control agreements that limit force balances under a variety of measures (e.g., SALT, US and Soviet START negotiating positions) would at least bound the problem of balance and allow trade-offs while maintaining overall limits. Proposals such as those of US Congressman Gore[10] to eliminate or keep MIRVed ICBM at very low levels would be even more effective.
– Some arms-control measures could possibly provide for survivability of silo-based ICBM, so that they could contribute to the perceived balance of force size while avoiding vulnerability problems detrimental to deterrence. A concept contributed by US Congressmen Aspin[11] and Gore[12] might accomplish this in the following way. An emerging technology that could improve silo survivability is the technique of 'super-hardening' – making silos invulnerable to all but a direct hit or a very near miss.[13] At the same time, new guidance technologies (terminally-guided re-entry vehicles, mid-course guidance update techniques) may produce accuracies so good as to defeat super-hardening. Thus, an arms-control aproach that halted development of these guidance technologies could, in conjunction with silo super-hardening, help to restore silo-based ICBM to a level of survivability more healthy for deterrence, while at the same time allowing the cost advan-

as to keep the West's force size up to that of the Soviet Union.
- The West (perhaps followed by the Soviet Union) could, as a matter of policy, de-emphasize the importance of force size as a measure of balance, while continuing to emphasize the importance of qualitative differences as a means of balancing forces. While appealing in principle, in practice this option raises the following dilemma. Force size balances are easy to compute and easy for the public to grasp, even if they can be very misleading measures of capability and deterrence. Measures reflecting capabilities more accurately — for example, potential to destroy sets of targets of interest by forces remaining after a variety of attack scenarios — are much harder to calculate and much more difficult for the public to decipher, but may be much more relevant to deterrence.

Conclusions
For silo-based ICBM alone, no plans seem likely to solve with great confidence this system's increasing vulnerability. But looking at the rest of the West's forces as they are evolving, it may be that this increasing ICBM vulnerability is becoming less important, at least in terms of achieving the fundamental objective — deterrence. The West's forces are expanding and diversifying in ways that seem to transform the silo-based ICBM from the unique centrepiece of nuclear forces that it was in the 1970s to only one element among a complex, expanded set in the 1990s.

Whether silo-based ICBM vulnerability is still a cause for concern depends very much on what one believes about the roles that nuclear forces need to play to preserve deterrence, and how effective other, especially newer, forces will be in compensating for silo-based ICBM in these roles. In particular:

- If 'assured destruction' of a high portion of Soviet industrial/economic targets is sufficient for deterrence, then other forces would seem adequate.
- If retaliation against hardened military targets (e.g. ICBM silos) is needed for deterrence, but retaliation need not be quick, other forces would again seem adequate.
- If retaliation against softer military targets (e.g. Soviet conventional forces) is sufficient for deterrence, then other forces would seem equal to ICBM in capability.
- If quick retaliation against hardened military targets is needed for deterrence, but if future SLBM (estimated to be capable of destroying these hard targets) can survive attacks and have a command-and-control mechanism capable of quick responses, then silo-based ICBM would again seem unnecessary.

Thus silo-based ICBM vulnerability would seem to be a problem only if one believes that the capability to destroy hardened military targets is necessary to deter Soviet aggression, that such destruction must occur quickly, and that future SLBM will be inadequate to the task.

These conclusions rest on the presumption that forces other than silo-based ICBM would survive a Soviet attack in substantial numbers and be able to retaliate. A possibility that could undermine this presumption is a Soviet capability for an effective barrage attack against *all* of the West's strategic forces. For some, such barrage attacks are technically infeasible or politically undesirable for the Soviet Union to pursue, and therefore unimportant in the deterrence equation. For others, however, this potential threat deserves to be addressed — through arms-control limits to keep forces below levels needed for barrage attacks or through ballistic missile defensive measures to thin out the massive number of warheads needed to execute a barrage attack effectively — or through both these means.

Finally, silo-based ICBM (independent of their vulnerability) already make a major contribution to commonly-used measurements of US (and Western) peacetime force size compared to that of the Soviet Union. For the future, in order to achieve growth in these measures to match the Soviet Union, silo-based ICBM probably give the greatest increment in force growth for a given expenditure. Since these measurements do not usually account for, among other things, the vulnerability of forces to attack, their adequacy as useful measures for deterrence is unclear.

Nevertheless, they do seem to affect public perceptions of which side is ahead or behind in the 'balance' of force size. Thus, if the United States wanted to catch up to or exceed the Soviet Union in the force-size balance, silo-based ICBM would seem to be a cost-effective way of doing so. Such an approach, however, could ultimately undermine deterrence because of these weapons' vulnerability to attack.

NOTES

[1] The notion of describing US strategic forces as a 'hexad' stemmed in part from a discussion with Dr Joel Resnick of Science Applications, Inc., in which he noted the evolution of US strategic forces to a 'hedged triad' (i.e. silo-based ICBM hedged by mobile ICBM, SLBM by SLCM, penetrating bombers by ALCM-carrying bombers).
[2] Alan C. Enthoven and Wayne K. Smith, *How Much is Enough? Shaping the Defense Program, 1961–9* (New York: Harper and Row, 1971), p. 207.
[3] The notion of threatening Soviet conventional forces (especially the Red Army) as a useful mechanism for deterrence is based on discussions with Lt-Gen. (ret.) Glenn A. Kent of the Rand Corporation.
[4] Phillip Shabecoff, 'Grimmer View Painted of Nuclear War Effects', *New York Times*, 30 October 1983.
[5] Theodore H. Moran and Peter A. Wilson, 'A New Strategic Arms Agreement', *SAIS Review*, Winter/Spring 1984, p. 119.
[6] Moran and Wilson, present one particular arms-control formulation to keep warheads well below the 17–20,000 threshold estimated as necessary for a barrage attack capability. Any one of a number of alternative arms-control proposals (including the US START position) could also cap warhead levels below this.
[7] *Soviet Military Power 1984* (Washington DC: USGPO, April 1984), pp. 22–31.
[8] See for example, *Military Posture FY 1985*, The Organization of the Joint Chiefs of Staff, p. 27 and *An Analysis of Administration Strategic Arms and Modernization Proposals* (Washington DC: Congressional Budget Office, March 1984), p. xvi.
[9] *Strategic Forces Technical Assesment Review, Executive Summary* (Washington DC: US DoD, 31 March 1983), pp. 13–14.
[10] Albert Gore Jr, 'A New Proposal for START Talks', *Congressional Record*, 4 August 1983, pp. E4045–8.
[11] Walter Pincus, 'New Silo Hardening Tests Could Reopen Missile Basing Debate', *Washington Post*, 11 May 1984, p. 15.
[12] Albert Gore Jr, 'Super Missiles: Their Relationships to Military Security and Arms Control', *Congressional Record*, 26 April 1984, pp. E1794–E1795.
[13] Edgar Ulsamer, 'The Prospects for Superhard Silos', *Air Force Magazine*, January 1984, pp. 74–7.

DATA ANNEXE

Figures A–D (pp. 35–6) show the strategic nuclear force structures for the West and the Soviet Union over the period from 1974 to 1994. These figures are not intended to serve as measuring devices for the balance of forces between the West and the Soviet Union. Rather they are intended to portray a general sense of the distribution of types of forces available to both sides over time.

Forces for the West include all those capable of striking Soviet territory. Forces for the Soviet Union include all those capable of striking the continental United States (assuming no forward basing in locations outside the USSR, such as Cuba). The figures use weapons-carrying capacity as a measure of force size.

Figures A and C show forces in 1994 under an assumed START arms-control agreement consistent with the current US negotiating position. Figures B and D assume no arms-control restraints.

Forces in the graphs for 1994 are only illustrations of a few of very many possibilities. While the actual numbers of weapons could vary widely from those shown (especially in the 'no arms control' cases), the graphs probably depict accurately forces as a diversified mix of an increased variety of force types.

The figures break forces into the following major categories:

- Silo-based intercontinental ballistic missiles (silo ICBM).
- Submarine-launched ballistic missiles (SLBM).
- Bombers that will penetrate enemy defences to a point at or very near their target before delivering their weapons (P. bombers).
- Small, single-warhead ICBM based on mobile launchers (mobile ICBM).
- Ship- and submarine-launched cruise missiles (SLCM).
- Air-launched cruise missiles carried on bombers (ALCM).
- A variety of Western theatre nuclear forces (land- and sea-based tactical aircraft, British and French SLBM, *Pershing* and cruise INF missiles) that are capable of attacking targets in the Soviet Union (Western TNF).

All figures highlight portions of the forces that constitute the traditional strategic 'triad' of silo-based ICBM, SLBM and penetrating bombers. Upper portions illustrate those additional forces that could be considered 'strategic' in the sense of being capable of attacking the US or Soviet homeland.

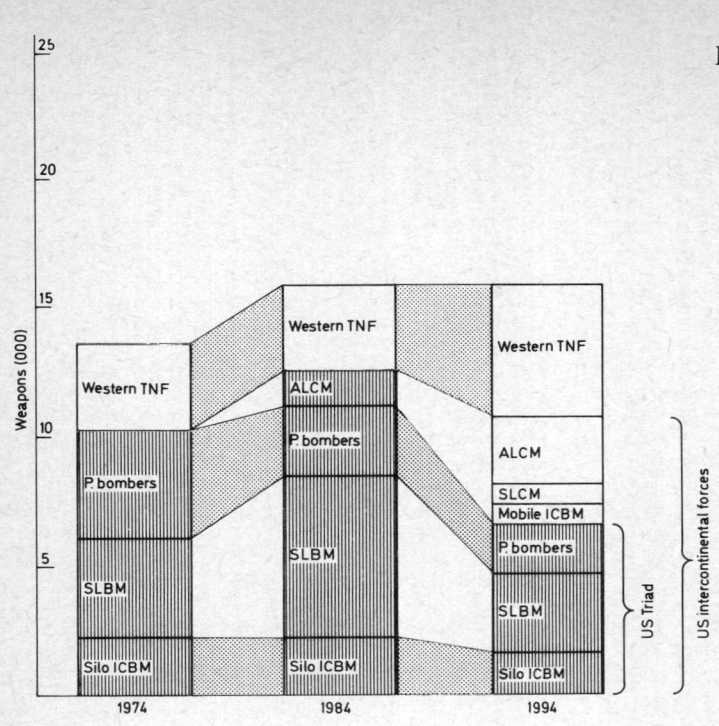

Figure A: Weapons deliverable on Soviet territory
(assuming US START build-down position in 1994)

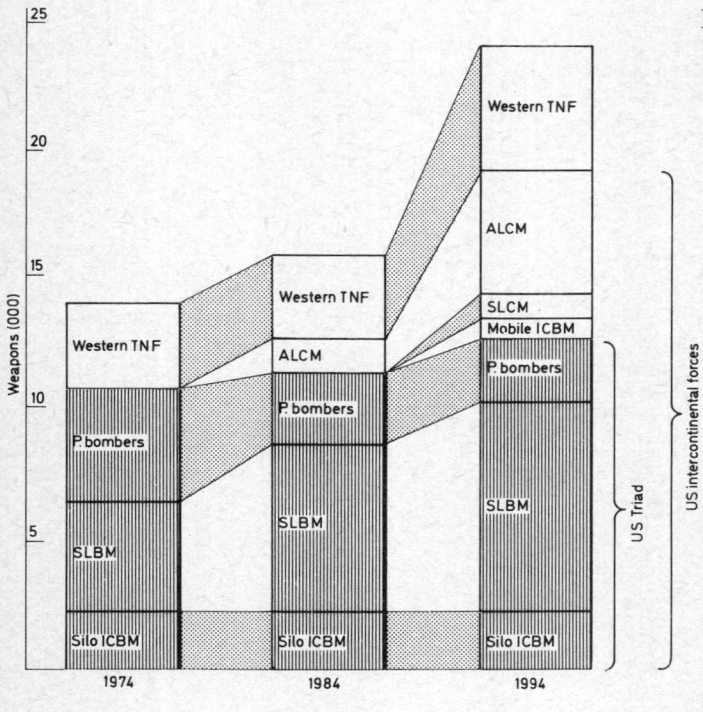

Figure B: Weapons deliverable on Soviet territory
(assuming no arms-control restraints in 1994)

35

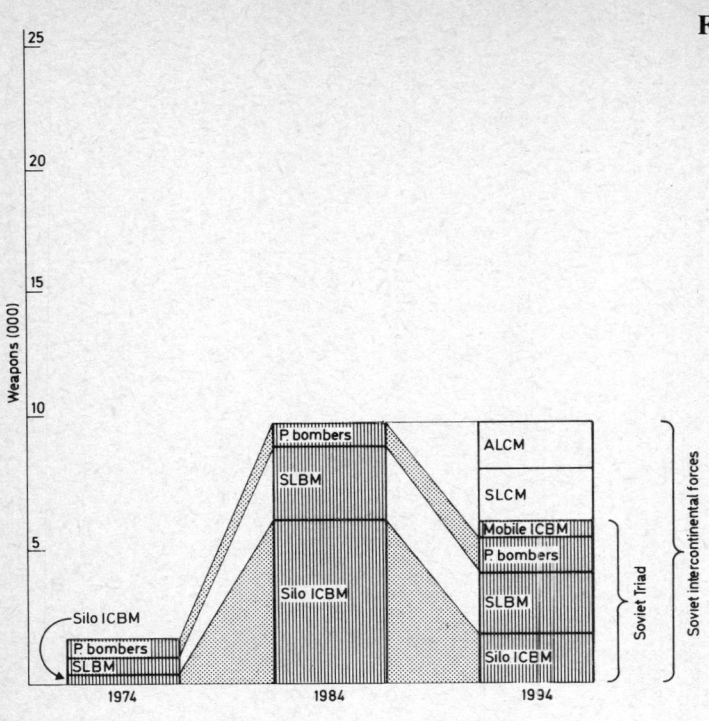

Figure C: Weapons deliverable on the continental US
(assuming no US START build-down position in 1994)

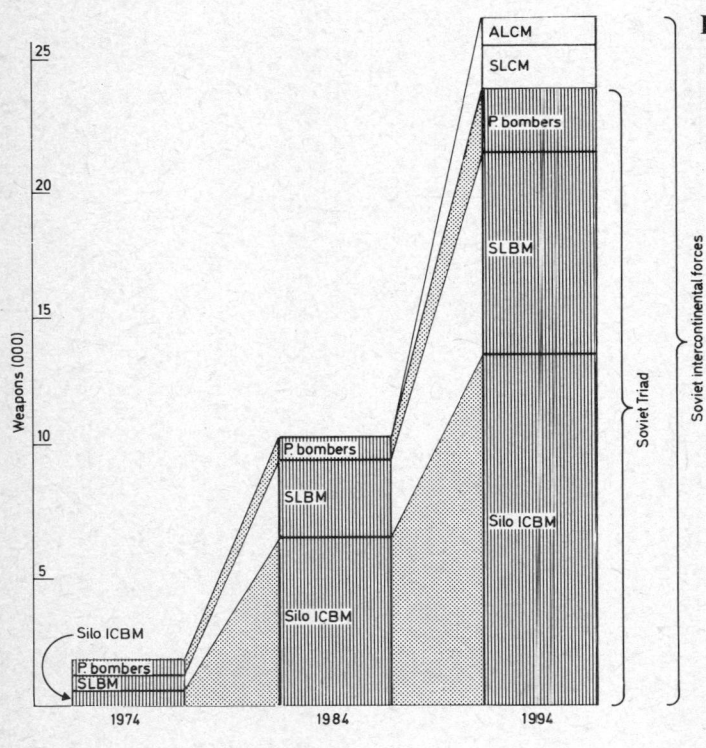

Figure D: Weapons deliverable on the continental US
(assuming no arms-control restraints in 1994)

Sources of Data: Figures A–D

Source	Data Category
Collins, John M., and Thomas Peter Glakas, *US Soviet Military Balance Statistical Trends, 1970–1981 (As of 1 January 1983)* (Washington DC: Congressional Research Service, October 1981, updated 1 August 1983.	All 1974 force data except as noted below. British, French, Western TNF 1984 force data extrapolated from 1983 data.
'Rationale for the 1979 NATO Decision to Deploy New Long Range Theatre Nuclear Forces' (Washington DC: US DoD, 1979).	British force data for 1974.
Finch, Louis C., *START Ballistic Missile Warhead Portion of the 'Build Down' Proposal* (Washington DC: Congressional Research Service, 17 January 1984).	US and Soviet ballistic missile forces in 1984 and 1994 under START.
An Analysis of Administration Strategic Arms Reduction and Modernization Proposals (Washington DC: Congressional Budget Office, March 1984).	US and Soviet bomber forces in 1984 and 1994.
Soviet Military Power 1984 (Washington DC: USGPO, April 1984).	US and INF forces in 1994.
The Military Balance 1983–1984 (London: IISS, 1983).	Extrapolation of data as of July 1983 for British, French and NATO forces for 1984.
Moran, Theodore H., and Peter A. Wilson 'A New Strategic Arms Agreement', *SAIS Review*, Winter/Spring 1984.	US and Soviet intercontinental forces in 1994 under no arms-control restraints.
Bowen, Alva M., *Navy Nuclear Armed Cruise Missiles* (Washington DC: Congressional Research Service, 9 May 1984).	US nuclear-armed SLCM in 1994.

Technological Development and Force Structure Within the Western Alliance: Prospects for Rationalization and the Division of Labour: Part I

DR INGEMAR DÖRFER

Emerging Technologies – The Initial Reaction

The new or emerging technologies (ET) useful for deep strikes behind the enemy lines include:

- Advanced non-nuclear submunitions.
- Accurate, long-range delivery by surface-to-surface missiles or by air-launched stand-off missiles.
- Information processing and distribution techniques.[1]

An impressive array of new weapons are being developed, produced and even introduced into NATO's forces. Submunitions include the German MW-1 and the French *Durandel* and BAP-100 dispensers. There is also the British JP-233 system and the *Stabo*, *Skeet*, KB-44 and MI-FF submunitions.

Of the delivery vehicles, the Vought Multi-Launch Rocket System (MLRS) is being bought by the United States, Britain, Germany and Italy, co-produced by companies in Europe.

Out of the US Army's *Assault Breaker* Programme and its successors have come the following surface-to-surface missiles: *Patriot* T-16, *Lance* T-22, *Pershing* II, CAM-40 *Trident Boss–Axe* Joint Tactical Missile System (JTACMS). New surveillance and target acquisition systems include the Joint Surveillance and Target Attack Radar System (JSTARS) (funded in FY 85 with $200 million in R&D) and Joint Tactical Fusion (JTF) (funded with over $100 million). A Joint Tactical Information Distribution System (JTIDS) is being incorporated into the airborne warning and control system (AWACS) and air defence sites. Satellite command, control and communications systems include *Milstar* and the *Navstar*/Global Positioning System (GPS). Information processing is enchanced by new technologies such as very high speed integrated ciruits (VHSIC), supercomputers and short-wavelength lasers.

Clearly in all these technologies, except that of unguided submunitions, the United States has the lead, hence many of the political and economic complications connected with ET.

Ever since Secretary Weinberger took the first ET Initiative at the meeting of NATO Defence Ministers in June 1982, the reaction of the Europeans has been pointedly cool. The British *Statement on the Defence Estimates 1983*, for example, spends most of its only page on 'New Technology, New Tactics' pointing to the problems and complications involved in introducing such technologies:

> 'Nevertheless, the ideas discussed in this essay might, if realised, lead to a major improvement in NATO's conventional capability. It will be important for the Alliance to study them closely and examine ways in which they can be turned into realistic and specific proposals.[2]

Whether by negligence or design the *German White Book* on Defence of October 1983 omits almost all discussion of ET.

The NATO machinery has meanwhile been set in motion. In November 1982, four areas were selected for study by the Committee of National Armaments Directors (CNAD). An American effort in December 1983 to select 30 weapon system programmes under development as 'ET programmes' was rejected by the Europeans. In April 1984 NATO accepted eleven areas for ET application. As a precondition, each had to be supported by at least four nations. The eleven areas are:[3]

1. New IFF (Identification Friend or Foe) systems.
2. Submunitions dispensers for fixed targets.
3. Electronic Support Mission (ESM) systems for the passive detection of enemy aircraft and vehicles.
4. MLRS with precision-guided submunitions (PGSM).
5. Automated 155mm precision-guided munitions (PGM).
6. Battlefield target acquisition system.
7. Electronic jamming system for tactical aircraft.
8. Short-range anti-radiation missiles.
9. Artillery locating systems.
10. Stand-off surveillance/acquisition systems.
11. Self-protection system for battlefield helicopters.

Strictly speaking these are hardly 'emerging' but are rather advanced technologies with a momentum of their own. As always in NATO, these systems are being developed by individual nations with national funding, whether they are specially designated by NATO or not. The CNAD selection is the outcome of a process of bargaining among NATO nations that has virtually no impact on the viability, usefulness or survival of the particular system developed. 'Rank does not intimidate hardware' proclaims Augustine's Law Number XXII.[4] The glorification of some of these systems as 'ET' will add to the NATO machinery but not to the defensive capability of the Alliance.

What then is the purpose of new military technologies? Already on this point there are different opinions within the Alliance. In the US Army, new technology will help the Army to strike up to 150 km behind enemy lines (as in AirLand Battle). SACEUR, Gen. Rogers, wants to deliver a Follow-On-Forces Attack (FOFA) on stationary military targets up to 300 km (and preferably 400 km)[5] beyond the forward edge of the battle area (FEBA). The US Director of Defense Research and Engineering (DDR&E) and the European Security Study (ESECS) group also believe that *mobile* targets can be successfully hit at this longer range.

The missions necessary for the forward defence of Western Europe can be summarized as:

– Counter-air;
– Interdiction;
– Attack on echeloned and mobile follow-on ground forces;
– Defeating massed armour in the zone of contact.[6]

It is clear that most Europeans want to hit the first echelon before they hit the second. West Germany in particular must be able to do that to uphold the principle of forward defence but most other countries have no wish to be over-run by the first echelon in any case.

Prior attention must be given to halting the massive momentum of the *first echelon*. If this means making less imaginative use of new technology which yet has to be deployed, they say, so be it. The first need is to stop the machine in its tracks, hopefully by every available *tactical* device available on the shelf now – particularly in short-range target acquisition, in concealment, and in night fighting – but also by an increase in the *quantity* of basic consumables proved necessary by the colossal rate of attrition in recent wars elsewhere.[7]

The greatest challenge to the strategic concept of deep strike is offered by analysts such as Steven Canby and David Greenwood.[8] If the Soviet Operational Manoeuvre Group (OMG), as explained by Christopher Donnelly,[9] is the main Warsaw Pact *modus operandi*, as they claim, the second strategic echelon is not especially important. To strike the first echelon remains important but, if the new Soviet mode of attack is probing and fluid, this is best done with robust systems demanding little by way of preprogrammed strikes or distant real-time target acquisition.

The Requirements of Doctrine

According to some calculations, the introduction of tactical nuclear weapons saved NATO 70 divisions and 7,000 combat aircraft during the 1950s, 1960s and 1970s. Can ET do the same for the 1990s?

Flexible Response, introduced as MC 14/3 in 1967, had been discussed for several years before its adoption. Half a generation has passed since then and the Soviet Union has attained nuclear parity and (some would say) achieved local conventional superiority.

Although the ability to respond flexibly is in doubt under the new circumstances, a nuclear doctrine designed to accommodate sixteen sovereign nations is a delicate thing and should not be tampered with. A good defence doctrine for the Alliance should meet the following criteria:

- Deterrence;
- Reassurance;
- Crisis stability;
- Detente;
- Uniformity;
- Service compatability.

Deterrence
ET is intended to reduce the risk of early nuclear escalation and thereby increase the credibility of keeping the war conventional. Here the Allies have to tread a fine line. If conventional war becomes too credible, a Soviet attack that risks nothing worse than conventional destruction in Western and Eastern Europe could seem to be worth the gamble. Yet anything which ends in stalemate would be likely to have tremendous political repercussions in Eastern Europe. ET should thus be designed to prevent a *quick* Soviet victory while avoiding NATO's first use of nuclear weapons. This would give back flexibility to Flexible Response. In the back of some European minds is the suspicion that America will use her traditional strength – technological superiority – to disengage from Europe. The American impulse to solve political problems through technology might lead to bringing the troops home while leaving the machines behind. To the Reagan Administration, Europe may not be that much more important than the rest of the world, where American presence also is needed.

In practice, of course, things are moving in precisely the opposite direction. Intermediate Nuclear Forces (INF) are being deployed while ET are still only on paper. Nuclear coupling is being assured as long as a moderate number of cruise missiles and *Pershing* IIs are deployed in Europe. On the other hand, too large INF combined with a substantial ET programme would tend to weaken coupling. Although the Germans have paid lip service to the concept of deep strike, they are quick to point out that it is not a new strategy.[10] The French interest in new technologies has logically been channelled in the direction of new European missiles. Given French strategy, it is only to be expected that France's future deep strike would be nuclear, to be executed by the *Hadès* system.

Reassurance
The European public is still somewhat preoccupied with INF and nuclear weapons generally. Even though the Peace Movement is on the wane everywhere, except perhaps in Holland, any new major deployment of weapon systems in West Germany will make it flare up again. Since the missiles carrying the new ET munitions can be dual-purpose, they will reassure Western publics no more than the Warsaw Pact. Any deep-strike strategy will be depicted as aggressive by many in Western Europe and will undoubtedly be accompanied by another propaganda offensive directed from the Soviet Union.

Another key group that has to be reassured is the West German government. A deep-strike strategy could seem to imply also defence in depth and the temporary abandonment at least of forward defence. The Warsaw Pact would be fighting 100 km further from its main airfields and supplies while NATO disrupts its second strategic echelon and infrastructure.[11] Although this may make much military sense, it makes no political sense to Bonn.

Crisis Stability
Some of the missiles that can be used for deep strikes are obviously more destabilizing

than others. This goes especially for conventionally-armed cruise missiles and *Pershing* II since it is very difficult to verify the nature of the warhead. So powerful now is the arms-control paradigm in Western thinking that such considerations are always at the forefront when new weapon decisions are taken. Yet a certain double standard prevails. Arms control has not been a consideration in the Soviet deployment of SS-20, -21 and -22 missiles. Even though self-restraint is in Western interest, the same should be demanded from the Warsaw Pact.

ET missiles can be destabilizing in other respects too. The tempo of ET warfare is likely to be so fast and violent that little time will be left for reflection.[12] The temptation to conduct pre-emptive strikes is increased and thus also the likelihood of nuclear escalation. The ability of longer-range ET weapons to hit command-and-control centres at a distance of 400 km also adds to the uncertainty.

Detente
Selective detente remains the policy of the Federal Republic of Germany and most other West European nations. The notion of striking hundreds of targets in Eastern Europe is not consistent with that spirit. Again it is easy to lose perspective. There will be no strike unless the Soviet armies move West. As Sir Ronald Mason has pointed out, the idea of being able to distinguish between offensive and defensive weapons systems (as the German and Danish Social Democrats now attempt to do) rapidly becomes meaningless.[13] The detente issue is also one of selectivity. Certainly, as one technological enthusiast has stated, all of Europe can be divided into kilometre squares. But the question is not 'is the square filled or empty?'[14] One should rather ask 'whose troops are in the square?' 'Whose troops or civilians fill adjoining squares?' One major Western political goal in any Warsaw Pact offensive is to discourage the East European troops, to separate them from the Soviet troops. Selective deep strikes against fixed targets and choke points could serve this purpose. Indiscriminate strikes would not. Since NATO's main strategic purpose is deterrence, not warfighting, a strategy of discrimination could have a discouraging effect on Eastern belligerency.

Uniformity
Like nuclear doctrine, a comprehensive doctrine for deep strike cannot be introduced piecemeal. Since C^3I resources will be dominated if not monopolized by US forces, and since the doctrines are so dependent on C^3I, routines for sharing and allocating target acquisition data will have to be established. The NATO air defence system based on NADGE and AWACS but with individual *Luftwaffe*, RAF and USAF air defence squadrons as well as national troops manning the missile belts could be used as a model. Since the new technologies will be introduced over a period of fifteen years there will be time to formulate a comprehensive plan, combined with the restructuring of other ground and air forces on the Central Front and elsewhere.

Ultimately it must be assumed that deep-strike forces will be under the command of every corps but if, in an intermediate stage, only the two American corps have such missile-based forces, interim arrangements will have to be made.

Service Compatability
It is DDR&E rather than the US services that has been interested in ET. The US Army has a large conventional acquisition programme underway and Tactical Air Command frowns upon programmes that do not involve pilots. In due time the services will have to reconcile the problem of an Army supporting system that is dependent on target acquisition handled by the Air Force. Also the Allied Air Forces in Europe have different philosophies. The German MW-1, designed for the *Tornado*, began development in 1969 and will be deployed in 1985. Like the RAF, the *Luftwaffe* plans to use runway penetration munitions carried over the target by manned aircraft. The USAF, disliking the idea of overflying airfield defences, cancelled the British JP 233 runway munition because it wants stand-off weapons only. While waiting for these stand-off systems and ballistic missiles, West German strategists, such as Gen. Schultze, are advocating more submunitions

for the aging combat aircraft of Western Europe.[15] Before NATO forces are wholly restructured, a mix of *Tornados* carrying new submunitions and American ballistic and cruise missiles carrying similar payloads will form the backbone of deep strike forces in Europe.

Budgets, Procurement and Priorities

Gen. Rogers, SACEUR, claims that the ET systems can be procured at a budget that increases 4% a year as compared to the present NATO goal of a 3% real increase per year. What does this mean?

In 1982 NATO Europe spent $102 bn on defence, according to a GAO study. The United States spent $107 bn on European defence.[16] If Gen. Rogers refers to the European members of NATO, he in fact calls for an additional $68 bn over ten years, this being the difference between a 3% and 4% real growth. This figure is some five times higher than those quoted by Cotter and Wikner:

Donald Cotter (in 1983): $ 9.4 bn
Fred Wikner (in 1984): $13 bn[17]

Assuming that a deep-strike capability will cost between $10 and $50 bn, how will that money be raised?

In 1984 only four of the European Allies reached the 3% goal in NATO, whereas the United States may be shown to have reached a figure of 9%.

ET will not save money by replacing nuclear weapons with cheaper systems. Since all NATO financial planning is only the sum of national planning, ET funding has to come out of the national defence budgets. Here the prospects are bleak. France and Britain are modernizing their nuclear forces at considerable cost. The planned re-equipment of the British Army and the *Force d'Action Rapide* will consume much of British and French defence budgets. The West German defence budget is already overcommitted to conventional weapons systems. Without a restructuring that would eliminate the need to acquire 200 combat aircraft, there is no space in the West German budget for ET. The smaller members of NATO have not taken much part in the ET debate. They are not in favour of deep strike. To most of their governments ET spells 'Extra Trouble'.

Thus while $0.5 bn is allocated to R&D for deep strike in the US FY 85 defence budget,[18] the European figures are much more modest. More characteristic is the joint $2 million American–British–German long-range stand-off missile project, funded only over an 18-month trial period.

The European military R&D budget is currently more than 50% of that of the US.[19] In the field of command, control and communications (C³) and electronic warfare, the European effort is substantial and here the Europeans can achieve results. A family of firms 'agrees to co-operate on the right weapons systems at the right time with the right expertise' to quote the Chairman of Fiat.[20] This philosophy is shared by Malcolm Currie in his report to NATO. It is not shared by European defence corporations if they fail to see an operational requirement for the end product. Indeed, the plethora of American corporate initiatives, with the bewildered Europeans being offered a *Stabo* in September, a *Skeet* in October, a *Boss* in November, makes one look for some order and a sense of priorities. The reasons for European scepticism are well known. The two-way street of American–European arms transfers is 7–1 or 3–1 in American favour depending on whose statistics you read. 'Europe will not buy ET systems from America'[21] says Richard De Lauer (DDR&E), without realizing that it might not buy ET systems from Europe either. Inherent in the reluctance to get on the American ET bandwagon is, of course, also the hardening American position on export controls over high technology and uncertainty concerning the final shape of the Export Administration Act. Despite assurances that ET components will *not* end up as items to be considered by COCOM, American reluctance to grant technology release has made potential European producers wary of too much dependence on overseas suppliers.

Even without a grand programme to enhance technology, particularly in the deep-strike form, the considerable military R&D resources of Western Europe could be better harnessed. The recent suggestion of the

North Atlantic Assembly to create an advanced European Research Agency, a European DARPA, merits attention. Such an agency would then complement rather than duplicate the American DARPA programme and would concentrate on programmes such as electronic warfare and tactical target acquisition that have specifically European applications.

Above all there is a need for realism and priorities when it comes to ET. Cost estimates are surely too low. Technological optimism is also rampant when it comes to schedules. As noted already, the German MW-1 submunition, conceived in 1969, will become operational *only in 1985*. The *Assault Breaker* programme itself was delayed between 1978 and 1981. ET systems could become operational in due time if funded, but certainly not by 1990.

Solutions
After this rather gloomy survey of the problems and complications created by ET in NATO planning, one must ask what is to be done. The most urgent task for NATO is now to create a viable conventional defence (based on Flexible Response) on the Central Front in Europe. Three complementary methods are suggested.

— Use ET selectively;
— Increase efficiency through marginal reforms;
— Improve the division of labour through restructuring.

Selective Emerging Technologies
Obviously the capability of the West is improved by rapid advances in information processing and distribution techniques. The risks of putting all the eggs in one electronic basket should be clear to NATO planners but a great deal can be done to improve NATO's ability to handle information despite Soviet counter-measures and to deny information to the Warsaw Pact.

Of the deep-strike technologies under consideration, it seems sensible to target the 44 Warsaw Pact Main Operating Bases[22] (MOB) that are located within 300 km of the Inner-German border. The lethality of Pact air defence systems makes it prudent to withhold manned aircraft for other missions, such as striking the Dispersed Operating Bases (DOB) after they have recovered Pact combat aircraft. Also choke points, such as bridges, are sensible targets for conventional missiles. Bearing in mind political and psychological ramifications, clever targeting could achieve remarkable results in disrupting the enemy's westward march.

A deep-strike strategy not dependent on highly sophisticated target acquisition systems or real-time communications could release many Western combat aircraft to close air support and air defence.

Marginal Reforms
Marginal reforms can act as force multipliers and not least in the field of air defence. Although the US is able to deploy 1,500 additional combat aircraft to Europe in wartime, only 300 will be properly sheltered and serviced under current conditions. The improvement of air bases and their protection is one of the marginal reforms suggested by Robert Komer in a $13 bn package.[23] Other such improvements suggested by Komer are: enough war reserves to sustain at least 30 days of fighting; an improved infrastructure; defensive barriers; and larger infantry reserves.

Restructuring
But Komer does not go far enough. Why settle for 12–25 additional infantry reserve brigades when many more could be created?

It is important to point out that we are speaking here of *reserve* forces, created out of the pool of European men who already have done their military service and have been returned to civilian life. The best system in current use is the Dutch RIM system. Therefore West German statements of a shortfall of 100,000 men in the future *Bundeswehr* miss the point when it comes to these reserve units.

Even though the direct personnel costs are thus kept to a minimum, costs for additional equipment will have to be met. As explained, the tight defence budgets of Western European nations will allow for little or no real increases in expenditure. Thus the additional costs for Army units have to be met through restructuring. The process of restructuring is facilitated both by the marginal reforms suggested by Komer and by the deployment of some, but by no means all, of the ET systems under investigation.

An obvious target for reform might be some of the smaller navies of Western Europe. Two-thirds of the German, Danish, Dutch and Belgian naval budgets go towards destroyers or frigates and naval air force. Between them these navies have 57 destroyers and frigates performing functions that could be performed equally well by the US Navy and the Royal Navy. Yet a closer look makes it clear that the effort is hardly worth the price. The annual savings achieved by abolishing these functions are about $4 bn, not much compared to the total European NATO budget of about $100 bn. The Belgian Navy is so small that the cost savings would be marginal. The Dutch Navy is one of the finest in the world and to abolish most of it would not be very cost-effective, not to mention the emotional and moral trauma involved. The German and Danish surface navies, in addition to their wartime tasks, play an important political role in showing the flag in the Baltic. So too does the German naval air force. Since the four *Marine fliegergeschwader* are in the process of receiving their *Tornados*, any restructuring of this force will in any case take 20 years or more.

Restructuring the European air forces may be more promising.[24] Belgium, Denmark, the Netherlands and Norway are now receiving (or have received) 348 F-16 fighters and have ordered more. West Germany needs some 200 new combat aircraft beginning in 1990. At the same time only 1,500 (out of a total of 5,500 American combat aircraft available) deploy to Europe in war to enhance the peacetime force of 850 US combat aircraft in Europe and the Mediterranean. Instead of procuring 450 new aircraft at a cost of $15 bn, Belgium, Denmark, Holland and Germany could allocate the money to Army equipment. The USAF could deploy six more wings (432 aircraft) to Europe in peacetime to replace the air resources of these four West European nations. It will cost no more to operate these air wings in Europe than in the US. The process can be achieved through the natural phasing out of obsolete fighters; substantial national fighter forces would remain in all four nations after the change. The experience of the USAF fighter squadron at Soesterberg (in Holland) shows that the concept works well. Since the number of fighters in Western Europe would be the same after the switch and since some deep-strike systems would in any case release air resources to air defence, the overall air/counter-air situation will look better.

In the course of such a restructuring – the transition of six European air wings to American wings – many of the lessons learnt in connection with the West German–American *Patriot-Roland* and the British–American *Rapier* deals can be implemented, to save money and allocate Allied resources more rationally. Leasing, operating and maintenance of joint weapon systems belong to such reforms.

However, the real gains would come from the additional combat forces created out of Army reserve manpower. Using the air force savings, the European nations could create an additional twelve West German, three Dutch, and two Belgian divisions for the Central Front. The Canadian Battle Group currently in an unsound location, should be moved and augmented to assist in the defence of Schleswig-Holstein. With additional West German, Dutch and Belgian brigades in forward positions, a Pact surprise attack would be less attractive and the arrival of combat divisions from the United States in time would begin to seem much more credible. Clearly all this will cost money. Canada should provide more than the 'modest strengthening of conventional forces'[25] advocated by Harold Brown. The other nations should use the resources released by their air forces, reduced under this scheme by 50%.

Conclusion

New technology as such is not necessary for restructuring NATO. But its introduction in modest doses, as advocated here, will open the Alliance to new forms of co-operation, of role specialization and of reallocation of resources that can be beneficial. In the meantime a combination of American political insensitivity, European technological timidity, American impatience and European indecisiveness can lead to a situation that certainly will not be saved by technological fixes, emerging or not.

NOTES

[1] Donald R. Cotter: 'Potential Future Roles for Conventional and Nuclear Forces in Defense of Western Europe' in *Strengthening Conventional Deterrence in Europe: Proposals for the 1980s*. Report of the European Security Study (ESECS) (London: The Macmillan Press, 1983), p. 219.

[2] *Statement on the Defence Estimates 1983* (London: HMSO, 1983), p. 24.

[3] *Aviation Week & Space Technology*, 16 April 1984, p. 28.

[4] Norman R. Augustine: *Augustine's Laws* (New York: American Institute of Aeronautics and Astronautics, 1984), p. 126.

[5] *Aviation Week & Space Technology*, 21 May 1984, p. 57.

[6] Cotter, *op cit.* in note 1, p. 220.

[7] *Diminishing the Nuclear Threat. Nato's Defence and New Technology* (London: The British Atlantic Committee, 1984), p. 34–5.

[8] Steven L. Canby: *The Operational Limits of Emerging Technologies* (Washington DC: The Wilson Center, 1984). David Greenwood: 'New Defence Possibilities and Their Affordability' in *Defence Papers. A Transatlantic Debate over Emerging Technologies and Defence Capabilities* (London: The Economist Intelligence Unit, Special Report No. 172, 1984).

[9] Christopher N. Donnelly: 'Soviet Operational Concepts in the 1980s' in *Strengthening Conventional Deterrence in Europe, op cit.* in note 1.

[10] Defence Minister Manfred Wörner in *Armed Forces Journal International*, December 1982, p. 73. Also 'German Defence Minister says "No"' in *International Defence Review*, November 1983, p. 1,556.

[11] *Op cit.* in note 7, p. 365.

[12] Johan J. Holst, *Some Reflections on Alliance Strategy and the Problem of Command, Control and Communications (C³)*. (Oslo: Nupinotat nr 284(B), October 1983), p. 15–17.

[13] Sir Ronald Mason: 'Emerging Technology in Defence: Real Gain or False Economy?', RUSI, June 1984.

[14] Fred Wikner: 'Soviet Military Strategy and the Role of Modern Conventional Forces' in *Defence Papers, op cit.* in note 8, p. 19.

[15] Franz Joseph Schultze: 'Rethinking Continental Defense', *The Washington Quarterly*, Spring 1984.

[16] Quoted by Richard Halloran in *International Herald Tribune*, 21 July 1984, p. 1.

[17] Cotter, *op cit.* in note 1, p. 252; Wikner, *op cit.* in note 8, p. 21.

[18] Caspar W. Weinberger, US Secretary of Defense, *Annual Report to The Congress FY 1985* (Washington DC: USGPO 1984), p. 128.

[19] Vitalij Garber: 'A New Defence' in *NATO's Fifteen Nations*, Special 1/1982, p. 66.

[20] Giovanni Agnelli: *More Effective Defence Investments*, Shapex 83, Mons, 1983.

[21] Richard DeLauer: 'The American Programme' in *Defence Papers, op cit.* in note 8

[22] *Armed Forces Journal International*, November 1982, p. 55.

[23] Robert W. Komer: 'A Credible Conventional Option: Can NATO Afford It?' *Strategic Review*, Spring 1984, and *Maritime Strategy or Coalition Defense?* (Cambridge, Mass.: Abt Books, 1984), Chaps 8 and 9.

[24] See Steven Canby and Ingemar Dörfer: 'More Troops, Fewer Missiles', *Foreign Policy*, Winter 1983–84.

[25] Harold Brown: *Thinking About National Security*, (Boulder, Colo., Westview Press, 1983), p. 107.

Technological Development and Force Structure Within the Western Alliance: Prospects for Rationalization and the Division of Labour: Part II

JOHN ROPER

The relationship between military doctrine, resources and technological development and their implications for defence procurement and for structure are complex enough within any single nation. Within an Alliance of sixteen nations, in all of which factors of geography, industrial capabilities and budgetary pressures operate in different ways, the potential of new technology to assist in improving deterrence and defence is parallelled by its potential to create and aggravate intra-Alliance tensions.

Over the last two years there has been a growing, if not always harmonious[1], chorus of voices arguing for an increased emphasis on non-nuclear defence within NATO. The theme is by no means new, nor are the suggestions that new technology could facilitate non-nuclear defence. Ten years ago in 1974, Dr Malcolm Currie, then Director of Defense Research and Engineering (DDR&E) in the US Department of Defense, testified to Congress that 'a remarkable series of technological developments have brought us to the threshold of what will become a true revolution in conventional warfare'.[2] In the years immediately following, many of the issues we are now discussing were fully considered both in the IISS and elsewhere.[3] This discussion was overlain in the remainder of the 1970s by the debate over NATO's LRTNF modernization but it has now come back to centre stage for four reasons. These have been: first, the public debate in Europe on the relative roles of nuclear and conventional forces following the 'dual-track' decision of December 1979 and the initial deployment of cruise and *Pershing* II missiles in Europe in 1983; second, the further development of new technology and its relevance to defence and deterrence in Europe, as indicated by Gen. Rogers' introduction of Follow-on-Forces Attack (FOFA) on 1982,[4] Secretary Weinberger's Emerging Technology (ET) initiative at the Bonn NATO Summit in June 1982 and in the technical papers submitted to the European Security Study (ESECS);[5] third, the doctrinal debate in the US Armed Forces resulting in the publication of the US Army's 1982 field manual (FM 100-5) introducing the ideas associated with 'AirLand Battle'[6]; and fourth, increased awareness of the growing superiority of Warsaw Pact forces on the Central Front.[7]

In considering technological development, NATO is not primarily considering incremental improvements in technology which have, of course, occurred regularly and will continue to occur in virtually all of the roles and missions of the armed forces of the members of the Alliance but which, in the light of developments of Warsaw Pact technology, no longer permit NATO forces to retain the qualitative edge to compensate for their quantitative deficiencies. Rather, what has gained attention is the application of fundamentally new (and largely untried) technology to achieve conventional unmanned deep attacks on both fixed and mobile targets, together with more effective conventional battlefield firepower and in general an enhancement of C^3I and counter-C^3I capabilities. Much of the new technology available for these functions 'greatly enhances the stability of the defences against mechanized assault', most of it being 'oriented to anti-manoeuvre firepower'.[8]

Doctrinal Implications
In examining the impact of new technologies on the Alliance, one must examine their doc-

trinal implications and in particular their effect on the existing consensus and compromise on Flexible Response and forward defence. Some of the arguments for the introduction of new technology and more effective conventional defence have been based on perceived inadequacies in existing doctrine.[9] Others have argued that it is precisely by restoring effective conventional options that the doctrine of Flexible Response will regain credibility. Problems over doctrine within the Alliance will arise if new technology is seen as a method of substantially modifying Flexible Response. As Josef Joffe has argued,[10] although certain Europeans might be reassured by a move to a declared 'no first use' policy which enhanced conventional capacities might make possible, others would see this raising of the nuclear threshold as a significant reduction of effective deterrence which they would find anything but reassuring.

There has always been an ambiguity in different interpretations of Flexible Response and, since its adoption, European concern about the delicate relationship between deterrence and defence. Europeans have always wanted nuclear weapons to be as prominent as possible in their role as deterrents and as distant as possible if deterrence fails and war occurs. In the early 1960s, 'McNamara's efforts to enhance NATO's conventional forces, however, found little support in Europe. Opposition was based at least in part, on the premise that a strong conventional defence posture would imply a lack of confidence in nuclear deterrence, and effectively open the way to a "decoupling" of the US strategic forces from the defence of Western Europe'.[11] In the 1980s West German officials have made it clear that conventionalization must not lead to the loss of any nuclear options.

One aspect of the compromise is that, while in the United States Flexible Response is often seen as a set of vertical options, the rungs in a rigid ladder of escalation which are followed sequentially, in Europe it is more frequently seen as a lateral set of options which can be tailored to respond at an appropriate level to any attack made by an opponent. The analogy might be closer to a hand of cards available to NATO's political and military leadership from which they can select appropriate options to deal with enemy attacks. Strengthening conventional options by means of new technology would mean that there would in more cases be non-nuclear options that could be employed. This would have the desirable effect, *inter alia*, of strengthening intra-war deterrence. What worries Europeans and could cause stress in the Alliance is the suggestion that conventional cards could in some way be substituted for nuclear ones as that would be seen as an overall weakening of deterrence.

European ambivalence to any change in NATO's force structure, nuclear or conventional, which might have the effect of strengthening our defences is one aspect of a general ambivalence to which Robert Jervis has recently referred: 'Statesmen are torn between supporting deterrence by underlining the threat that what the other side values be destroyed if major war breaks out and the desire to minimize damage if conflict actually erupts'.[12] In other words Europeans have been divided between welcoming military developments which can be shown to make overall deterrence more credible, and resisting them on the grounds that, if deterrence failed, they would be more likely to suffer. In the context of the current debates, these old dilemmas reappear and although some may argue that new technologies 'will help NATO to implement more successfully the old strategies',[13] they are equally likely to reopen the debate on the ambiguities in those old strategic doctrines.

Apart from the fear that increasing theatre credibility, whether conventional or nuclear, will lead to some form of decoupling from US central strategic systems, the other aspect of NATO doctrine that appears to be at risk from new technology and the new doctrine that accompanies it is forward defence. It has also been seen by many in the United States as a compromise, accepted for the sake of understandable West German concerns but not as providing the basis for a credible conventional defence and therefore, in spite of our acceptance of Flexible Response, providing little more than the traditional 'tripwire' for an early use of nuclear weapons. Some interpretations of recent American operational doctrine have suggested that AirLand Battle, with its greater stress on manoeuverability, will involve military activities on both sides of the Inner-German border. They are likely to be opposed in Europe and particularly in Germany by a wide spectrum of opinion.[14]

On the other hand, Philip Karber[15] has argued that none of the concepts involved in AirLand Battle, FOFA or Deep Attack 'offers an alternative to a forward defence strategy'. They all have in common 'an attempt to gain operational *depth* for the theatre by carrying the air-war across the inter-Bloc border, a rationale that makes sense only as a complement to forward defence and an implicit dependence on forward defence for their success'. This may not necessarily reassure European public opinion for, while NATO has always had plans for air-interdiction, the increased stress on this will appear to conflict with NATO's claim to be a defensive Alliance and there is no doubt that, in spite of the Warsaw Pact's own offensive force posture, the Soviet Union will attempt to make the most of the concerns of Western public opinion about a strategy that is increasingly seen to be based on air and missile attacks on East Germany or elsewhere in Eastern Europe. The political unacceptability of this can be seen by Joffe's remark 'with the Federal Reublic in the vanguard, the West Europeans will fight tooth and nail against a doctrine that would seek to deter the Soviets by threatening the East Europeans and hence the very ethos of *Ostpolitik* and detente'.[16] Military logic may thus argue for defence in greater depth or operations across the inter-Bloc border but politically both would imply heavy costs, particularly in Western Germany: defence in depth because it would put at risk such a large proportion of the area of the *Federal Republic*; a more active forward defence because it would appear unacceptably aggressive.

Some have argued for increased emphasis on conventional defence in the interest of reassuring Western publics[17] but the particular proposals outlined earlier do not appear to be the best ways of doing this. They would present a further opportunity for intra-Alliance tension to arise in that, while they might have a reassuring effect in European countries at some distance from the inter-Bloc boundary (including the United Kingdom), they could have the opposite effect in West Germany. Further intra-Alliance tension could be created if the development of new conventional technologies were perceived in Western Europe as destabilizing East–West relations. The proposals have already been described by the USSR as providing the basis for a new arms race, although the proposed conventional versions of the Soviet SS-21, SS-22 and SS-23 shorter-range ballistic missiles will provide the WTO, possibly before NATO, with many of the capabilities which are here discussed. Conventionalization may thus reopen the tensions within the Alliance between the advocates of dialogue or defence as our first priority.

New Technology and Resource Constraints
Irrespective of their effects on doctrine, new technologies are also argued for as a method of helping to solve NATO's problems of limited resources. At the simplest level the increased lethality and accuracy of 'smart' weapons are cited as indicating the scope for economy. In spite of the increased cost per round, their increased effectiveness is believed to lead to economies. Two recent studies of the costs of strengthening NATO's conventional forces have produced different assessments. Donald Cotter's figure of 'a *minimum* ten year cost of less than $10 billion'[18] included an assumption that 900 CAM-40 missiles based on the *Pershing* II could be acquired for $2 million each (for a total of $1.8 bn). The ESECS steering group were wise enough to double the sum and suggested a figure of '$20 billion (with a possible variation of 50% higher or lower)'.[19] This is equated with an increase of from 3%–4% in annual real rate of growth in defence spending, a figure which has also been quoted by Gen. Rogers[20] although, as Karsten Voigt points out, 'the 4% real increase in defence expenditure requested by Gen. Rogers refers to fulfilment of the NATO force goals for 1983–8; it does not include new technologies for Deep Attack'.[21] An

earlier analysis by Seymour Deitchman[22] suggested that a higher figures would be needed to achieve a credible deterrent in Western Europe. It took into account only to a limited extent the possibility and costs of Deep Attack.[23]

In fact, instead of increasing the 3% target to 4% as suggested by Gen. Rogers, NATO Ministers have decided that there is little value in setting unattainable goals and may well not continue the 3% target beyond 1986. New conventional technology will therefore have to compete for a share of a defence budget which in real terms will be virtually static in much of Western Europe and which will be growing much less fast in the United States. US Treasury Secretary, Donald Regan, is now expecting that yearly increases in 'defence spending authority are likely to average 3% to 4% after adjustment for inflation'. Others are anticipating zero real growth of defence spending in the United States by the end of the decade.[24]

In these circumstances there will be high opportunity costs for any new projects, particularly as new conventional technologies are unlikely to bring any significant savings on nuclear progammes, are largely directed to the Central Front and are unlikely to have immediate benefits for either the flanks or maritime activities of the Alliance. They will therefore be competing with funds urgently needed to improve readiness and sustainability within the existing conventional forces of the Alliance and, in the absence of significant progress in increased conventional effectiveness, for funds to maintain and modernize the Alliance's battlefield nuclear capabilities. This can be clearly seen from the debate in the US Senate in July 1983 on Senator Nunn's amendment to transfer $50 million from the funding of a new nuclear shell for 155mm artillery to the provision of new improved conventional munitions.[25] Sen. Nunn, in arguing for this relatively small change, made much of the fact that in the Senate debates in the first half of 1983, $413 million had been cut from a range of projects contributing to new conventional technology without any complaint from the Department of Defense. 'Deep strike has been defeated by bureaucratic squabbling between OSD [the Office of the Secretary of Defense] and the services and among the services themselves . . . In constrained budgetary environments the services have traditionally placed a higher emphasis on procurement of ships, tanks and other weapons platforms than on munitions themselves.'[26] Sen. Nunn subsequently pointed out the circularity of the present situation: 'We cannot get the conventional forces that we need because we are spending so much on nuclear forces. Because we cannot get the conventional forces we need, the generals and the admirals rely more and more on nuclear forces and early use of nuclear weapons'.[27] If in the United States, at a time when defence expenditure was growing so rapidly, it was difficult to get adequate funding for new conventional technologies, and if 'service parochialism' backs existing systems rather than a new approach, then the prospects for them in a harsher budgetary climate looks rather slim unless Presidential authority gives them an overwhelming priority.

Even if Defence Ministers were prepared to face up to the opportunity that new technological solutions provide to make radical changes in force structures (for instance by not proceeding with a policy of replacement of 'like with like' in the case of manned aircraft), it would still be some considerable time before any resources would be freed for expenditure on new technology. A strong case would be made for the retention and replacement of traditional conventional systems for use outside the Central Front. Missile-oriented systems have much less flexibility in use than many of the existing manned aircraft. While there would be little savings on other systems, the introduction of new systems would bring the inevitable 'bow wave of training maintenance and logistic support'[28] associated with any new equipment and at a higher cost than that which it has replaced. There seems to be no evidence that, in the medium term at least, the proposals for new technology will in any way ease budgetary pressures. If anything, by making budgetary pressures tighter they may preclude other things being done which might be more cost-effective. Unless the publics and Parliaments of Western countries can be persuaded of the relative cost-effectiveness of this expenditure, they are unlikely to support the extra resources required, or support a transfer from existing programmes, all of which have strong service and industrial lobbies behind them.

New Technology, Rationalization and Division of Labour

It has been suggested that, in spite of the doctrinal problems outlined above, and because of the budgetary restraints, the move to a new generation of weapons systems and new military concepts would increase opportunities for rationalization and the division of labour within NATO. Walther Stützle, discussing the question in 1977, suggested that as 'the military implications of new weapons technology . . . tend to favour a force structure that is mission-oriented . . . One consequence could be that under the concept of integrated forward defence in the Alliance the present system of defence areas being allocated to specific national forces would be replaced by an allocation on a mission-orientated basis . . . it would not be possible for every ally to participate in every mission'.[29] Sen. Nunn went further. In a lecture in 1983 he argued that 'to implement properly the new Army-Air Force doctrine of AirLand Battle, our forces must emphasize manoeuvrability and flexibility, lighter reinforcements, special operations forces, communications and second echelon attack. The Allies, however, must increasingly provide the basic ingredients for Europe's initial forward defence, including heavy ground forces, more effective utilization of their vast pool of trained reserves, and the possible employment of barrier defences. In short, if US forces in Europe are to assume the primary responsibility for disrupting and destroying Soviet second echelon forces, European units must assume the primary responsibility for holding the first echelon in check'.[30] Sen. Nunn's rather radical views on a division of labour have not received particularly wide circulation nor do they have any public backing from the Department of Defense. They would require very substantial changes in Europe and would presumably be opposed by the European Allies, who have always stressed the political importance of the presence of US troops amongst those providing forward defence. If it were put forward as a concomitant of the introduction of new technology, it would probably provoke substantial resistance. On the other hand, some of the sensors and surveillance capabilities associated with Deep Attack technologies are such that they would have to be common to the whole of the Central Front rather than operated on a national basis. They and the data fusion system that would process the information on a real-time basis prior to disseminating it could perhaps be funded on a basis comparable to the AWACS aircraft.

In another way there will be an inevitable division of labour arising from the growing asymmetry in equipment between the various corps on the Central Front. A recent estimate has suggested that 'throughout the 1980s there will be a growing gap between NATO armies in their respective levels of technology; indeed, across the Central Front some national corps will be as much as two generations behind their adjacent Allied units'.[31] This will inevitably lead to some *de facto* division of labour. It also suggests that in some ways new technology may prove to be the opposite of a force multiplier.

New technology can in some instances be incorporated in new equipment capable of being operated and maintained at lower levels of skill than is required by the present generation of equipment. That does not, however, always occur and, if higher skill levels are generally associated with new technology, this must be recognized as presenting particular problems for those armed forces largely manned by conscripts who inevitably cannot reach the same training levels as those serving for longer periods. These differentials in national equipment and possibly in skill levels suggest that, in spite of improvements across the Central Front in C³I, the progress to rationalization, standardization and interoperability (RSI) will be a slow and painful process.

It is likely that in a limited number of specific projects – namely the eleven endorsed by the Conference of National Armament Directors (CNAD) in the spring of 1984 (see Paper by Ingemar Dörfer) – there will be an opportunity for Alliance collaboration. While at first sight these projects would appear to have some chance of ensuring a more satisfactory 'two-way street' in arms trade across the Atlantic, there are already signs that most of the traffic will continue to flow one way, although there is considerable variation in the degree of imbalance among the European Countries. Richard De Lauer's (DDR&E) recent call on America's European allies 'to organize their [defence] industries and their markets on a scale more comparable to the US, otherwise the structure for co-operation can be neither efficient nor viable', is understandable and finds an echo from many Europeans, who would also agree with his statement that 'co-operation is perhaps only realistic between two relatively equivalent partners'.[32] The present reality is, of course, very different. The United States has a defence market 50% larger than that of all her Western industrial allies put together. It is a market twice as large as that of France, West Germany and Britain who together make up three-quarters of production in Western Europe. The United States spends more than twice as much on defence R&D as all of her allies.[33] There is therefore a significant variation in scale even if the Europeans were able to translate the discussion of the IEPG into effective defence industrial co-operation. In fact, the problem is much more difficult because, in addition to different technical competences among different European defence industries, there is also a significant range of missions undertaken by different European members of the Alliance who therefore have quite different requirements. Some European members of the Alliance maintain capabilities to operate out of the NATO area, on the flanks and on the Central Front. The majority, however, are only concerned with either the Central Front or one of the flanks. European co-operation in defence procurement, which is seen as a prerequisite for effective *Alliance* co-operation in procurement, is therefore much easier to talk about than to achieve.

While the response to the Weinberger ET initiative prepared by the IEPG in the spring of 1984 was an important step forward (in that it included a European conceptual analysis for the potential of new technology as well as a detailed list of all projects under consideration by the European members of the Alliance which involve the application of new technologies), it is a long way from the common decision-making and perhaps eventually common funding within Europe which is probably necessary if Europe is to become something remotely approaching a 'relatively equivalent partner of the United States'. It is virtually inconceivable that this can be achieved in time to be relevant for the present consideration of new technology. In the meantime the variations between European countries as to industrial competences as well as defence requirements, which in many ways is greater than that between Western Europe as a whole and the United States, is going to make equitable collaboration across the Atlantic very difficult.

Conclusion
There are no doubt some things that can usefully be done with new technologies but there is also, as has been indicated, no magic solution for the Alliance's internal strain arising from them. Secretary Weinberger, in his January 1984 report to Congress on Standardization of Equipment in NATO, claimed that 'Technology is revolutionizing the conventional battlefield and offers the Alliance the high ground of increased performance and efficiency for marginal increases in development or production costs. We can use our technology to enhance affordability, cost-effectiveness, interoperability, maintainability and reliability'.[34] This contrasts with the more cautious approach of Geoffrey Pattie, then British Minister of State for Defence Procurement, who represented a widespread European view when he argued in February that emergent technology, 'is *not* a strategy, real or surrogate. At best the emerging technologies will enable us selectively to convert what is technologically feasible into what is operationally cost-efficient and relevant. At worst, the emerging technologies can become costly potential capabilities looking for work to do . . . I believe there are very real constraints on the extent to which, and the rapidity with which, ET can be exploited for defence purposes'.[35]

In coming to its decisions on which items of the new technologies should be incorporated into new defence projects, the governments of the Alliance must develop more effective mechanisms for assessing the claims of those who argue for new technologies. With limited resources and a growing threat, the case for rationality in decision-making in defence procurement is greater than ever. If Europeans override their reservations about the value of these proposals in the interests of assisting current arguments over burden-sharing, they may find that – not for the first time – they have been sowing dragon's teeth.

NOTES

[1] The range and diversity of those supporting conventional defence is discussed in Josef Joffe 'Stability and its Discontent: Should NATO Go Conventional?' to appear in *Washington Quarterly*, (Fall 1984), vol. VII, no. 3.

[2] Malcolm R. Currie, *Statement to the House Appropriations Committee, Department of Defense Appropriations for 1975* (Washington DC: USGPO, 1974), Part 4, p. 450.

[3] See Richard Burt, *New Weapons Technologies: Debate and Directions*, Adelphi Paper no. 126 (London: IISS, 1976); Johan J. Holst and Uwe Nerlich (eds), *Beyond Nuclear Deterrence: New Aims, New Arms* (New York: Crane Russak, 1977); *New Conventional Weapons and East–West Security*, Adelphi Papers nos 144 and 145 (London: IISS, 1978); and Sen. Sam Nunn and Sen. Dewey F. Bartlett, *NATO and the New Soviet Threat, Report to Senate Armed Services Committee, Jan 24th 1977* (Washington DC: USGPO, 1977), p. 20.

[4] Gen. Bernard W. Rogers, 'The Atlantic Alliance: Prescriptions for a Difficult Decade', *Foreign Affairs*, (Summer 1982), vol. 60, no. 5, pp. 1152–3.

[5] *Strengthening Conventional Deterrence in Europe: Proposals for the 1980s* (London: The Macmillan Press, 1983), pp. 209–53 (hereafter ESECS).

[6] US Army Dept. Operations, *Field Manual* (FM) 100-5 (Washington DC: 1982).

[7] See Philip A. Karber, 'To Lose an Arms Race' in Uwe Nerlich (ed.), *Soviet Power and Western Negotiating Policies*, vol. I (Cambridge, Mass: Ballinger, 1983).

[8] Philip A. Karber, 'In Defense of Forward Defense', *Armed Forces Journal International*, May 1984, p. 47.

[9] 'The doctrine of "Flexible Response" needs to be replaced. The new technology offers the opportunity to do so'. Marshal of the Royal Air Force Lord Cameron in the Foreword to *Diminishing the Nuclear Threat: NATO's Defence and New Technology* (London: British Atlantic Committee, 1984).

[10] Josef Joffe, *op. cit.* in note 1.

[11] Karsten Voigt, *Draft Interim Report of the Sub Committee on Conventional Defence in Europe, North Atlantic Assembly* (Brussels: May 1984).

[12] Robert Jervis, *The Illogic of American Nuclear Strategy* (Ithaca, NY: Cornell UP, 1984), p. 48.

[13] Christoph Bertram in Adelphi Paper no. 144, *op. cit.* in note 3.

[14] Josef Joffe, *op. cit.* in note 1.

[15] Philip A. Karber, *op. cit.* in note 8, p. 46.

[16] Josef Joffe *op. cit.* in note 1. Interestingly, the reverse side of this argument is seen on the relatively mild protests in Eastern Europe about NATO's LRTNF deployment which is seen as threatening the Soviet Union rather than Eastern Europe.

[17] Michael Howard, *Deterrence, Consensus and Reassurance in the Defence of Europe* in Adelphi Paper no. 184 (London: IISS, 1983), p. 17–26.

[18] ESECS, *op. cit.* in note 5, p. 240ff.

[19] *Ibid.*, in note 5, p. 35.

[20] *Ibid.*, in note 4.

[21] *Ibid.*, in note 11, p. 10.

[22] Seymour J. Deitchman, *New Technology and Military Power: General Purpose Military Forces for the 1980s and Beyond* (Boulder, Colo: Westview Press, 1979), pp. 185–204.

[23] But see also Seymour J. Deitchman, *Military Power and the Advance of Technology* (Boulder, Colo: Westview Press, 1983), pp. 173–98.

[24] *Wall Street Journal*, 5 June 1984, p. 39.

[25] *Congressional Record*, US Senate, 3 July 1983, pp. 9852–62.

[26] *Ibid.*, pp. 9854–85.

[27] *Ibid.*, p. 9859.

[28] Philip A. Karber, *op. cit.* in note 8, p. 49.

[29] Walther Stützle in Adelphi Paper no. 144, *op. cit.* in note 3, p. 27.

[30] Sam Nunn, 'The Need to Reshape Military Strategy' in *CSIS Significant Issues Series*, vol. 4, no. 5 (Washington DC: CSIS, 1983).

[31] Philip A. Karber, *op. cit.* in note 8, p. 49.

[32] Quoted in the *Financial Times*, 4 May 1984.

[33] Herschel Kanter and John Fry, *Co-operation in Development and Production of NATO Weapons*, IDA Report–R-253 (Arlington, Va: IDA, 1980), p. S-6

[34] Caspar W. Weinberger, *Standardization of Equipment within NATO: Tenth Report to the US Congress* (Washington DC: DOD, January 1984), p. 1.

[35] Geoffrey Pattie, 'Emerging Technology: the Need for Reality', address to *The Economist* seminar, 19 February 1984.

New Technology, Stability and the Arms-control Deadlock: Part I

PROF. WOLF GRAF VON BAUDISSIN

Technical developments bringing about relevant increases in the efficiency of reconnaissance and C^3, as well as in the effectiveness of weapons are commonly put under the heading 'New Technologies'. Their effect is that they engender completely new weapon systems. Rapid progress in electronics especially has brought about long range and 'intelligent' systems, quick to react, whose greater destructive capabilities could not have been imagined without improved accuracy and effectiveness.

What lie at the heart of more recent strategic thought are conventional arms systems which have already been enhanced by the implementation of 'New Technologies', or which are still in the process of being developed. I only need to mention two keywords: 'the Rogers Plan' and 'the AirLand Battle doctrine'. As to nuclear weapons, foreseeable technological developments – if not already introduced into hardware – are of at least similar importance to the trends in the conventional sector in so far as their effects on strategic stability and the process of arms control are concerned. In this context I should also mention the planned American ballistic missile defence (BMD) programme.

Spectrum of Consequences

The 'New Technologies' now being applied raise a number of questions for NATO's military strategy as well as for arms control:

– Do these 'New Technologies' open up new military options either by conferring an enormous increase in the efficiency of known and ordinary weapons or by truly new systems?
– Will these options change current military strategies?
– Do we have to worry about a destabilizing effect or will the present technological trend have a stabilizing effect with regard to deterrence and security?
– What is the outlook for arms control and does the new setting help make this process more effective?
– Will new aims and objectives have to be laid down for arms-control talks?
– Do we have perhaps to reconsider the whole approach – possibly in the sense of preventive arms control?

Naturally the implementation of new weapon systems also poses questions as to their tactical, structural, logistic and budgetary effects. Besides that, public debate of the *Pershing* issue has made very clear how strong an effect arms decisions may have, not only with regard to individual countries and their domestic situations, but also with regard to the relations within an alliance as well as to the process of detente. Thus, anyone interested in making fair judgments will not be able to disregard the fact that arms decisions have many consequences. One is likely to arrive at the possibly puzzling conclusion that the results of innovational processes in arms technology often seem to contradict each other. That which commends itself tactically may be questionable in strategic terms and may not be at all conducive to further arms control; what appears to be a welcome way out of domestic political confrontation can turn out to be unfavourable in terms of Alliance politics and detente.

Conventional Land and Air Forces

With regard to conventional land and air forces, certain trends in arms technology are already apparent. On the one hand – as with precision-guided munitions (PGM), for example, – these weapons are suitable for reinforcing anti-armour defence at the forward edge of the battle area (FEBA); on the other hand, with increased range it may be possible now to engage also the follow-on units ('deep interdiction'). To be able to use PGM effectively, the necessary 'real time' systems for reconnaissance and C³ are either under development or are already in production.

One should surely welcome any development which makes the conventional component of NATO's defence more effective, provided that this guides deterrence in a 'downward' direction. Another reason for welcoming such a development is that it may also create the conditions enabling a reduction in the number of tactical nuclear weapons.

On the other hand, we must be careful not to overestimate the deterrent effect of a wholly conventional defence. The aggressor has the initiative, and can more or less decide not only the form, intensity, and scope of operations, but also on when to bring hostilities to an end. To a considerable extent, conventional combat takes place on the territory of the party attacked. After only a very short time even conventional combat will bring devastation to such densely-populated and highly vulnerable geographic areas like that of Central Europe.

Furthermore, a fully conventional defence inherently brings with it the danger of decoupling conventional and nuclear forces as well as the danger of making the nuclear-strategic potential of the United States appear to become uncoupled from Europe. The Alliance's political as well as its strategic unity would then be in doubt. The nuclear commitment of the United States towards her non-nuclear partners in the NATO alliance could, under these circumstances, thus be narrowed simply to undertaking retaliatory strikes in reaction to the first use of nuclear weapons by the Soviet Union. As long as the aggressor therefore abstained from using nuclear weapons, he could even begin to contemplate a major attack against Western Europe while counting on the possibility that his territory would remain a kind of sanctuary.

In the face of defence budgets expected to rise by at most 4% in real terms, it seems impossible to try to make up for the Warsaw Pact's conventional supremacy simply by introducing more effective conventional weapon systems. Possible savings in the nuclear sector could not offset the total increase in cost. Furthermore, experience seems to show that the procurement of more sophisticated weapon systems usually turns out to cost more than preceding generations.

The considerably-improved outlook for deep interdiction will probably not confer much advantage either. It could even turn out to be rather harmful. This is one example of how a decision may look good from a military point of view, but be judged to be unhelpful when its political implications are taken into account. A decision for deep strike may help to validate the Soviet allegations of 'Western Revanchism', the political slogan that is meant to invigorate the integration of the Soviet empire.

Thus there is room to argue that, with regard to land and air forces, 'New Technologies' will produce a change in the meaning of conventional warfare because many of them do provide possibilities for deep-strike missions. Hence the term conventional warfare could begin to acquire a new meaning. Conventional weapons could transcend tactics and affect the operational level, if not the strategic level, of warfare.

Naval Forces
At sea it is already difficult to distinguish strategic from non-strategic weapons and this makes for fundamental problems. The nuclearization of several naval weapon systems – most notably cruise missiles – widens the scope of 'non-strategic' weapons which can have strategic impact:

– Over 90% of all modern SLCM and long-range SLGM are either nuclear-tipped or dual-purpose;
– Many of the newly-developed ASW, surface-to-surface anti-ship missiles and air-to-surface anti-ship missiles are nuclear-tipped or dual-purpose, not to speak of nuclear depth charges for ASW and plans to use ICBM as ASW weapons;

- The variety of nuclear-capable weapon-systems in the naval field, as well as their sheer number, have consequently – although tragically – nourished the assumption that nuclear warfare at sea may be less dangerous because of less collateral damage, may be easier to limit because of fewer military items involved, and thus, may be more feasible;
- In professional papers, naval commanders have begun to discuss how nuclear warfare at sea should be best conducted. Consequently, the focal question is not so much *which* nuclear weapons should be used in naval warfare, but *how* they are to be released for use;
- Since long-range SLCM can be launched from ordinary torpedo tubes, this weapon system, formerly tactical, has become an instrument of strategic importance and presents a crucial problem of verification. Who in the future will know, or dare to judge, whether a submarine on patrol in the Baltic does or does not carry nuclear-tipped cruise missiles in its torpedo-tubes?

'New Technologies' may also affect the invulnerability of the sea-based second-strike nuclear capability in rather dramatic ways. The cornerstone of our deterrence system may thus tend to erode over time, although in an unbalanced fashion:

- New sonar devices, sophisticated and long-range sound-surveillance systems, integrated information systems, bottom-mounted hydrophones, refined air-borne ASW sensors, improved ASW sensors and weapons on surface ships, an extended and modernized capacity to install ASW mines at choke points which can be activated from land-based command posts will, together with many other factors, tend to mean that the sea areas in which submarines can effectively be detected and destroyed get larger and larger;
- Strategic submarines in confined areas can no longer be considered reliable second-strike forces. This becomes even more evident when concepts like aerial nuclear 'sanitation' or nuclear barrage bombing around choke points are contemplated;
- The adoption of such concepts by both sides would not only render SSBN forces more vulnerable but would reward strategies which pay special attention to the decisiveness of the 'first salvo'.

Furthermore, recent plans to extend the operational areas of US/NATO ASW forces to the northern seas and the northern Soviet littoral – including efforts to enhance the ability of US attack submarines to operate under ice – must increase the Soviet Union's fears that her second-strike SSBN will be locked up and destroyed within her adjacent seas, possibly by pre-emptive attack.

Besides the sea-based second-strike option being put in jeopardy by new technology, both ICBM and C^3 are also endangered to an increasing extent. The chances are growing that the fixed land-based systems of both sides could be eliminated by using 'offensive' systems pre-emptively or preventively. In this scenario, the reciprocity of deterrence would be destroyed by the build-up of 'defensive' systems. Thus the existing strategic stability could become unstable.

Ballistic Missile Defence

At first sight a viable BMD system, like the one planned by the American Strategic Defense Initiative (SDI), could not do better in epitomizing the ideal characteristics of the defence. Taken on its own, it does not threaten any foreign power. On the other hand it would seem to be suitable for warding off nuclear attacks. However, seen in combination with offensive nuclear potential, the odds are that strategic defence will break up the stability provided by mutual deterrence, for it will permit nuclear attacks while promising at the same time to fend off the other side's ballistic missile counter-attack. According to the logic of deterrence, the United States' BMD deployment can only precipitate new Soviet arms production in order to prevent this situation from arising or at least in order to forestall an American option of this kind.

Given mutual mistrust, the build-up of such a potential can only be looked upon as an attempt to create an option for a nuclear first strike.

Apart from questions of money and technical viability, the critical question with regard to a BMD system lies in the countermeasures which would have to be expected from the Soviet Union. We have at least to reckon with greater dynamism in arms production. The decisive factor in evaluating the effects of a US BMD system lies with the Soviet elite and its perception of the system's potential. Even though there might be objective grounds for not considering a BMD system destabilizing (taking into account the technical problems which might make it rather unsuitable for the task originally assigned to it), the Soviet elite's propensity to think in worst-case terms is only too well known (even if this approach is barely distinguishable from that of some discerning people in the West).

Arms Control
Leaving aside that in all probability the introduction of such new technologies will not present their users with reliable capabilities to be able to strike first, to decapitate the other and to be able to survive, the processes of detente and arms control have suffered badly from new technical developments. Against this background, arms control is becoming all the more urgent. The more intense becomes the qualitative dynamism of arms production internationally, the more important arms control becomes as an instrument to reduce the manifold dangers which arise from it.

It will not be easy for the parties concerned to decide on whether and how to take up the process of arms control again for it is a very complex issue. Matters which should really be dealt with objectively have again become questions of prestige. As to power politics and strategic considerations, pre-nuclear concepts have been revived as has ideologically-induced mistrust. A judicious reconciliation of expectations and ways and methods with today's reality is just as necessary as striving for more empathy.

However, adapting the original approach of arms control to today's dynamism of arms production is also necessary. The characteristics of this rapid process are mainly qualitative, that is they are precipitated and controlled by the progress of technological development.

Once production has begun it becomes a sheer impossibility to estimate the number of weapons already produced or to find out where the storage depots or the locations of deployment are, let alone take into account the fact that many weapons can be quickly transferred to their launchers over great distances.

A further problem is the marked gap in quality between the different generations of weapons. Criteria for command and control, as well as for certain standards of measurement, become dated more quickly than treaties can be negotiated and signed. Furthermore, it is not only that these highly-sophisticated systems are composed of hundreds of important components, but also that their operational potential can be varied fundamentally by exchanging small components. Criteria guiding arms-control negotiations have just not kept pace with the technological process. That is why I recommend Preventive Arms Control.

Preventive Arms Control
Until now, weapon systems already in operation or ready for deployment have for the most part been the subject of negotiation. This approach proved to be inadequate as these weapon systems are hard to compare. Thus, it became extremely difficult to agree on mutual reductions. Each side presses his opponent to abolish just those which the other is particularly interested in maintaining. Even if agreements to reduce the actual numbers are reached, the loss in quantity can quite easily be counteracted with improvements in quality. Also, the diplomatic process simply cannot keep up with technological progress, and this often reduces the real impact or significance of any agreement.

Thus, I think that a much more promising approach would be to negotiate systems *before* production has begun, an approach I call Preventive Arms Control. Planned systems would become the centre of negotiations rather than those systems which are already operational. I realize that this approach may considerably restrict the sovereignty of the countries involved, but it would also make stable security much more attainable.

The advantages of negotiating armament programmes not yet operational are evident. Each side would have less of a vested interest in the retention or deployment of planned programmes. Both sides would therefore be more willing to mutually abandon certain technologically-advanced systems. This approach would also increase the chances for a slow-down of production and a reduction in deployment of sophisticated weapon systems. I would even venture to say that this negotiating procedure would have the positive influence of limiting research and development. If this were indeed to occur, the destabilizing tendency to modernize would be restricted.

This preventive approach to arms control, significantly different from current concepts, should be handled routinely. Depending on the particulars of the planned weapon systems, discussions could occur in the regional context of the CSCE, among the members of the alliances themselves, between NATO and WTO, or bilaterally between the superpowers. The structures for these negotiations already exist to some degree. Thus, they would serve as platforms for the exchange of information, data and proposals. They could even serve as verification agencies.

The Brussels Double-Track Decision has been the first opportunity to adopt preventive arms control as a negotiating approach. Unfortunately, it was offered under very unfavourable circumstances, as the USSR had already begun the SS-20 programme. A genuine 'preventive' approach to the negotiations was therefore impossible.

Conclusion

With regard to the process of arms control, good opportunities were wasted in the past. The first phase of arms control, from the end of the 1960s until the middle of the 1970s, could easily have been pursued, not only with regard to all levels of negotiations, but also with regard to nearly all kinds of weapons and armaments. One then had to deal only with a definable number of systems and with characteristics which could be verified to a greater or lesser extent by agreed procedures. R&D could still be overseen without much difficulty.

As to the future, the problems seem certain to become considerably more complicated. Decreasing transparency of arms production programmes promotes mutual mistrust. In order to justify excessive arms production, the two sides all too quickly have to resort to the existing lack in transparency. This not only weakens international stability as a whole, but also the stability within the systems. In this context I am less worried about the much-quoted danger of war and more about an increasing cold-war psychosis which has again brought about the confrontational patterns of thought which governed the second half of the Nineteenth Century. I am also anxious about the epidemic psychosis of fear which has taken hold of – I can't say why – the larger part of the younger generation. This psychosis leads not only to their rejection of the existing systems of security, but to their defying our political systems as a whole, which are held to be responsible for the creation of the present security condition. A rational approach towards security policy calls more urgently than ever for thoroughgoing arms control – if with different approaches and measures. Given secure second-strike capabilities, transparency and inferiority in parts may carry little risk. However, what mainly governs how rational an approach is taken regarding security policies and the extent to which certain risks are accepted is the overall political climate. Only stability provided by a climate of detente can produce the necessary conditions for decreasing the undoubtedly real feeling of being threatened. This stability will also help to establish the idea that the renunciation of force is not only an obligation of international law but also the minimum common denominator which conditions the further existence of industrial societies. Not until detente makes progress at last will the question of military strength be of secondary importance. Only then will it become quite clear that the mutual knowledge of intentions, strategies and means does not lead to weakness but to strength.

Ten Theses
By way of conclusion I suggest that the following ten theses should guide those concerned with arms-control policy:

1) New Technologies are neither good nor bad. Their introduction will have differing impacts on political, strategic and structural problems. The modernization process has therefore to be thoroughly controlled.

2) New Technologies are not a short-term threat to existing strategic stability. Concrete risks have to be expected on a medium- or long-term basis, however, unless the qualitative arms dynamics can be controlled in international co-operation. Nevertheless, misconceptions and suspicions – whether justified or not – will destabilize the international conditions; they will make arms control an illusion and justify measures which seem to promise new and unilateral strategic options.

3) Some of the emerging technologies would seem to offer options which turn away from the existing mutual self-deterrence of MAD. They could encourage a strategy of preventive aggression in the framework of old-fashioned defence concepts or at least they can provoke suspicions, particularly in the USSR where strategic thinking still follows rather conservative tendencies.

4) The modernization of the conventional component discussed in the context of 'no-first-use' of nuclear weapons, should emphasize the aspect of qualitative and quantitative verification. Otherwise the MBFR negotiations will never achieve stabilizing results. Dual-purpose systems, as well as Insertable Nuclear Components, should eventually be cancelled. The introduction of cruise missiles, particularly of SLCM, will have to be considered very critically.

5) In general, it should be the purpose and aim of arms control, which is a long and complicated process, to make any kind of war – not only nuclear war – in Europe as unlikely as possible. Conventional war will not only be the first stage leading to nuclear war, but after a certain period, it produces nuclear-like catastrophes for the societies directly affected.

6) The release of sea-based tactical systems has also to be placed under stricter political control. Otherwise, the mere existence of these weapons and the inclination to use them in naval warfare will destabilize the political and strategic situation in any crisis. Nobody can be interested in a conventionalization or depoliticization of any kind of nuclear weapons. Conventional weapon systems specified for deep interdiction missions should also be subject to release by political authorities for their use too will have a strong political impact.

7) Only Preventive Arms Control, undertaken continuously in permanent fora (i.e., negotiations on armament programmes before production has begun) will offer the chance of checking the incalculable and technologically determined process of arms procurement. The experience of the Antarctic, Seabed and ABM Treaties encourage the belief that systems which are not operational are easier to abandon. Preventive Arms Control would result also in a certain degree of mutual transparency which will tend to support political stability. Conditional freeze agreements as well as *moratoria* may help to stabilize requirements before or during negotiations.

8) Arms Control has stabilizing effects only if it is seen as co-operation in spite of fundamental incompatibilities in other fields. Such an approach can only be expected after today's confrontation has been overcome.

If both sides are *really* interested in a resumption of arms-control negotiations, it should not be too difficult:

– To exchange in the Stockholm CDE a 'No-first-use of any Weapons against any State' for some concrete CBM, which might be better renamed as 'Distrust Reducing Measures';
– To agree in MBFR in Vienna the ceilings already negotiated;

- To put all nuclear systems in and around Europe which have ranges between 800 and 5,500 km into one basket (admitting that the previous approach has been too narrow and that no real technological differences exist today);
- To turn the quite promising negotiations in the 1970s on CTB (Comprehensive Test Ban), space and chemical warfare into binding agreements.

The real barriers are political:
- Prestige has become more important than facts;
- Some governments conduct detente, security, and arms-control policy chiefly with respect to domestic opportunities.

9) The NATO Allies should remember their commitment under the Harmel formula and try to begin a new detente process on the basis of existing second-strike nuclear capabilities.

10) Both sides – East and West – must learn that their security depends on the other's feeling unthreatened. Only stable systems – internally as well as externally – are calculable and reliable; only they can make durable compromises and enter fruitful co-operation.

Conventional Force Development and New Technology: How Real are the Gains in Prospect?

HENRI CONZE

The introduction of new military technologies has always been the priority of every nation, of every human group, anxious to ensure survival. That is true whether we are speaking of defence today or the conquest of hunting territories in the past. Nothing seems fundamentally new in the present trends. Mankind has always searched, and will always search, for ways of improving conventional forces, using what are now called 'emerging technologies', considered by some to be the corner-stone of the Free World's defence in the next decade.

If we do not care enough, if the urgency is absent, the present debate in the Alliance is liable to have some negative consequences for our defence. On the other hand, the conditions governing the introduction of new technologies in the next generation of weapons are in some ways quite different to what they were in the past. As an introduction to the real matter of this Paper, it is important to examine these two points.

I believe that the present debate could be counter-productive if its short-term result were simply to delay or to cancel the introduction of systems based upon technologies, existing or emerging, in areas where we really cannot afford to wait any longer. In the C^3 area, for example, civilian administrations have already replaced mechanical switching systems by fully digitalized ones. The same effort should be made for defence by taking advantage of *existing* technology in full-scale production.

Other areas in which we could and should go ahead now include low-altitude air defence, identification of friend and foe (IFF), and fixed and protected target neutralization. Do we have to wait for completely new systems in order to fulfil an urgent need when, on a national basis or in co-operation, systems exist, are fielded or almost fielded? Some recent decisions, such as US Air Force and *Luftwaffe* base defence with the Franco-German *Roland* system, or the future Mobile Subscriber Equipment of the US Army where two systems are in competition – the Franco-Belgian *RITA* (already fielded) and the British *Ptarmigan* (which will be fielded soon) – demonstrate the dangers of postponing important decisions because of the potential of new technologies. Here the search for the best would seem to be the enemy of the good enough. However, we need to be careful.

On the second point, I am convinced that the present debate on new technologies could be fruitful if it triggers serious reflection on the way our defence can be improved by the rational development of new technologies and their introduction in our forces. In my mind these conditions are related in the following statements.

There is certainly some kind of 'development-production' cycle in the field of armaments. Initially equipped with World War II armaments, in the 1960s the Free World developed new systems, taking into account the enormous progress made in the electronics field, for example. Now we are almost at the end of the production phase of systems designed in the 1960s, and we are again at the stage where a large number of decisions have to be taken on the development of new systems. The decisions taken now will undoubtedly define the status of our defence in the 1990s, and probably beyond 2020 when we remember that a system can remain in service for 30 years, or more in some cases. For example, the KC-135, designed in the mid-1950s, will be in service beyond 2010 with the present re-engining programme based upon the US–French CFM-56 engine.

The real issue, then, is to develop, select and produce the best possible technologies for military equipment which will be in service for more than thirty years. At the same time, as in the electronics field for example, even two years may give rise to an enormous qualitative gain. Here then is a quite new element in our decision-making process, highlighting some of the difficulties of the present debate on emerging technologies. We already have examples. Faced with determining future air-to-air missiles, between a system designed in 1979 and another designed in 1983, a reduction in missile weight of about 50% could be obtained due simply to improvements made during that period on solid-state transmitters. Given that a system is obsolete as soon as it enters production, what policy can one adopt, except never to decide? Would it be better to accept more frequent and more radical mid-life improvements in order to take advantage of technological breakthroughs? Maybe we also have to develop international co-operation more than we have in the past. Technology is certainly more and more costly, and the share of Research and Development (R&D) in the total life cycle cost of any system is rapidly increasing. We may assume that the ratio of R&D (as an average, because this ratio is not the same for a rifle or for a fighter aircraft) will increase from about 10% in the 1970s to about 30% in the 1990s.

That means that co-operation, which has mainly been handled case-by-case in the past, depending on a given political situation or industrial opportunities, has now to become a general rule. It is obviously true for Western Europe, and efforts made within bilateral or multilateral *fora*, such as the IEPG have to be understood not only as demonstrating political will but also as a necessity, as the only way to ensure the acquisition of key technologies and the development of crucial systems while maintaining independence of decision for each participating nation. I am convinced that this evolution has to be considered also by the US. Even for the US the cost of any development and the risks for the companies involved are such that we have to wonder if unrestrained competition will last much longer. How many companies are now building civilian wide-body aircraft? How long will it take for the same situation to arise in fighter aircraft or missiles? Ten years? Twenty years? No more to my mind.

We must therefore be sure to establish priorities and maintain strict control when deciding future armaments. Moreover, if potential adversaries could procure these technologies in less time (and at less cost) than the Free World, we should be worse off than before.

National control of priorities and international co-operation are both necessary, but they ought not to be incompatible. Unfortunately they sometimes are. Nations do tend to keep to themselves the new technologies which would, if shared, assist the Alliance, believing that they are themselves better protected in this way. This seems particularly to be true of European officials at high levels.

I would like, at this stage, to mention something which is not always understood by officials, mainly on the Western side of the Alliance. Technology is shared more across the Atlantic than is usually known. Some recent attempts at co-operation between US and Western European companies – such as MLRS (Multiple Launch Rocket System) Phase 3 and the CFM-56 engine – have demonstrated that both sides can benefit from real co-operation. Industry-to-industry co-operation must be encouraged. Will it be? Any embargo, such as the one imposed on France in the early 1960s, is likely to have unpredictable results. What would have happened to *Ariane*, EURODIF, nuclear energy and so on if, at that time, the US Administration had permitted co-operation? The embargo, if I consider its results for France twenty years after, was beneficial. But would it be sensible to play that game again?

A final problem is to get the services to see new technology not simply as providing a one-for-one replacement of obsolete equipment but as a way of redefining operational concepts, if necessary involving the revision of roles and missions. If we fail in that, we shall fail to gain much of the benefit of new technology. We know that we are up against history and the facts of inter-service rivalry, but it is possible to show – as in the recent fielding in the French forces of a new tactical fully-digitalized, secure, mobile, redundant communications system – that this has increased efficiency enormously in ways that a simple one-for-one replacement of an old system could not have done. The reason is that this replacement has taken place simultaneously with a new look at operational procedures.

Practical Questions for Policy
So far I have tried to define the limits and constraints which tend to impede the introduction of new technologies in conventional armaments. Now we need to consider:

- Which are the really new technologies?
- What are the main conventional systems affected by these new technologies, and how can improvements to them modify the deterrent posture of the Free World?
- What are the political, military and financial implications of introducing new technologies?

New Technologies and Application to Systems
Fundamental technological breakthroughs can be anticipated in:

- electronics;
- software;
- sensors;
- new materials.

It would be absurd to separate those four areas, even if they correspond to different scientific disciplines, because they have to play a similar and complementary role in the development of our future defence systems. What is the actual problem? Summing up, it corresponds to what we may call the problem of 'real-time' management of many different objectives.

Real-time Acquisition and Recognition of Targets. The goal here is to develop high-speed electronic components and associated software able to dispose of small, smart munitions capable of detecting and hitting the most vulnerable point of any target. The technologies relevant to this mission are: Very High Speed Integrated Circuits (VHSIC); Submicronic Components; Very Large Scale Integration (VLSI); flexible and adaptive language; and miniaturized sensors (infra-red, millimetric wave radar, solid-state transmitters etc.).

Electronic Warfare. Here the need is for real-time electronic counter-measures and counter-counter-measures capable of preventing any enemy electronic intrusion or jamming, or assist one's own electronic intrusion or jamming – again the technology relates to electronics (VHSIC) and software.

C^3I. We need to be able to see, react, decide and act. Critical to these functions are future C^3I systems and, again, we are looking for 'real-time' technology, that is to say VHSIC, VLSI and software. To give some idea of the scale of the problem, we are asking that something weighing less than one kilogram should do the same job as a late-1960s CDC 6400 computer (weighing tons) – and we want hundreds of thousands of these instead of hundreds. And we want this new system to be more reliable than a CDC 6400 computer. Finally, of course, we must be able to afford hundreds of thousands of them.

Lastly we must not ignore the remarkable qualities of new materials. Development of ceramics, carbon-carbon or quartz phenolic three- (or more-) dimensional structures, will make possible the development of completely new engines, missiles or armour.

New materials and new computing power will revolutionize future generations of all kinds of missiles and fighters, allowing reduced weight, more manoeuvrability, shorter time of flight, etc.

The Evolution of Conventional Systems. New technologies generally, and especially those listed above, will chiefly affect systems needing high computational capability (in virtually real-time), mobility, security and reduced vulnerability. Those systems are:

C^3I. Communications technologies, such as spread-spectrum and frequency agility, digital transmission and switching, and microcomputer automated data processing, will allow much better security, survivability and reliability and help to solve interoperability problems. It is necessary to emphasise that fire-and-forget weapons and a full multi-targeting capability are conceivable (only) if new C³I systems are developed, because of the complexities of command and control associated with these systems. Solution of these complexities will also allow a shorter reaction time and improved battlefield management.

Defence against the First-Echelon and Follow-on Forces. Smart munitions or sub-munitions, able to detect mobile or fixed targets and to hit them at their weakest points, will give the capability to defeat attacking armoured forces at much longer ranges and with less loss in terms of men and equipment. Those munitions will be delivered by fire-and-forget missiles – short-, medium- and long-range, ground-to-ground or air-to-ground – giving, for example, a complete stand-off capability to aircraft. Those systems will be day-and-night, all-weather capable. Target acquisition is also a critical area. Real-time surveillance both of the battlefield itself and far beyond FEBA will be possible, both from the ground (by being able to collect all available information, by processing it and disseminating it using microcomputers and digitalized C³) and from airborne and satellite platforms.

All these systems will, of course, face enemy counter-measures. Diversification of sensors (optical, infra-red, millimetric) associated with sophisticated signal processing will confer some real protection against ECM, but to have the lead in these technologies will be crucial.

Air Warfare. A major step will be the careful integration of all the elements relating to air warfare or counter-air capability, namely active and passive measures, C³I, air-to-air and ground-to-air systems, and identification of friend and foe (IFF). On the assumption that the enemy will also develop stand-off capabilities, a parallel priority will have to be given to the development of anti-tactical missile capabilities and to countering all systems assigned to the neutralization of choke points and the destruction of runways, radars, etc. Another important development will be to give a real multi-targeting capability to air platforms, thus fostering their intrinsic military value and reducing their vulnerability.

Concerning these three major areas, listed above, the Alliance is not just sitting and doing nothing at the present time. Important programmes, the more recent ones involving emerging technologies, have already been decided upon and are in progress. Some examples include: MLRS Phase 3 (co-operation between Western Europe and the US); a new generation of anti-tank weapons (France, West Germany and Britain and, possibly, some other European countries); AMRAAM and *MICA* air-to-air missiles; the French RDX radar; the *Mistral* surface-to-air short range missile; *RITA* and *Ptarmigan* (already mentioned); and the C³ *STRIDA* system for the French Air Force. Fortunately, free world nations do have not to wait for the conclusion, if any, of the debate on emerging technologies.

Political, Military and Financial Problems
These aspects of the problem are in fact rather closely connected and have to be discussed as a whole. Of course each nation of the Free World, each social or political group, has its own perception of this batch of problems, depending on its geographical, economical or budgetary situation. However, instead of trying to find an impossible compromise between them, or even to describe them, I shall limit myself to the presentation of French views, or at least what appears to be views of almost all French political circles.

The French do not deny the necessity of disposing well-equipped and well-trained conventional forces. This has to be done to accord with our doctrine and with the strategy of Flexible Response adopted by nations belonging to the NATO military organization. Nor do we deny the military necessity of developing conventional weapons which are more accurate and more efficient. But we consider that it would be counter-productive to base our defence only on technological leadership. Our common experience during the last thirty years has been that, every time, the Warsaw

Pact has been able to close transient technical gaps. The disproportion of conventional forces between them and us is such that it would not be realistic to believe that we could bring about a drastic change in the existing ratio of conventional forces. This is the main reason why we consider that nuclear deterrence has been and still is the best way to prevent any conflict.

We fear that there is some misunderstanding in this debate, especially when dealing with some official declarations to the effect that the nuclear threshold could be raised by the introduction of new technologies. We believe that any conflict in Europe, whether conventional, chemical or nuclear, would be a holocaust. Any conflict, even a so-called conventional conflict, even with promises of 'no nuclear first use', would probably turn into a nuclear conflict. Our goal therefore has to be the prevention of *any* conflict. In order to do that, France needs a strong nuclear deterrent. Giving it up or weakening it would mean war or slavery. We totally reject both alternatives.

This position, which has been the French position for twenty years, has been stressed by French authorities recently. We have consistently taken the view that it is highly dangerous to postpone the deployment of new nuclear INF on the grounds that conventional deterrence based upon emerging technologies is feasible.

This danger arises especially because:

– The Free World cannot dedicate, as the Soviets do, 12–13% of its GNP to its defence.
– An average three-year period of conscription, such as obtains in the Warsaw Pact, is not feasible in the West.

Thus the Western Alliance cannot, in principle, accept the idea of a sustained conventional conflict. We believe that, whatever the technological evolution, the Warsaw Pact will continue to retain an important conventional advantage.

Nevertheless we recognize that deterrence is indivisible. We must therefore retain the ability to respond to any kind of possible crisis. That means that we must be in a position to deploy credible conventional forces. We must modernize them in case a tactical or strategic nuclear response would not appear to be credible, for example because disproportionate for a given crisis.

This, to my mind, gives us some idea of the objectives that should be given a high priority when considering the introduction of new technologies. Besides efforts made in C^3I and air warfare, we should aim to neutralize armoured forces in the combat zone and beyond the FEBA. There are many targets which are now assigned to nuclear weapons because current weapon technology is inadequate or appears to be so. It would be highly desirable to be able to attack such targets with conventional means. Developing and fielding precise, stand-off, fire-and-forget weapons will certainly fill such a gap and foster defence against attack, thus limiting the risks of crisis escalation.

The financial aspects of this effort are obviously crucial. Many figures have been published. What is the reality? It is true that technology is costly: the real cost of production of modern equipment increases at a rate somewhat above fiscal inflation. This tendency will continue. The share of R&D in total life cycle costs is also increasing drastically. It is therefore true that system replacement will cost much more in constant currency than in the past. Yet adaptation of concepts, possibly involving the transfer of missions, will lead to possible reductions of manpower, of logistics and of maintenance costs. Co-operation could also save for each nation a large part of R&D expenditures and reduce overall production costs. What will be the final result of all these contradictory tendencies? That will obviously depend on the results of trade-offs, of political will, and so on. We can only say that the future is very unpredictable.

I shall try to demonstrate at this stage the very tight connections between the conceptual, financial and political aspects of the introduction of new technology in conventional armaments. I have chosen a very simple example, now an issue of debate, known as the counter-air problem. I do not want to make any judgment on that issue but, to simplify, I will assume that the supporters of a missile solution are right.

How can one neutralize for three days an airfield some 1,000 kilometres beyond the potential FEBA? With present weapons, except nuclear, almost the only way is to drop bombs of World War II type, except the recent (and limited) introduction of new types of runway denial weapons such as *Durandal* or BAP 100. What is needed? About twenty or thirty bombs delivered by ten or fifteen aircraft. Those aircraft have to be protected against fighters and air-defence systems by friendly fighters and ECM and ECCM aircraft.

The order of magnitude of the investment to deny one airfield is thus the cost of about fifty aircraft, that is to say $2 bn as a marginal cost (not including R&D), if we consider not only the aircraft and their weapons, but also the cost of pilot training, air-base defence and so on. The same job, with the same efficiency, can be done with one missile, say a US *Trident* or French M-4, with terminally-guided versions of the anti-runway *Durandal*. I do not say that those systems are especially well-suited for that mission nor that we do not need aircraft. The problem is not there. But marginal cost of one of these missiles, including the necessary infrastructure, is about $20 m, that is to say one hundredth of the airborne system cost. Whatever the exact figures, even with errors of a factor of two or three, the result is an order of magnitude at least in favour of the missile system. But an aircraft is an air force system, whereas a missile system will probably be deployed by the Army. Yet the same missile could carry a nuclear warhead (as can aircraft), which raises an awesome political problem of deployment. But it is difficult to move from the present situation, where we are trying to prevent a third world war with third-world-war platforms equipped with second-world-war weapons utilized within first-world-war concepts, towards a more realistic and coherent solution.

From what has been said here, it may appear that I am at least sceptical about the actual importance of new technologies. The problem is not to play down the place of technology in the evolution of the defence that we forecast, but rather to understand that the problem we are faced with is neither new nor revolutionary. The Alliance is only trying to do what France has always done. France has always given priority to defence, and has always tried to take advantage of the technical efforts of our people. Nothing is new under the sun, except perhaps that we are now able to fight without the sun, even without the moon during the night, and that we will be able to manage any kind of situation in real-time. It will not be a revolution but an evolution, and this evolution will take time and money. How much money we cannot say. There are large uncertainties in the figures. It will depend on how clever we are and whether we can find the optimum trade-offs between concepts and equipment and whether we can combine our efforts while at the same time maintaining the independence of our separate nations.

However I do not believe that it is in our interest to let anybody think that a short-term technical revolution could drastically change the military balance between the two Blocs. Nor will new conventional weapons technology permit us to relax our efforts in the nuclear field. If those two propositions are not clearly perceived, I am convinced that the gains in prospect from new technologies would turn out to be negative.

New Conventional Force Technology and the NATO–Warsaw Pact Balance: Part I

DR STEVEN L. CANBY

Can emerging technologies offset NATO's inferiority in combat strength in Europe? Proponents say yes – and for only a 4% real increase in defence spending. They argue that we are at the threshold of a new age in warfare – that of the electronics. Microelectronics undeniably offer revolutionary capabilities in sensing and processing data. The *technical* question facing this conference is whether emerging technology can be translated into a significant *military* advantage. If so, major *policy* issues arise regarding technology transfer, intra-Alliance arms co-operation, crisis stability and so on – all of which are correspondingly moot if the technology cannot be so translated.

History suggests that, at least between European countries, technological advantage has not been decisive. It is transitory in nature; technology is readily copied and countered. It is soon incorporated into the forces of both sides. The advantage comes from recognizing its potential impact upon such factors as strategy, doctrine and organization – which may take years to recognize and still longer to be proved and imitated by opponents.

New technologies will obviously change the *techniques* by which things are done in war, but they will change neither the *nature* of these things (e.g., gathering intelligence, commanding, striking, protecting and moving about) nor the *principles* according to which these things are done (surprise, concentration, economy of forces, security, etc). These will remain as important as they have always been, regardless of the technology in use. Indeed as long as war itself remains what it is, i.e., a violent struggle among politically organized groups of people, these fundamentals will stay unchanged.[1]

Nor can the new technologies be expected to benefit the defence over the offence. Contrary to the volumes written on this topic, technology is neutral. The sword and the shield are illustrative. Without the sword, there is no defence; without the shield, there is no attack. Sensing technologies would appear to aid the defender for the defender is putatively in position and well-entrenched while the attacker must move and expose himself. The pitfall in that argument is that the positional defender cannot survive in this age of firepower dominance. The defence, too, must be based on movement (and elusiveness); if not, the defender will be destroyed by fire, enveloped, or defeated in detail by forces with greater initiative. This has been the criticism levelled by reformers against NATO's *implementation* of its otherwise valid concept of forward defence. NATO corps now tend to subscribe to a more fluid, German style of war based on the counter-attack. The problem is that NATO lacks the operational reserves to execute its (newly) agreed doctrine. The new technologies address the issue of inadequate NATO reserves by attempting to reduce the availability of opposing reserves.

Unfortunately the concept generally is operationally flawed.[2] Deep attack on aircraft runways is potentially effective only on Day 1; thereafter it is little more than Harassment and Indiction (H&I) fire. Deep attack on choke points like river crossings is only marginally effective, and not effective at all against backed-up forces. Against Follow-on Forces, which has been its principal thrust, deep attack is likely to be totally ineffective. This Paper explains in detail the reasons behind this extraordinarily strong statement.

Emerging technologies applied to the deep attack of Follow-on Forces (FOFA) *cannot* be effective, in principle or practice. FOFA is a concept beyond the capabilities of technology. Its infeasibility transcends the many limitations of the specific equipment proposed. It is necessarily a preprogrammed, deterministic system. Such systems cannot operate in uncongenial, adaptive and unpredictable environments. Comparisons citing the scepticism overcome in such programmes as *Polaris* miss this invalidating distinction.

The military argument for deep attack is that NATO's forward forces can hold frontline Warsaw Pact forces, but cannot match subsequent incoming Soviet reinforcements.[3] If these reinforcements could be destroyed *en route* or significantly reduced through the use of high-technology weapons, the Pact could be held and possibly defeated piecemeal. This argument, however, is derived from an incorrect understanding of Soviet operational methods. The high-quality lead echelons, not the follow-on echelons, must be stopped from *enveloping* (as opposed to frontally assaulting) NATO's defending formations.

The second argument of this Paper is that the emerging technologies, which are to perform deep attack, are not operationally up to the task. Electronics has made it possible to sense and hit targets at great distances, while munition payloads can be subdivided into many small but lethal submunitions. However, the guidance technologies are easily countered and the munitions themselves are readily defeated by simple adaptive behaviour.

For the goal at hand – offsetting numerical superiority (in teeth units) by technological superiority – the new technologies fail on four counts:

– Technology can be a trap;
– The Soviet operational method has been incorrectly analysed;
– Technical and operational feasibility are not synonymous;
– Counter-measures exist.

The Technology Trap

In strategic warfare, technology dominates, and much can be mechanically calculated. In conventional warfare, while such calculations are common, they are often spurious. Even one-on-one air-to-air combat calculations have proved to be wrong, suggesting the importance of intangible factors. As the scale descends from equipment-oriented and formal warfare to light-infantry and guerrilla warfare, especially in close terrain, increasing importance must be given to such intangibles as uncertainty, surprise, training, tactics, adaptability, national character and the like. These factors make war an *art*, not a science.

Throughout the ages, the introduction of a qualitatively new weapon has been heralded by the prognosis that war will never again be the same. To date, these predictions have always proved false. There is no reason to believe that tactics will not adjust to precision weapons. Historically, armies have adjusted – or perished. As Michael Howard reminds us:

> I am tempted indeed to declare dogmatically that whatever doctrine the Armed Forces are working on now, they have got it wrong. I am also tempted to declare that it does not matter that they have got it wrong. What does matter is their capacity to get it right quickly when the moment arrives.[4]

A technological solution to a military imbalance caused by numerical inferiority can be practically achieved only if the technological leader improves the performance of his forces at costs equal to, or less than, those incurred by his opponent. Otherwise, a vicious spiral is initiated. Even better technology is needed to compensate for ever-diminishing numbers of troops and weapons. Relative combat capability suffers further as equipment becomes more complex, the supporting 'tail' becomes larger, and training is curtailed because of operational costs. Clearly this has been the trend of recent decades.

The proposition that technological sophistication can offset numbers can be tested. In close terrain, sophisticated weapons can actually be disadvantageous. This is most apparent in high mountains, large forests and deep snow. At night, armour is vulnerable to infantry even in open terrain. In these not uncommon circumstances, technologically sophisticated weapons simply cannot cope with an enemy presenting *ambiguous* and *deceptive signatures*. In World War I, on the open, heavily-manned, and firepower-dominated terrain of northern France, the Germans discovered (in 1918) that high-quality *light* troops (followed by regular forces) could infiltrate, collapse and defeat entrenched defences, whereas ever heavier artillery fire could not. The discovery that ambiguity, deception and surprise could neutralize co-ordinated defensive fire underlies the German use of armour.[5] It is a discovery that many have yet to appreciate; indeed, it is the very antithesis of the engineering approach to war. It also helps to explain why technology is so often focused on the trivia of the obvious to the exclusion of the more conceptual but larger pay-offs available from revised tactical methods.[6]

Blackboard strategists often portray combat as one-on-one duels, an appropriate cartoon for medieval Europe and Homeric Greece. Modern combat is a semi-organized, confused *mêlée* of many-on-many. In such contexts, the advantages of sophistication tend to be lost, and tactics, training, numbers, organization and the like tend to dominate.

Sophistication can be tested, too, against analytical models. In the United States, forces have been structured and evaluated in one variation or another on the basis of Lanchester's formula:

$$K(red) (Nr)^2 = K(blue) (Nb)^2 + C$$

where quality (K) is a linear parameter and numbers (N) are squared parameters. Among its implications is that, in comparing the British Army of the Rhine and the Soviet Third Shock Army, British technology must be 4 to 9 times better than the Soviet technology to offset Soviet superiority in combat power, even though the two forces are roughly equal in personnel strength.[7]

This example applies equally to NATO's other corps, as well as to NATO overall. Even though NATO is not outnumbered and, if one includes French home-based forces, actually outnumbers Pact forces, NATO technology using the Lanchesterian formulation must be 4 to 9 times better. It can be argued (erroneously) that the defender – in this case NATO – obtains an additional multiplicand of 3. The defender's inherent 3-to-1 advantage multiplied by a technological edge could then offset the square of the force ratio. The pitfall in this formulation is that the 3-to-1 rule is a micro-argument, valid only in one-on-one frontal engagements. It is not valid for the total theatre nor against thrust and manoeuvre tactics. The rule is only valid against armies attacking across-the-front, as occurred in World War I and again on the Western front in 1944–5.

In the manoeuvre model of war now gaining favour in the United States, effectiveness is determined by combatant numbers and overall force quality. Firepower *per se* is not a major determinant. *Surge* firepower remains important but *sustained* firepower does not. The latter simply leads to unnecessary destruction and imposes large logistical demands for resupply and for maintaining lines of communication (LOC). Numbers provide command flexibility, while organization and tactics allow small, high-quality lead forces to obtain tactical advantages that can be subsequently exploited, pursued and consolidated by lower-quality follow-on forces. In the manoeuvre model, highly sophisticated forces statically occupying positions of apparent great strength and relying on firepower and attrition will be quickly enveloped, and the integrity of their defence destroyed, by elusive manoeuvre forces. This is precisely how the Soviet Union plans to operate against NATO forces with their much publicized Operational Manoeuvre Groups (OMGs).

The Form of the Threat Does Matter
Ironically, while the OMG thesis is now in vogue, the significance of the concept has not been understood and its meaning for deep attack has not been grasped. A prominent example comes from Gen. Rogers himself:

In order to *breach* ACE defenses rapidly and maintain the momentum of the offensive, Warsaw Pact doctrine calls for the commitment of forces in *successive* waves, or echelons, always keeping great pressure on the defender and seeking to *mass* sufficient forces for a *breakthrough*. Pact forces can be expected to employ highly mobile exploitation formations at army and army group (front) levels. These combined-arms forces, called Operational Maneuver Groups (OMG), are designed to penetrate deeply into the rear of NATO's defense in order to seize critical objectives, cut lines of communications and to limit the ability of NATO forces to respond, especially with our theater nuclear forces.[8] (Emphasis added)

Unfortunately, this conception of Soviet tactics and operations is no longer valid.[9] OMG are more than mere high-quality, second-echelon exploitation groups that come into play *after* a breakthrough. Rather, the OMG system is a means to amend the entire breakthrough process. It is a probing (and subsequently irruptive and exploitative) operational method that seeks natural fissures in the opposing array. This is a qualitatively different and tactically more advanced method than the World War II procedure described above. In that method, a breakthrough is akin to a dam breaking from the exertion of great pressure and a subsequent torrent that carries all before it. It succeeds by the momentum of the torrent. The new method is like probes from a pitchfork with subsequent exploiting forces following paths of least resistance. By not recognizing these qualitative distinctions, all too many have adopted the terminology and form of the OMG method while the content of their argument remains that of 1944.

The Soviet concept of offensive ground operations calls for the establishment of multiple, *phased* axes of advance. Each axis is to achieve *predetermined* space-and-time objectives for divisions and armies in second and third echelons as well as forces in contact. In this way the attack is intended to keep *pressure* on the defensive forces in depth and to *exhaust* their capabilities over a relatively short time. To succeed, the Pact must 'force' rates of advance with *precise* timing of *massed* suppressive fire (artillery and air) and inflict '*massive blows*' with echeloned motorized rifle and tank formations. Additional and simultaneous Soviet operations would include suppression/annihilation of NATO's headquarters, aircraft, nuclear storage sites, major logistic depots, communications, etc., by aircraft and missiles throughout the depth of the theatre.

The concept rests on a survivable '*top down*' command, control and communications system, plus *detailed pre-planning* and *timing* of reinforcements. Precise tasking of combat manoeuvre and logistical support units is also required, thus limiting the flexibility of the lower-level field commanders.

The Soviets echelon their ground forces to lessen their vulnerability to nuclear attack. Reinforcement depends upon meeting rather *precise timetables* to achieve certain norms for local, but overwhelming, *force ratios* in selected *breakthrough* areas. The Front commander has authority to subordinate forces to those field armies achieving success. The whole operation is vulnerable to disruption and delay by successful NATO attacks on divisions and armies in second and reserve echelons. Thus NATO could exploit the inherent vulnerabilities in the Soviet offensive operational concept.[10] (Emphasis added)

In the FOFA 'hold the second-echelon at risk' concept, the Soviet Union must *mass* in order to break through. Thus, as long as the threat of conventional and nuclear firepower forces dispersal, the Soviet Union will have insufficient force to break through. If the Soviet forces do try to break through, they must concentrate and disperse quickly in order to minimize their vulnerability. This calls for detailed planning and precise timing in road movement (each division nowadays has thousands of vehicles) and in fire support. Clearly, disrupting this plan can cause significant delays – delays which can mean that opportunities are not exploited and attacking forces themselves may be left unsupported and vulnerable to counter-attack.

Secondary advantages for the Rogers' concept accrue, too, from the USSR's putative need to mass. First, massing obviously provides larger arrays and easier detectability. Smaller formations blend more easily into the background. Earlier detectability allows more time for accurate weapons targeting and delivery. Second, massed forces must attack on *predetermined* axes. Small, high-quality forces can more readily change direction; large forces cannot do so, because their support requirements are restrictive. To concentrate large formations rapidly, organic support must be slim to prevent road congestion. Consumables and support must be prepositioned. Surprise becomes difficult to obtain and large forces are required instead. Third, given the assumption that the Soviet forces would concentrate divisions on narrow fronts, their following replacement and exploitation units must be stacked in depth behind each other. In the Rogers/Cotter scheme, the weight of this mass moving forward gives the Soviet system its momentum and power; it is also the source of its vulnerabilities.

If this *were* the Soviet operational method, then deep attack might seem a reasonable solution. Clearly in this method second echelons are vulnerable to attack by fire and are likely to be the decisive exploiting element. But, as brought out by Donnelly, this is *not* the current Soviet battle plan. Their new OMG system significantly reduces *all* the vulnerabilities that Rogers, Cotter, and their followers hope to exploit. Nor, for that matter, would deep attack have been effective against the German *Panzer* tactics in World War II – an operational method from which the USSR has obviously drawn heavily in developing her OMG method.

In the classic German method of 1939–42, there were no massed, breakthrough battles. The Germans usually *leaked* their way through (the flowing-water method), the tanks following high-quality armoured reconnaissance. By relying on 'cutting edge' *Panzer* formations and reconnaissance to avoid strength, the Germans did not need mass heavy logistical support at the point of penetration. Self-contained columns permitted rapid shifts along and between axes as events unfolded. Follow-on forces of progressively lesser quality consolidated the gains of the lead forces. Nor did the Germans have need for detailed planning; indeed, they had neither the time nor the staff for it.

The OMG method captures the operational attributes of the German *blitzkrieg*.[11] Neither is a system keyed to smashing breakthrough battles. Exploiting echelons of forward forces become reserves. These are, of course, still located behind forward forces, but their mission is more general, rather than preassigned, with a corresponding change in locale. Exploiting reserves are more spatially and laterally distributed than second echelons and 'flow' according to developments rather than being echeloned in depth along predetermined axes. Mission assignments and axes are determined by events. As Hines and Petersen note:

> leading echelons . . . would advance in dispersed march formations and on multiple axes . . . Once weak sectors were identified, the Soviets would hope to quickly penetrate forward defenses . . . cutting off and isolating divisions.
>
> In effect, the deep operation seeks to destroy the enemy's defenses with several deep finger-like penetrations that are controlled by a single powerful hand rather than the driving fist of a *frontal* assault.[12]

In the OMG method, breakthrough battles are no longer necessary. The low density of opposing NATO forces is such that there will almost always be gaps to probe, widen and pass through. If NATO forces are fully deployed, gaps may have to be created from 'soft spots' in the NATO array.[13] In this case, OMGs will be fully deployed only after other formations have developed a soft spot and enveloped defenders along main axes. High-quality OMGs are not to be wasted in avoidable combat. However, it is most likely that NATO will not be fully deployed. In a pre-emptive attack, as is much discussed in relation to OMGs, NATO will by definition not be fully deployed or perhaps not deployed at all. In this case easy-to-develop gaps exist from the start, and OMGs may themselves be the lead element, lesser-quality formations following in their wake, providing back-up and consolidation.

Against the OMG method, the putative benefits of the Rogers' Plan disappear. There is no need to plan for a breakthrough with divisions massed forward on narrow frontages backed up by deeply-stacked second-echelon armies. There is no elaborate timetable required for road movements and fire support.[14] There is no momentum to be 'altered by attacking high value, second echelon targets, reducing his ability to mass and build up momentum'. Interdiction does not 'reduce the attacker's alternative by disrupting his ability to execute his intended plan'.[15] Forced dispersion is no longer a value in itself. On the contrary, the new methods *presume* dispersion.

There are no longer predetermined axes. Many units will be probing for gaps – only those gaps with the greatest potential will be subsequently developed and become the channel for funnelling exploiting OMGs and still larger follow-up forces, for rolling-up defences and consolidation. Nor can this more flexible system be so easily disrupted by targeting a 'top-down' command system. Subordinate commanders have greater latitude.[16] Many units are available for probing and exploiting; co-ordination requirements are reduced.

Unfortunately the situation is worse for the Rogers' Plan than just the disappearance of its posited vulnerabilities. In the OMG method, the deep second echelons – as in the original German model – are no longer the dangerous element. It is the *extended* first (operational) echelon that is now critical. The damaging force is the 19 line divisions of the Group Soviet Forces Germany (GSFG). The reinforcing formations from the Western Military Districts (MDs) assume the character of the space-consolidating *Wehrmacht* horse-drawn infantry. These serve a vital function, but they are redundant in numbers, and few are first-line combat units. It is true that, if the reinforcing 'second *operational* echelon' could be eliminated, the first echelon would be left unsupported and vulnerable. However, this vulnerability could only be exploited if the defence mounted large-scale counter-attacks to contain and destroy the overextended Soviet OMG thrust. It goes without saying that, if NATO had the forces for this capability, it would not need the deep attack capabilities in the first place. This is recognized by Soviet planners. As Donnelly states:

> what all contributors to discussion in the Warsaw Pact press emphasize nowadays when referring to the concept of the Mobile Group is that a formation with a relatively higher speed and greater inherent flexibility

than other formations presents the best means of achieving a rapid penetration into the operational depths of a modern defence of the style proposed by NATO. When that defence, if hastily established, possesses little in the way of operational reserves and no provision for a strong second operational line of defences, the premium on a rapid breach and rapid advance into the depths becomes immediately obvious. Such an advance at an early stage (day 1 or 2) of the battle would not only cause NATO serious problems of control, but would make the use of nuclear weapons very difficult, and would pose a serious threat to security of NATO's nuclear weapons themselves.[17]

In short, the Rogers' Plan would be ideal from the Soviet standpoint: it optimizes the advantages of the new OMG method. The vulnerabilities it seeks do not exist, while it is itself uniquely vulnerable to the OMG concept. Once OMGs enter the NATO rear, targeting by the deep attack apparatus becomes very difficult: there is too much mixing of forces to be able to hit OMGs with confidence, and the OMGs will be destroying the C^3I infrastructure required for attacking deep.[18] There would be little time to deliver many weapons on the approaching reinforcements, and success is in any case irrelevant if NATO defences are collapsing. It is the GSFG that must be destroyed. These are the OMGs which ease the way for the Soviet mass and subvert the power of fire. Stop them from enveloping NATO's front, and the Soviet attacking forces pile up on themselves and the NATO mission of defence is essentially accomplished.

Technical and Operational Feasibility Are Not the Same
The central issue in deep strike is the importance and ability to interdict (destroy, disrupt, and delay) the Soviet second *operational* echelon. Attack ranges are out to 300 kilometres.[19] Deep attacks on fixed points like rail marshalling yards are not in question.[20] Attacking runways and choke points, like bridges, may be difficult but is similarly not in question; however attacking the follow-on forces delayed at these choke points *is* in question.

The second operational Front clearly originates from the Western MDs of the USSR. In the putative forms of the threat, these are the replacement, reinforcement, and exploitation echelons for the forward breakthrough forces. They are forces in transit. Often they will be in assembly areas at rest or waiting for road clearance.

Interdiction has long been a major task for tactical air forces. Battlefield interdiction (isolation of the immediate battlefield) has on occasion been successful. Deep (sometimes termed 'supply') interdiction on land has never been notably successful in halting the flow of material – there are too many hides and too many alternative routes. Nevertheless, air forces have long sought to locate, strike and destroy opposing ground forces before they make contact with friendly forces.[21] The problem has been two-fold: poor target acquisition and inadequate munitions.[22] Emerging technologies might appear to have removed these constraints. For targeting, there are:

- Signal sensors and airborne movement detection radar (and other sensors) with the ability to locate enemy units – either transmitting or moving – quickly and accurately.
- Low-cost digital data processing systems and display systems permitting real-time processing of operationally significant information to be provided to commanders quickly.
- Grid systems allowing the integration of information and locations on NATO forces and Soviet–Pact forces referenced to a common grid.[23]

As for munitions, advanced area munitions and better dispensers can in theory reduce sortie requirements by a factor of ten to fifteen. For example, the following are calculated for a single breakthrough array:[24]

- 5,500 aircraft sorties expending 33,000 metric tons of gravity bombs; or
- 600 sorties using anti-armour unguided submunitions (3,000 metric tons); or
- 50–100 sorties using terminally-guided anti-armour submunitions (TGSM) (500 metric tons). (A metric ton of TGSM would have a kill effectiveness against company-sized armoured vehicles roughly equivalent to a low-yield fission or enhanced radiation (ER) weapon.[25])

Obviously TGSM have great potential. But can that potential be translated into operational capabilities? Weapons development is notorious for failed expectations at great cost. Too many US weapons have had kill probabilities of 0.9 in technical tests (usually programmed runs in the desert) yet have experienced kill probabilities of 0.09 or less in combat.

The Very Intelligent Surveillance and Target Acquisition (VISTA) Technologies

Deep attack of mobile ground forces requires the adoption of advances in the methods of real-time surveillance, automated targeting and information development.[26] The targeting methods attempt to turn mobile targets into 'fixed' targets by assessing past and present location and predictable future locations.[27] This information is then fed to precision-guided delivery systems with TGSM.[28] For the deep attack technologies, five problems exist:

- Cost
- Equipment reliability
- Equipment vulnerability
- System complexity
- Flawed logic

Clearly the technologies are expensive. Cotter estimates that only $0.9 bn is needed to *complete* RDT&E for deep attack of follow-on forces and $5.85 bn as the 10-year costs for equipment, missiles and manning. (The VISTA technologies comprise one-third of these totals.)[29] These are not full-cost estimates. When the systems are deployed, modifications will certainly become necessary to counter Soviet responses. These can be expensive and cannot legitimately be passed to other accounts. Cotter's equipment and operating costs are those of the *Army Force Planning Cost Handbook*, which reflect the direct incremental cost of a unit. They exclude a range of supporting costs which make functional costs many times greater. In addition large allowances must be made for component replacements for highly vulnerable equipment and for a serious underestimation (see Appendix) in the number of missiles required. Any estimate is therefore highly speculative.

The reliability of this complex equipment in a hostile environment is bound to be debatable. Not only are individual functions complex, but they must be combined. A failure in one component will bring down the system as a whole. To date, no demonstration has successfully combined all functions. Two VISTA components – SOTAS (Stand-off Target Acquisition System) and TACFIRE (Tactical Fire Direction) – have already been cancelled due to cost and marginal performance. Assuming that a system will eventually be made to work, its performance in a hostile and dynamic environment is still questionable. Testing conditions usually involve vehicle columns and parks against an open desert background.[30] In war, the system must cope with dispersion, terrain and town-masking, radio and radar silence, rapid movement, and passive and active countermeasures.

Equipment and system vulnerability are obvious. Moving target indicator (MTI) radars, for example, are line-of-sight sensors. They must be high (in the air) and relatively close to the FEBA in order to minimize terrain-masking. Airborne platforms will be very vulnerable to SAM and fighters. Electronic emission creates another vulnerability. VISTA depends heavily on receiving, assessing, and relaying data. The enemy, too, has detecting and home-on-target systems. Even assuming that technology can counter these threats, there remains vulnerability of terminals to ground attack, overt and covert, and the electronic security of the computer system. Worse, because many of the VISTA functions are so expensive, replacements and redundancy are limited. Repeated destruction of one link will bring down the system as a whole.

Science and unconstrained budgets can perhaps resolve these problems, but there are two hazards that cannot be solved technologically: *system complexity* and *system rigidity*. History indicates that simplicity and adaptability are essential to winning wars. Even an inherently simple and robust laser-guided artillery system can illustrate the pitfalls of complexity and rigidity. Moving targets are difficult to hit because too much time elapses between the call for fire and the actual impact of the round. Projectile flight typically requires half a minute, to which must be added several minutes for calling in and directing a gun. Even on a clear day, a vehicle moving at quite modest speeds (25 kph) will have passed outside the cone or footprint in which a projectile can be guided to the target. In cloudy weather the footprint will be smaller. If the terrain is hilly or covered, the observer-to-target line of sight may be broken. There is also a co-ordination problem. The artillery observer desires to minimize his laser spotting of the target in order to reduce his own exposure. Precise knowledge of the projectile's trajectory could reduce laser spotting to seconds but such co-ordination is difficult without providing yet more equipment for an observer whose survivability is dependent on being inconspicuous.[31]

Deep attack, as it is now conceived, would be vastly more complex and less adaptable to wartime dynamics than visually-confirmed guided artillery. Electronics replace the human observer for sensing, interpreting and predicting the enemy's whereabouts. Such technology is often termed 'brilliant' – but it would rank low on an intelligence (IQ) test. It can sense and process data faster than the unaided observer, but its fatal flaws are in interpretation and prediction. Machines can only be preprogrammed; the unexpected renders them useless, even dangerous. Reliance upon them puts a premium on adaptive enemy behaviour. Man is, of course, very adaptive. There is no way that the technology can remove these inherent realities. Whether in quantum physics (the Heisenberg Uncertainty Principle) or human behaviour (Hawthorne Effect), the very act of observation affects that which is observed.

Remote sensing proceeds from the false premise that 'we know the tendencies and patterns of threat units when they are deployed as they would be in a second-echelon formation'.[32] This supposition allows correlations to be developed so that raw data can be machine processed (and implicitly interpreted) and used for fire direction, combat formation and intelligence.[33] Correlations provide the basis for determining enemy behaviour, of which there are three general types:

- *Doctrinal Templates* are models based on enemy tactical doctrine. They generally portray his frontages, depths, echelon spacing and force composition, as well as his disposition of combat, combat support and combat service support units for a given type of tactical operation.
- *Situational Templates* are a series of projections that portray how the doctrinal templates will most probably appear when they are applied to a specific piece of terrain or an avenue of approach under specific weather conditions.
- *Event Templates* serve as models against which enemy activity can be recorded and compared. They represent a sequential projection of events that relate to space and time on the battlefield, and they indicate the enemy's ability to adopt a particular course of action.[34]

The manual continues:

> Once event templates have identified the enemy's general activities, the commander and the intelligence officer direct their attention toward specific areas or windows of interest. Comparing these windows with doctrinal templates, the commander can determine the enemy's options and possible course of action.[35]

Such thinking and procedures invite the enemy to deceive our programmed machinery. A functioning VISTA system must be able to detect and cope with deceptive and unanticipated behaviour on the part of the enemy. Automated command-and-control systems cannot draw correct conclusions from deceptive or unexpected data. Deception affects a battle at two levels. In a microscopic sense, it results in the expenditure of weapons on false targets. In the macroscopic sense, it results (through aggregation) in the misdirection of the command-and-control system (as above for event templates). While the first is important because it influences the rate of weapons exchange in a conflict, the second can be pivotal to the outcome of a conflict. It induces surprise and command paralysis.

The development of automated processing has led (or soon will) to a situation which *appears* flexible. Command and directional staffs can look at their data in any one of a wide variety of ways. Everything known about Soviet operational technique has been captured, it is hoped, by models; counters have been thought out in advance and the computer can draw on them virtually instantaneously. Unfortunately, these attributes provide flexibility only within the realm of the predictable. Consider two computers playing chess. Each has been given a set of rules and a repertoire of attacks and defences. As long as the rules are followed and the repertoires match, each computer is marvellously fast and flexible in its generation of response. Now, however, imagine that one computer adds an unfamiliar attack to its repertoire: it will win quickly and easily. The lesson generated by the analogy to warfare is that automated techniques are extremely flexible within the predictable – and that they are totally inflexible outside it. Electronic deception is analogous to creating a new move in chess. While we know it can be done, we cannot predict how or to what purpose it will in fact be used.

The use of highly automated command-and-control systems invites a variety of reactions, of which deception is only one. Dependence on a system and its potential importance in battle raises the value of its destruction to an enemy. From peacetime observation the enemy can develop countermeasures. If this response is not revealed until wartime, a counter-counter-measure may be foreclosed in a fast-moving war. The fallacy underlying this potential vulnerability is to allow such reliance on any system in the first place: more diffuse *organizational* means of data gathering and command and control would be more robust. Electronics cannot provide this robustness. Indeed, the attempt to do so will render its decisions 'bureaucratic': in the attempt to filter false information and to validate all decisions to avoid mistakes, it will make no decisions at all. Alternatively, so much information is sought that data demands are ever-increasing and the system is continuously faced with breakdown from data overload.

The discussion above hinges on a point whose importance goes beyond the question of automated command and control for FOFA. It is pertinent to any attempt to substitute automatic processing for human data collection, analysis and interpretation. The point is simply stated: automaticity implies extreme inflexibility wherever the enemy can discover – and operate outside of – the bounds of the predictable. Both sides in a conflict must adapt their behaviour to conditions created by the other side. Disallowing overwhelming advantage, the side which adapts most quickly and cleverly will win. If NATO relies on automatic processors, the Soviet Union could adapt her behaviour to the creation of inputs which at least confuse us, and, in the extreme case, defeat us. Alternatively, with our reliance on automaticity, we may deny ourselves the ability to behave outside the predictable. Man must often be eliminated from an automatic system. This is satisfactory if automation is sufficiently monitored. Only man, however, can ensure robustness and reduce the possibility of large-scale deception. In FOFA this check is missing. VISTA is an Achilles' heel. Its technologies can only work if the enemy does not know he is being watched or if the data collected is straightforward. Neither of these assumptions is valid. In this case, too, even the templates in use are invalid, because of a failure to grasp the significance of the OMG method.

Counter-measures and Munition Limitations

Munitions and their delivery systems have improved dramatically in the last decade. Nevertheless, the projected deep strike munitions will prove ineffective for six reasons:

– System mechanics and multiplied probabilities lead to low overall success;
– Targets are well within their own territory;
– Targets must be hit while in transit;
– Time lags exist between target detection and weapons delivery;
– Effectiveness depends on terminal guidance;
– Lethality of small warheads can be negated.

System Mechanics
Assault Breaker submunitions suffer from the phenomenon of linked probabilities. Success is low in the best of circumstances because of the many mechanical tasks that must be accomplished (ballistic flight, ejection, deceleration, search, track and strike). Brassey's table indicates a hit chance of only 14% and a firepower (F) or personnel (P) kill, given a hit, of 20%, yielding an overall non-catastrophic kill chance of 2.8% per submunition and 3.6% given successful delivery (2.8% ÷ 0.77). Cotter's own estimate is not much higher; he shows 288 terminally-guided warheads *destroying* 13 tanks, for a 'destroy' rate of 4.5%.[36]

Assault Breaker 'bus' missiles cost $600,000. The T-16 (*Patriot*) carries 14 TGSMs or 56 *Skeets*; the T-22 (*Lance*), 24 TGSMs or 96 *Skeets*. With so few expected kills per 'bus,' each F or P kill costs well over $100,000 and, with T-16s with TGSMs, $1m each.

Distance
On the immediate battlefield counter-measures are often difficult to orchestrate. Many are too awkward for combat. Where there is no contact with the enemy, the full panoply of counter-measures can be developed and used. In deep attack, second echelons out to 300 kilometres behind the line of contact are to be attacked. With no threat of direct ground attack, vehicles can move administratively and missile defeating features unsuited for combat can be added during transit. Examples are special plates for signature diffusion and for added protection, and non-combat loading of and minimal crews for armoured vehicles. The first reduces the already low chances of hit, the second reduces the power of already weak warhead charges, and the third reduces the

possibility of secondary explosions (the condition necessary for a catastrophic kill with small shaped-charge warheads).

The damage caused is likely to be repairable, temporary and of little operational significance. Additional rear echelon repair units can be spaced along the route to cope with projected damage. For minor vehicle damage to aggregate into significant damage in the deep rear, repair units would have to be swamped, requiring high rates of fire and therefore more firing battalions, missiles and VISTA infrastructure. Lesser rates of fire can, of course, be disruptive against closer-in forces concentrating for a breakthrough, as in the putative threat.

Transit
In deep attack, the targets are vehicles in transit. At any point in time, some will be at rest in assembly areas; others will be on roads moving forward. Forces in assembly areas are not so easily targeted. Positions cannot be precisely determined for attack, and armoured vehicles at rest cannot easily be attacked with submunitions. Assembly areas are in woods or, increasingly, in towns. Both mask the signatures necessary for acquiring targets. Trees and buildings also trigger and absorb the effects of small warhead submunitions.[37]

Reinforcing echelons are vulnerable to attack only during movement. This puts a premium on real-time intelligence and response. Detection and weapons delivery, however, can never be accomplished in real time. While VISTA would in theory be in real time, missiles in flight lead to time lags and to detection in flight.

Time Lags
The lapse of even a few minutes against moving targets on a road means the targets are likely to be outside the footprint (or cone of vision) of the incoming missiles since the moment of detection. Accuracy for other than area fire therefore requires mid-course correction. Otherwise, the target's location must be projected (guessed) or the target presumed to be one among many in a linear array moving across a targeted point. Mid-course correction capability adds to both the expense and complexity in an already complex weapons system. Moreover, even with data updates, missiles can be defeated by the simple administrative expedient of combining spacings between formations (a practice used in all armies) and variation of column speeds.

Specialized battalions control traffic in the Soviet Army. Controllers are spaced about a kilometre apart. In addition, the Soviet Union has many higher-level EW battalions. These could be assigned sectors along LOC axes. Besides such obvious counter-measures as jamming, these could detect incoming ballistic missiles (which take some 3 minutes to travel 90 km) and give 2–3 minutes' warning (including submunition dispersal and sensing). This data can be passed to the spaced controllers by radio, creating a cheap warning system keyed to an already existing means of traffic control. Counter-measures would entail speed changes, turns and the firing of chaff, aerosols and flares from column vehicles and from automatic mortars similarly spaced along the LOC. Changes in speed and course mean that impact points would be empty.

Countering VISTA and Terminal Guidance
Chaff raises the general issue of detection and target classification by long-range sensors and tracking by terminal sensors on the submunitions themselves. During detection and classification, decoys can draw attention and fire to erroneous targets. Once the missile is *en route*, decoys can create more 'targets' than actually exist, thereby lowering the kill probability (Pk) of individual submunitions.

False images can also be created to deceive the sensors and swamp and break down the VISTA system. Formerly false images on the battlefield were expensive – they had to deceive visual observation. Now they can be insubstantial. Images can be created by deceiving 'simple-minded' sensors and simulated electronically across a number of sensor modes. For example, the MTI radar detection system can be deceived and the entire system overloaded by the simple expedient of sending civilians or soldiers with corner reflectors on their caps jogging or bicycling in single file from town to town and forest to forest, thus appearing as innumerable columns of vehicles moving from hide to hide. In one known Soviet simulation technique, vehicles are made to appear to be moving down roads, when in fact there is nothing more than a line of (small and difficult-to-hit) radar reflectors (to overload signal processing) and emitters (to attract fire) strung parallel to a road like Christmas-tree lights.

Decoys can assume many shapes. Civilians might be forced to drive down roads to draw fire (consuming a limited inventory of expensive missiles) or be interspersed with military vehicles to deter fire. Or simple devices like corner reflectors for millimetre wave radars and flares and extended 'pipes' for infra-red sensors can be made more attractive than the real targets. Should the *Assault Breaker* weapons prove successful, previously destroyed vehicles may deflect weapons aimed at live targets. Then, too, most of the targets presented – trucks – are themselves quasi-decoys.

Decoys may be filtered out by greater sensor sensitivity, signal processing and multimode cross-referencing. In large missiles, this is merely a question of higher sensor cost – one cost among many. For submunitions, where the sensor is the dominant cost, the demand for greater sensor sensitivity can multiply the cost of each submunition significantly. There are other penalties as well. Greater sensing and signal processing capability means larger submunition diameters and therefore fewer submunitions per missile and smaller payloads.

Chaff and aerosols can blind the sensor, reducing its Pk to that of a random hit. Missiles carrying *Skeets* and TGSMs cost over $600,000 each, while chaff, aerosols and smoke are very cheap. They can be mounted on vehicles or fired from special launchers on signal. High-performance fighters now protect themselves against sophisticated air defence missiles with chaff and flares. Obviously, much denser chaff clouds can be fired from the ground to cover much slower-moving ground vehicles, and submunition sensors lack the sophistication of hyper-expensive air defence missiles.

Additional complications in terminal guidance are inherent from natural clutter, weather and terrain. In ground warfare contrasts are low, and signatures need only be reduced to blend into the natural environment. Paints and nets are well known for breaking visual contrasts; similarly they can be used for reducing IR and radar signatures. Other obvious complications include cloud cover and rain for IR-sensing TGSMs and ground winds for all terminally-guided submunitions. Local wind strengths and azimuths cannot be discerned at great distances. Yet, because most submunitions have retardants to slow the rate of fall so that the sensor can take its bearings, wind can blow these descending submunitions out of target footprints.

Besides the masking nature of town and forest, there is a problem with many European roads. Only autobahns offer clear sensings. Autobahns, however, are not good military highways; besides being exposed to observation, embankments inhibit movement off the road when attacked, in effect making them vehicle traps.

The better roads for military use are the old, tree-lined network still prevalent in the East. Trees diffuse the sensings of inventory IR sensors, while often being more attractive targets in the IR 8–13 micron band and for millimetre wave radars than vehicles themselves. Trees are also a natural frame for supporting special screens to complicate detection, blind terminal sensors and even triged-charge bomblets. Equally significant, bridges and chokepoints along the old road network are generally sited in or near towns. Vehicles queued at such chokepoints are naturally protected from detection, from terminal guidance, and from the warhead effects themselves.[38] Towns can 'absorb' large units waiting to pass congested chokepoints. The nature of the road net itself thus partially defeats one of the attractive features of deep strike: the destruction of chokepoints, followed by subsequent attack upon 'bunched' formations queued at the obstacle with submunitions. Instead, the requirement remains one of high-tonnage, high-explosive ordnance.

Finally, the only proven sensor, heat-seeking IR which is attracted to a vehicle's engine, has numerous limitations.[39] Heat signatures can be duplicated or diffused. For example, the heat from large engines can be diffused and made to appear small, while small engines themselves can be made undetectable and decoys made to appear everywhere. These are other limitations, too. Often, hotspots will not exist, and, when they do, special protection can be limited to a fraction of the total vulnerability area. Moreover, the primary target in any attack on follow-on forces – the tank – generally does not move forward in deep rear areas under its own power. To minimize wear, these vehicles are carried as much as possible on transporters and rail flatbeds. Most tanks can be expected to be so transported, while the lighter armoured vehicles move under their own power. Tanks on transporters obviously cannot be targeted. The transporters themselves must first be destroyed, which at a minimum consumes time and additional munitions.

Countering Small Warheads
The greater the number of small warheads, the greater their overall hit probability. But subdivision leads to smaller warheads and so less lethality, given a hit. Because warheads are small, they can be countered in ways not possible against larger warheads. Most must hit the target; a near miss is not sufficient. With the self-forging warhead variant of the shaped charge, the firing jet is initiated from several hundred feet. This causes loss of accuracy. Sighting (much like a pistol) cannot be accurate, and the penetrator is never entirely predictable about its axis.

The main problem with small warheads is that their terminal effects are by definition limited. The damage caused by the penetration will be relatively small. Equipment and personnel directly in the path of a shaped-charge jet or a self-forging fragment slug will be damaged or destroyed, but little other damage may occur. What is hit can generally be replaced or repaired. Severe damage and catastrophic kills require secondary detonation and fire. Without such secondary effects, small shaped charges and self-forging warheads are likely to do little more damage than a high-energy sniper's bullet. Against tanks, there is likely to be no effect, or at most a temporary firepower or mobility kill. Against thin-skinned armour and trucks, damage may amount only to entry and exit holes and to whatever lies between.

The effects from shaped charges can be countered by dissipating penetration power, reducing internal spalling and preventing secondary detonation and fires. Much of this is a matter of vehicle design. The M-1 tank, for example, has its munitions in compartments to reduce the chance of ammunition detonation, and blow out panels (to prevent catastrophic loss) if the munitions do detonate. Soviet tank designs could incorporate these safety features if they have not yet done so. Since the 1973 Yom Kippur War, much has been done (and considerably more can be done) to reduce spalling and secondary detonation and fire. Among the counters for the first are better metallurgical properties, absorptive liners, and crew and component compartmentalization and redundancy. Secondary detonations and fire can be reduced by desensitizing high-energy ammunition propellants, by using non-flammable hydraulic fluids, nitrogen- and foam-filled fuel tanks, and by incorporating halon fire suppressors.

Armoured vehicles incorporating these internal features have little chance of being catastrophically damaged by small shaped-charge warheads. For the case in hand, even current Soviet tanks can readily incorporate some of the above features. During administrative movements, tank ammunition and internal fuel need not be loaded and temporary absorptive liners/compartments could be added within the turrets. Even vehicles moving under their own power do not need full crews. Thus, lethality rates, given a hit, are likely to be much below those projected. Larger and more powerful submunitions will be required for more than negligible damage.

Tanks in the future will undoubtedly incorporate strengthened top armour, but it is obvious that the trade-off is less protection elsewhere. In administrative marches, however, top protection can be strengthened without paying a permanent penalty. Against small unguided bomblets like the M-42 (51mm) many devices could be introduced.

For example, blocks of removable ceramic armour and even sacks of children's marbles laid on top decks would be sufficient to defeat penetrating jets. Against larger submunitions, thin sheet-steel 'standoff' umbrellas could be mounted. In the future active armour will certainly defeat these types of threats.

In Conclusion

Deep attack of Follow-on Forces therefore falters on *all* counts:

- The underlying premise is false: NATO is outgunned but neither outmanned nor outspent. NATO's problem is organizational and doctrinal; marginal technological advances cannot overcome these self-inflicted wounds.
- Technology is being wrongly focused on difficult deep attacks, rather than on easier and more rewarding targets close to the FEBA.
- While the individual technologies may work, the many diverse components and distinct tasks have yet to be combined and demonstrated in a benign, much less a hostile, environment.
- Unless protective measures are devised, any deployed system, because of the emissions of its VISTA infrastructure, will have large signatures. Components will be vulnerable to attack, and so the system will be inherently vulnerable; cost will inhibit redundancy.
- NATO requires 4% more annually just to modernize current forces. The proposed technologies are additions. Costs using its proponents own claims of effectiveness are an order of magnitude greater than asserted (see Appendix).
- Submunitions do not have nuclear equivalence in a deep strike role: effects are too limited and too readily countered.

These alone cast doubt on the desirability and feasibility of the concept. But, even if the technology worked perfectly and invulnerably, the concept remains *operationally* infeasible. The concept depends on a three-link chain:

- The enemy must concentrate for breakthroughs;
- Command and control must be robust and not subject to deception and jamming;
- Submunitions must have high *hit* probabilities and high *damage* rates, given a hit.

All must hold, yet *none* do hold. Nor does even a workable concept necessarily enhance deterrence and stability. FOFA strengthens NATO's strengths and weakens further NATO's weaknesses. If the system is deployed, NATO could be weakened conventionally if resources are directed away from forward forces. Should the Soviet Union conclude that the system is effective (i.e., that the technologically superior West must know something she does not), the obvious counters are pre-emptive surprise and heretofore concealed counter-measures. In addition, because NATO's nuclear threshold could appear to be lowered because its (early) tactical nuclear capabilities would be enhanced (the same VISTA infrastructure and missiles are used for both), the Soviet Union could logically conclude that Follow-On Force Attack is a mere Trojan horse for nuclear weapons and that NATO is in reality returning to a tripwire strategy.

NOTES

[1] For a detailed discussion, see Martin van Creveld, *Technology and War*, C&L Associates, Inc., July 1984.

[2] This concept is also variously known as *AirLand Battle 2000*, *AirLand 2000*, the Rogers Plan, Follow-on Force Attack, Hold the Second Echelon at Risk, Defense in Depth and Strike Deep. Two distinctions are worth noting. (i) *AirLand Battle* and *AirLand Battle 2000* are distinctly different. *AirLand Battle* is the new official doctrine for the tactical use of American tanks and infantry formations; it is in principle similar to French, German, and Dutch army tactics. *AirLand Battle 2000* is an extension of the old American style of attrition warfare. (ii) *Counter Air 90* (attack on Soviet main airfields with submunitions) is technically distinct from attack of second echelon ground forces. Runways are known, fixed targets. Their attack is in principle straightforward and could have a high military pay-off. (Its political feasibility given *Pershing* II INF is another question.)

[3] For an alternative *organizational* approach, stressing that, since NATO already matches Warsaw Pact forces man for man and significantly outspends the Pact, NATO could in fact generate the requisite combat numbers to obtain conventional superiority, see Steven L. Canby, 'Military Reform and the Art of War', *Survival*, May/June 1983, vol. xxv no. 3, pp. 120–27.

[4] Michael Howard, 'Military Science in an Age of Peace,' *RUSI Journal*, March 1974, p. 7.

[5] For a development of this theme, see Steven L. Canby, 'Light Infantry Perspectives,' Infantry Commanders Conference, Ft Benning, GA, 7 March 1984; *Infantry*, July/August 1984, pp. 28–31.

[6] Misused technologies readily coming to mind include C³I, 'stealth' aircraft, the M-1 *Abrams* and air defence tanks. For an alternative approach to technology, based on operational value, see Steven Canby, *Classic Light Infantry and New Technology*, C&L Associates, December 1982.

[7] The Soviet advantage varies from equal logistic lift and quantity of infantry to twice the armour and six times as many artillery weapons. Christopher Donnelly, 'Soviet Operational Concepts in the 1980s,' in *Strengthening Conventional Deterrence in Europe*, Report of the European Security Study (ESECS) (New York: St Martin's Press, 1983), p. 135.

[8] Gen. Bernard W. Rogers, '"Strike Deep": a new concept for NATO', *Military Technology*, vol. vii, no. 5, 1983, p. 40.

[9] For a development of the OMG thesis, see Christopher Donnelly, 'Soviet Operational Concept in the 1980's,' *ibid.*, pp. 105–36. Donnelly's thesis was first openly published as 'The Soviet Operational Maneouver Group: A New Challenge for NATO', *International Defense Review*, vol. 9, 1982. For an early formulation of the essence of this thesis, see Steven Canby and Edward Luttwak, *Operational Methods in Armored Warfare: Declared, Revealed, and Imputed*, C&L Associates, Inc., November 1978; and Steven Canby, *Soviet Operational Methods of Armored Warfare: Rigid or Flexible? The Evidence*, C&L Associates Inc., June 1980. 'The above-probing resembles the OMG except that there is no presumption of high quality or initiative for the probing and exploiting groups, rather it is a "command push" system deriving flexibility from the large numbers of units available. Unit flexibility is obtained by battle drill.'

[10] Donald R. Cotter, 'Potential Future Roles for Conventional and Nuclear Forces in Defense of Western Europe,' in *Strengthening Conventional Deterrence in Europe, op. cit.* in note 7, pp. 213–14.

[11] Substantive similarity exists between OMGs and German 1939–42 *panzer* groupings. This similarity, however, excludes technique (Russians are not Germans) and the popularized visualization of OMGs as mere disruptive raiders with little direct connection to main forces. Much of the Mobile Group discussion has been confused by Russian terminology which has Cossack origins. Cavalry-like raids may be the translation but it is not the meaning of the OMG method. Cavalry-like raid tactics are not (and were not) viable against a defence with strong mobile reserves of its own (as for instance in I German Corps in NORTHAG today). OMGs and Forward Detachments are precursors for the main body. Fracturing defending resistance requires rolling-out and moving far ahead of the main body. To be sure these attacks have the micro attributes of many raids, but their totality is considerably more, and it is misleading to view them as such.

[12] Lt-Col. John G. Hines and Phillip A. Petersen, 'The Conventional Offense in Europe', *Military Review*, April 1984, pp. 4, 7.

[13] 'Soft spot' tactics are techniques developed by the Germans in 1918 to penetrate the dense Anglo-French fronts in Flanders. Sometimes known as Hutier tactics, they are the forerunners of Guderian's methods.

[14] Donnelly, for instance, notes that rolling barrages (which are often the pace setters for breakthroughs) are now replaced with short (4–5 minutes) but heavy (on-call) successive fire strikes as a means of neutralizing the enemy. *Ibid.*, p. 131.

[15] Gen. Donn A. Starry, 'Extending the Battlefield,' *Military Review* (March 1981), pp. 41, 38. Gen. Starry commanded TRADOC from 1978–81.

[16] Donnelly, *op. cit.* in note 7, p. 128.

[17] *Ibid.*, p. 122.

[18] Interspersed OMGs can of course be hit with TGSMs fired from any number of observer-controlled devices. Here the three links which make deep attack inoperative do not hold. 'Attack shallow' is less sensitive to the unfolding of the Soviet attack, automated C³I is not required, and TGSMs are more difficult to defeat. 'Deep' can be defined as more than 50 km forward of the line of contact. It is the distance at which opposing artillery (e.g., MLRS) and counter-attacks cannot interfere with the preparation of units in assembly areas, and forces in movement have time to prepare for ground combat.

[19] Cotter, *op. cit.* in note 10, p. 215.

[20] Note that these targets are fixed and are area targets. Fixed targets do not require VISTA; area targets do not require terminally, guided point detonation. Nor are small warhead shaped charges being used. For area targets at ranges of several hundred kilometres, current technologies provide CEPs that are small enough to preclude the need for terminal homing. River crossings are

difficult targets. Bridges require repeated targeting with terminally-guided, large explosive warheads. The crossing sites themselves require repeated attacks to prevent repair and the deployment of new equipment. Many fixed targets are also very high value targets. Airbase attack (*Counter Air 90*) can be important for deterrence and warfighting. It offers a way to cripple the Soviet air force should they precede a surprise attack with a massive air onslaught. An attack on all runways (and parts of Autobahns) simultaneously on Day 1, while most aircraft are airborne, would prevent the USSR from reconstituting her air force for some time, and then at much reduced strength. The limitation is the relative ineffectiveness of the runway munitions. Cratering submunitions have empirically not worked out. Less demanding submunitions for potholing runways and for delayed mining are too easily countered. Damage is easily repaired and mines are readily swept. Nevertheless, because of the timing involved, the scheme has potential. (Large warheads can destroy runways, (by causing 'heaving') but cannot be delivered in the quantities required simultaneously.)

[21] Brig. Gen. John E. Ralph, 'Tactical Air Systems and the New Technologies', in G. Kemp (ed.), *The Other Arms Race* (Lexington, MA: D. C. Heath, Washington, 1975), p. 31. Gen. Ralph at the time was Director of Doctrine, Concepts and Objectives, DCS&O, Department of the Air Force. This article is perhaps the best articulation of USAF intent and views.

[22] *Ibid.*, pp. 29–30

[23] Donald Cotter, 'NATO Theater Nuclear Forces: An Enveloping Military Concept,' *Strategic Review*, Spring 1981, p. 51.

[24] *Ibid.*, p. 50.

[25] *Ibid.*, p. 50.

[26] Cotter, *op. cit.* in note 10, p. 225.

[27] *Ibid.*

[28] *Ibid.*

[29] *Ibid.*, p. 243.

[30] For an account of the many artificialities in the *Strike Deep* test programme, see Michael Gordon, 'Highly Touted Assault Breaker Weapon Caught Up in Internal Pentagon Debate,' *National Journal*, 22 October 1983, pp. 2152–7.

[31] For a detailed discussion of the operational limitations of the *Copperhead* system, see Steven Canby, *Terminal Guidance on the Battlefield: Obtaining its Potential Payoff*, (Santa Monica, CA: Technology Service Corporation, May 1975).

[32] Starry, *op. cit.* in note 15, p. 43.

[33] The process by which incoming information is collected, combined and correlated is termed 'fusion'. Fusion allows computers 'to correlate, interpret and display an unfolding battle in real time so commanders can select the optimum response to a specific class of targets'. It is accomplished by the 'systematic processing of numerous elemental sensor reports through self-correlation, cross-correlation, and aggregation'. ('Aggregation is the computer-assisted process of indentification of parent units based on 'sense' or known data about subordinate entities'.) Eldon Mangold, 'Joint Tactical Fusion', *National Defense: Journal of American Defense Preparedness Association*, December 1983. This article typifies industry (and much academic) thinking in 'hi-tech' C^3I. It is an engineering, mechanical approach to war that views war as a science and therefore as predictable and deterministic. There is little appreciation of the *art* in war, which of course leads to unpredictability and indeterminism. This distinction is fundamental yet unappreciated in discussions of command and control. If war is science, command and control are amenable to preplanning and centralization, like the British at the Somme in 1916 or in the US Army's more recent *Active Defense*. If war is art, command and control functions best in a system which accepts loose control and attempts to exploit developing opportunities. For a discussion of these two approaches to war, see Martin van Creveld, *Command*, C & L Associates, 1982; and John Boyd, 'Organic Design for Command and Control', unpublished.

[34] *FM 100-5: Operations*; Department of the Army, August 1982, pp. 6–8.

[35] *Ibid.*

[36] 'Potential Future Roles for Conventional and Nuclear Forces in Defense of Western Europe,' *op. cit.*, p. 232 and R. E. Simpkin, [Antitank], RUSI and Brassey's Defence Yearbook 1982 (Oxford: Brassey's, 1982), p. 159. Cotter's paper in this collection clarifies 'destroy' as a mobility (M) kill. M kills are defined as disablement for up to 30 minutes. This can be fatal on the battlefild, but not in the deep rear. Obviously this is not nuclear equivalence.

[37] 45% of Germany is classified as close terrain. Poland is somewhat more open.

[38] Where such protection does not exist, inexpensive shelters for negating these effects could be constructed.

[38] There may also be a fatal limitation. Some question whether the heat from a Soviet T-62 tank is sufficient to activate IR sensors in the 3–5 micron band. The very artificial testing which has been done (e.g., in deserts, known wind conditions, submunitions dropped from helicopters, etc.) have been against ancient M-47 gasoline-engined tanks. These have two red-hot exhausts mounted on top of an open grille over the engine. The hotspots on the T-62 and later-model Soviet tanks are well-shielded, probably making them vulnerable only to very expensive I^2R sensors.

[40] 'Potential Roles for Conventional and Nuclear Forces in Defense of Western Europe,' *op. cit.*, pp. 225–31.

[41] Industry estimates for missiles components are: $200,000 Missile including initial guidance; $80,000 Mid-course correction (desired by the USAF but not the US Army); $50,000 Submunition dispenser; $280,000–350,000 Submunition (14 TGSMs or 14 SDVs with 4 *Skeet* each) cost for 16 in. diameter T-16 missile (*Patriot*); $480,000–600,000 Submunitions (24 TGSMs or 24 SDVs with 4 *Skeet* each) cost for T-22 (*Lance*)

[42] *Soviet Army Operations*, Department of the Army, April 1978, pp. 2–11 to 2–47.

[43] The larger T-22 missile works more favourably for Cotter's example. It requires only 3 missiles per company. This translates into destroying 1,000 companies or 19.2 divisions' worth of line equipment.

[44] Cotter's example raises questions. His primary example using the Multiple Launch Rocket System (MLRS) states that 288 *Skeets* destroy 13 tanks, a kill

probability of 4.5% per *Skeet*. His widely reproduced Table 2 states that 50–60 strikes of a 'salvo of two surface-to-surface missiles per company sized target' destroys 60% of a Soviet armoured division of 3,000 total vehicles of 1,800 vehicles. Two salvoes of T-16 missiles (56 Skeet) times 55 strikes is 6,160 *Skeets*, or a kill (=destroy) probability of 29% per *Skeet*. If TGSMs are used, each TGSM (2 × 14 × 55 = 1,540) kills 1.17 vehicles! These numbers are absurdities. Yet since Cotter contends, only 3,000 long-range corps support weapons systems in Central Region are required, these *are* the required inputs for an appreciable effect. If in Cotter's example 55 strikes of T-16 missiles destroy 60% of a division, 3,000 missiles destroy 60% of 27.3 divisions (all arms and services).

There are other questions in this calculation as well. Cotter apparently assumes 55 company groupings per Soviet division. There are 107 company groupings in just the combat arms, exclusive of engineers and other support. Hence there is no way that 55 strikes can destroy 60% of a division. Second, his measure of effectiveness (divisions destroyed) is puffed up by the criterion of 60% destroyed equating to eliminating a division from the order of battle. Though widely used by wargamers in the US, it is a questionable criterion off the battlefield. In the deep strike case, divisions suffering such losses can be consolidated into small divisions or amalgamated with other remnants. The disruptive impact is minimal if a surfeit of divisions remains or if command relationships can be consolidated during movement forward. Actual reduction in the Warsaw Pact order of battle is now 0.6 × 27.3 = 16.4 divisions. If Cotter is assuming that a salvo of two missiles destroys 60% of 55 company groupings which form a quarter of a division's total company groupings, destruction totals 4 divisions.

[45] There are 3,000 vehicles in a Soviet division. Line companies have 10 tanks/armoured personnel carriers, except for the independent tank company, which has 13 tanks.

[46] Vehicle discrimination cannot be resolved by greater sensor sensitivity and better fusion techniques. Such proposals are high-cost traps rather than potential solutions.

[47] Cotter allocates another 2,000 missiles for destroying the air defence systems and follow-on forces at chokepoints *en route*. These munitions have much the same limitations as discussed for destroying the second echelon. Since all the above examples were based on 3,000 missiles, the additional 2,000 missiles would essentially raise all divisional kills by two-thirds.

[48] Ten or more firing battalions per corps *with support* approaches the manning and financial cost of a division. The NATO Corps averages 3 divisions. By implication *unless manpower is also increased*, the NATO Corps changes to 2 line divisions and a deep attack missile division. The cost of the emerging technologies is on top of this organizational cost.

Appendix

Proponent Cost and Effectiveness Estimates

Under the best of circumstances, as for instance those outlined by D. Cotter, deep attack is not cost effective.[40] Deep attack missiles are expensive, and kill probabilities are low. Cotter's cost estimate per missile is $600.[41] His kill probabilities for the relatively large and expensive terminally-guided submunition (TGSM) are unstated. His destroy rate for *Skeet* is 288 *Skeets* for a 13-vehicle tank and mechanized company grouping, or 4.5% (22 *Skeets*) per vehicle. Brassey's *F* or *P* kill chance is 3.6%.

Using Cotter's example, 5 *Patriot* T-16 missiles (5 × 56 = 280 *Skeets*) are therefore required to destroy a Soviet tank/mechanized company column. A Soviet tank/mechanized division has 52 such companies.[42] Therefore, 260 T-16s are required to destroy the *line* combat elements of a Soviet division. Cotter's example posits 360 missiles per NATO corps. This number kills 72 companies or 1.4 divisions worth of line combat equipment. Cotter's 3,000 missiles for the whole Central Region destroy 600 companies or 11.5 divisions worth of line combat equipment.[43] Given that the Warsaw Pact could deploy more than a hundred divisions, this number is not significant. Moreover, even without the many complications wrought by Soviet actions against these firing units and Soviet efforts to protect themselves from their effect, Cotter's kill estimate of 11.5 divisions is high.[44]

First, while there are 52 line companies per Soviet division, there are an additional 55 divisional air defence and artillery batteries that have a similar armoured configuration. Sensors cannot distinguish between them. With the inclusion of other heavy equipment and transport, there are roughly 200 indistinguishable company groupings per Soviet division.[45] There are in addition many Army and Front units. Assuming all missiles arrive and successfully disperse in the target area, 3,000 missiles now destroy fewer than 3 Soviet divisions.[46]

Equally serious is a biased lethality estimate. 'Destroy' from submunition attack necessarily presumes that the target is a combat-ready armoured vehicle: that is, a vehicle filled with fuel, ammunition and crew. Major damage requires a secondary explosion. If the tank is not combat-loaded and fully crewed, catastrophic kill lethality is very much reduced. The 'lethality' that does occur (e.g., a mobility kill from hitting the engine or firepower kill from destroying weapon components within the turret) is repairable.

In the Cotter/Rogers deep attack model, it cannot be presumed that combat vehicles will be combat loaded. In fact, most tanks will be empty and will be moved on transporters. Actual lethality will thus be very much less than estimated. Damage that does occur is likely to be minor. If such repairable effects are to have a significant impact upon the overall battle, damage must be sufficiently widespread to saturate (expanded) Soviet repair capabilities, otherwise vehicle losses will be quickly reconstituted and the military effect will be almost nil (see note 36).

It can be concluded that 3,000 deep strike missiles are likely to have no appreciable effect in the Central Region.[47] More than an order-of-magnitude increase in missiles, firing battalions, and funding would be required to make a difference.[48] Even so, it is an open question whether much effect will be obtained. With the inclusion of counter-measures against the *Assault Breaker* submunitions, hit probabilities drop sharply to not much more than random probability, while 'destroy' probabilities against armoured vehicles *effectively approach zero*.

New Conventional Force Technology and the NATO–Warsaw Pact Balance: Pact II

DONALD R. COTTER

This Paper will centre on the policy implications of new and available technology for conventional force improvements for the defence of Western Europe. To develop a context for this discussion, specific missions which are in NATO's operational plans and which today rely to a large extent on the threat of the use of a significant number of nuclear weapons will be examined. In attempting to improve NATO's conventional posture and at the same time reduce dependence on the early use of nuclear weapons, an approach will be taken which envisages a range of technologies and the overall environment in NATO. This environment will bear heavily on the political, military, economic and technical feasibility of adopting conventional force improvements of one form or another.

Context
Defensive Missions
NATO is a defensive alliance and has since its inception structured its forces for defensive operations and not for operations which could be construed as offensive. In the early days of NATO, Western Europe faced a very large Soviet land threat resulting from a Red Army which was not reduced at the end of hostilities in Europe. While US and Allied forces demobilized shortly after 1945, the Red Army remained largely intact and in place in Eastern Europe. The Soviet Union took the opportunity to consolidate her political control over Eastern Europe. With the advent of the Warsaw Pact, she undertook a considerable modernization programme in all phases – ground, air and naval forces – to maintain her control, and to build a military machine which presents a large aggressive threat to NATO. Today, we see a threat which can be described as a five-component threat[1] to NATO.

The co-ordinated threat includes:

- *A central battle*, wherein NATO front-line forces must deal with a large and fast-moving attack undertaken on perhaps as many as six to eight major axes of advance. The initial attack would be complemented by mobile reserve and armed reconnaissance and fighting forces and the planned insertion of other reserve forces;
- *The reserve forces*, defined by SACEUR as the follow-on forces, are those echeloned divisions, armies and fronts which, according to Soviet doctrine, are intended for exploitation (Operational Manoeuvre Groups or OMGs) after a number of breakthrough operations have occurred against NATO's central battle forces;
- *Simultaneous independent air operations* against NATO's rear areas, largely aimed at the neutralization of NATO's air assets and destruction of NATO's nuclear weapons and reserve forces;
- *An independent surface-to-surface missile attack* (using a combination of chemical, conventional and nuclear warheads) against key NATO fixed facilities; and
- *Air defence operations* to be used against surviving penetrating NATO aircraft which would be used in retaliatory attack against Warsaw Pact airfields, nuclear weapon sites and key transportation points. The objective of the Soviet/Pact air defence system is to deny NATO counter-air and interdiction operations.

Deterring or defending against this five-component threat involves NATO responding with *nearly simultaneous* operations with *in-place capabilities*. While warning time is important for reinforcement and mobilization, readiness is the key to dealing with the five-component threat, if the integrity of NATO territory is to be maintained. Further it is emphasized that NATO must be prepared to *absorb* the first attack elements and then *respond*. All concepts in this Paper are based on response *after* massive air and ground attack are under way against NATO.

Today NATO relies on a variety of nuclear forces to deny Soviet/Warsaw Pact success. These include:

- Short-range nuclear missiles, artillery and atomic demolition munitions (ADM) for the central battle;
- Quick Reaction Alert (QRA) nuclear-armed aircraft and medium-range missiles to strike Pact airbases, nuclear storage sites, and to interdict key transportation points such as bridges;
- Nuclear-armed surface-to-air missiles (being drastically reduced) against the Pact's independent air operations; and
- Medium-range dual-capable aircraft against follow-on forces and suppression of air defences.

The application of technology in helping to accomplish these missions with conventional as opposed to nuclear forces will be examined.

The Environment
The consideration of conventional force improvements will be greatly influenced by long-standing political issues involving the conventional/nuclear dilemma. Any approaches which appear to either the NATO Allies or to the Soviet Union to be one of denuclearization of NATO will meet justifiably strong opposition. To many, deterrence of Soviet aggression against Western Europe has been successful solely because of a strong nuclear capability in NATO. However, others question the credibility of NATO's nuclear deterrent and, more particularly, the dangers which may exist because of an outmoded nuclear strategy based on an obsolescent and vulnerable nuclear posture. Thus, the political dimensions of an improved conventional capability in Europe must be played against the requirements for modernizing NATO's nuclear forces as well. The key issue in modernization is not *whether* a quality nuclear force is needed for NATO. Rather, the issues are what *mix* of systems and what *dispositions* of forces will provide the needed survivability and posture and be compatible with an improved conventional force.

In addition there is the question of limited economic resources and, more importantly, the demographic environment in Europe which will prevail in the late 1980s and 1990s. A decrease in available manpower[2] for military forces will be the norm in all NATO countries. Thus, NATO will have to rely on roughly today's level of forces in terms of ground divisions, air wings, logistic support and naval forces. Conventional force improvements could, at best, include only a small increment of additional manpower for traditional manning of tanks, infantry, artillery, etc. This problem is similar to that which occurred at the inception of NATO, when an attempt was made to define a force structure for a 'conventional-only' defence of Western Europe. The requirements for force levels defined in 1952 at Lisbon indicate a requirement for 96 divisions and 9,000 aircraft. These goals were soon reduced to about half, but with little hope on the part of West Europeans struggling to recover from World War II of ever meeting those objectives.

The appropriate decision, which was made in the mid-1950s, was to seek a solution to the manpower and economic resource problem in an 'emerging technology', that of tactical nuclear weapons. Alliance decisions taken during the Eisenhower Administration led to the substitution of nuclear weapons to fill the gap in conventional forces. A requirement of 15,000 nuclear weapons was defined to support a 'feasible' NATO force structure of 26 divisions (12 of which were to be from the FRG) and about 1,400 combat aircraft. New nuclear technology thus provided a substitution of nuclear firepower for conventional firepower at a 'saving' of 74 divisions and 7,600 aircraft.

Today, NATO has essentially the same conventional force levels but, of course, being much improved qualitatively, especially in terms of aircraft. The numbers of nuclear weapons in NATO never rose to the 15,000 projected in the mid-1950s. Deployments were truncated at about 7,000 and have since been reduced by withdrawal of 1,000 old battlefield weapons in 1979 as a result of the INF two-track decision. A further reduction of 1,400 weapons was approved by NATO ministers in October 1983, which will leave NATO with approximately 4,600 nuclear weapons including the 572 INF weapons. The majority of the remainder require modernization to achieve greater survivability and military effectiveness. Although NATO has generally fewer warheads (some 4,600 to 12,500) and missiles than the Soviet Union, NATO can provide an adequate nuclear force within the reduced numbers, provided appropriate modernization takes place.[3]

The Indispensable Nuclear Component
NATO nuclear weapons and forces, it must be emphasized, will still be an indispensable component of deterrence and defence. Without the realistic threat of the use of nuclear weapons, NATO can never achieve a credible conventional defence within its limited manpower and economic resources. An important principle, borne out by observing changes over the years in Soviet doctrinal patterns for survivable deployments, has been formulated: the realistic threat of the use of nuclear weapons will enhance NATO's ability to defend with conventional forces.

The effect of battlefield nuclear weapons, and, more important, the medium-range aircraft weapons, on Soviet doctrine and tactics when those weapons were first introduced in the mid-1950s, has been remarkable. The Soviet Union went through great restructuring of her large conventional forces to achieve survivability for conventional operations. She adopted a concept of dispersal and echeloning of forces which, while giving higher levels of survivability, introduced vulnerabilities and complexities in their operations.

To attempt once again, as was tried in 1952, to seek a 'conventional-only' defence, would require NATO nations to go on to an essentially wartime footing in peacetime. This is neither politically nor socially acceptable to free nations. In addition, as long as the Soviet Union possesses nuclear weapons, NATO and the US will require a nuclear deterrent of high quality. Thus, we are faced with a need to exploit technology for modernization of both conventional *and* nuclear forces for the maintenance of a credible forward defence of Western Europe.

Defining Force Modernization
In speaking of 'force modernization' we include:

- Hardware (missiles, munitions, communication systems, etc.) to increase military effectiveness;
- Deployment and basing concepts to improve survivability;
- Employment concepts (targeting) to enhance deterrence and direct defence;
- Declaratory policy which can serve both deterrence and reassure the public;
- Arms-control arrangements which can achieve stability.

Questions On Modernization
The questions to be addressed are then:

- Can technology provide new conventional options which are operationally feasible?
- Can NATO provide the economic resources neccessary for some level of conventional modernization which will allow less dependence by NATO on the early use of nuclear weapons?
- Will available and 'emerging technology' provide new and conventional options at reasonable costs and within essentially today's level of conventional forces?
- Can NATO, in a timely manner, provide a modernized *integrated* conventional and nuclear force within the political environment that exists in Western Europe?

The NATO–Warsaw Pact 'Balance'
Asymmetries
We need to consider all aspects of the balance in Europe. This must take into account not only the quantitative but also qualitative aspects. A number of significant asymmetries are present. First NATO is a defensive alliance which must be prepared to repel aggression. NATO not only faces superior forces which appear to be poised and capable of short-warning attacks but it

also relies on significant reinforcements from the United States. Next, the geographical asymmetry presents a severe disparity in reinforcement times and logistic complexity. The United States is 6,000 km distant from Central Europe, whereas the Soviet and Pact reserve forces are in close proximity (600 km) and contiguous to NATO's Central, Northern and Southern Regions. The US plans a huge air- and sea-lift which could take weeks to months to bring reinforcements in. Good fortune is essential, since we plan on ports and airfields in Western Europe being in our hands, intact and capable of receiving the men and materiel after a Pact attack.

Finally, differences in doctrine and concepts of operation are significant between a defensive NATO and a Warsaw Pact which is structured for offensive operations. Additionally, the Pact has the distinct advantage of standardized weapons, since most fighting vehicles and all aircraft and missile delivery systems are of Soviet design. Command-and-control doctrine seems to be standardized on the Soviet model and has benefited over the years from a large number of integrated command-and-control exercises and field trials.

NATO's Problem – Defence 'On the Cheap'
This should be contrasted to NATO's problems which are largely self-inflicted wounds. Not only is there a diversity of national doctrines but each of the nations holds back a large portion of its national forces from SACEUR's control. Some deploy only token forces in peacetime. Add to this the large diversity of aircraft weapon systems, ammunition and logistic systems. Although many pleas have been made for RSI (rationalization, standardization and interoperability), this has so far received little more than lip service over the decades. Lastly, while NATO has greater productive resources available to it, it seems impossible to win appropriate allocations for such simple things as ammunition, fuel and other consumables. The varying inventory levels of ammunition have been so serious that the Supreme Allied Commander, Gen. Rogers, has indicated that it might be the unavailability of conventional ammunition which could drive NATO to the use of battlefield nuclear weapons.

When NATO decided to substitute nuclear weapons for conventional forces it became addicted to buying deterrence and defence 'on the cheap'. Is there any serious intention of abandoning the nuclear 'trip-wire' and reliance on early (or even first) use of nuclear weapons? If not, then NATO will find itself in a dangerous situation, with only the choice between conventional defeat or nuclear destruction.

In pursuing new technology for conventional capabilities, we must therefore consider the feasibility, effectiveness and cost of new non-nuclear capabilities against these decades-old problems of nuclear substitution.

Conventional Technologies Needed for Various Missions
In considering the broad threat to NATO, we must construct a defensive concept of operations which can provide nearly simultaneous actions to blunt a Soviet/Pact attack and prevent loss of NATO territory while also maintaining conventional and nuclear reserve forces. There are five operational areas which will be considered. These are:

– Eroding Soviet/Pact airpower, including the defeat of Soviet independent air operations;
– Interdicting key lines of communication to delay and disrupt the ground attack;
– Fighting the central battle;
– Attacking follow-on mobile forces;
– Dealing with the missile threat to Western Europe.

Some important mission areas are not included in this discussion. For example, those of disrupting Soviet/Pact command, control, communications and intelligence (C^3I) capabilities by means of Electronic Warfare (EW), and that of maintaining NATO C^3I under attack.

Target Spectrum
The target spectrum covers two broad categories. The first involves fixed targets which are relatively large and whose locations are precisely located. These include the Pact airbases (main and dispersal), key interdiction points supporting major lines of communica-

Table 1: High-value Time-sensitive Targets in the Central Region

Range from intra-German border (km):	0–30	30–100	100–200	200–300	300–800	Total
Fixed Targets						
Main Operating Airbases (close air support and ground attack)	–	13	18	13	28	72
Choke Points (bridges, railyards, highway junctions)	12	10	40	51	78	191
Underground installations (nuclear weapon storage facilities, C^3, petrol, oil and lubricants)	5	27	54	33	43	162
Total	17	50	112	97	149	425
Mobile Targets						
Manoeuvre Units (motor rifle and tank)	409	124	294	96	198	1,121
Supporting Artillery Battalions	423	8	30	6	96	563
Tactical Ballistic Missiles (*Frog, Scud, Scaleboard*)	256	120	84	12	84	556
Critical Logistic Support	–	9	6	2	3	20
Total	1,088	261	414	116	381	2,260
Total Fixed and Mobile Targets	1,105	311	526	213	530	2,685

tion (bridges and choke points), command-and-control installations and fixed air defence units. The variety and depth of these fixed targets (from the inner German border) are set out in Table 1 above. The second category involves mobile ground force targets, most of the important ones within 30 km of the line of contact and others out to 100–200 km, including Warsaw Pact mobile tactical missile staging areas.

Fixed Targets Eroding Soviet/Pact
ERODING SOVIET/PACT AIRPOWER

The requirements for NATO counter-air operations are to:

- disrupt Pact air operations in their early phases;
- substantially reduce Pact attack sortie rates;
- complicate or deny Pact aircraft recovery and reinforcement operations.

Gen. Charles Gabriel,[4] former Commander of Allied Air Forces Central Europe, has pointed out that the Independent Air Operation (IAO) planned by the Soviet Union must be thwarted if NATO is to survive for a period of more than a few days. The problem is that NATO would lose most of its aircraft and bases to a successful Soviet IAO and therefore lose air superiority over defending forces. He estimated that, if NATO could successfully suppress about forty key Pact Main Operating Bases (MOBs), thereby reducing the Pact's ground attack sortie rates, air superiority could be maintained and counter-air and interdiction operations successfully mounted. The suppression of MOBs must take place within a very short period of time – a few hours or less. This attack must also be supported by a complementary action, namely to destroy Pact aircraft on the ground at other bases – mainly Dispersed Operating Bases (DOBs) – which would now have to be used if the Pact were to sustain the IAO.

MOBs are heavily defended and have shelters for aircraft; DOBs are relatively lightly defended and have few shelters. If MOBs were to be closed, the DOBs would be packed with follow-on aircraft; the IAO might have to be truncated or aborted.

Proposals for MOB suppression include aircraft and land-based ballistic or cruise missiles with runway attack payloads. These could have the effect of shutting down the bases for periods of hours to days, depending on the level of damage and the repair capabilities of the Pact. The crucial complementary operation, that of attacking unsheltered aircraft on DOBs, would be a much more effective way of defeating the Pact IAO.

In the words of Gen. Johannes Steinhoff, former *Luftwaffe* Commander, in contrasting the destruction of aircraft on the ground versus destroying aircraft in the air with aircraft or missiles: 'It is better to destroy the wasps in their nest than to catch them one at a time in your hand'.

Under the postulated concept[5], the main objective for the counter-air mission is the suppression of those MOBs which support Pact offensive ground-attack operations. There are at least five options for executing this mission with non-nuclear forces, the last three involving ballistic missiles:

- *Attack by manned aircraft.* (This is a current option.) It is estimated that four aircraft with JP-233 runway attack munitions would be required per runway. These would be accompanied by about 6–8 protective aircraft (MIGCAP, ECM, defence suppression, etc.). Attrition estimates for the attacking aircraft run from 20% to 50% against heavily defended MOBs.
- *Attack by cruise missile.* Five cruise missiles of the medium-range air-to-surface missiles (MRASM) type or GLCM are estimated to be needed per runway.
- *CAM-40.* This is a 40-inch solid rocket booster using the *Pershing* II single- or double-stage rocket. Based in West Germany, the single-stage system could cover the closer 57 MOBs and 48 DOBs. The two-stage version could pick up the remaining 16 MOBs and 20 DOBs in Eastern Europe. The CAM-40 would have a terminally-guided 'bus' filled with kinetic energy penetrators (KEP) fused to explode beneath the runway. It is estimated that three CAM-40 missiles would be required per runway or taxiway.
- *Boss/Axe.* This is a larger booster based on the *Trident* missile. A larger payload similar to the CAM-40 KEP could be carried. One missile per runway would be required.
- *Total Air Base Attack System* (TABAS). This is a very large multiple booster system carrying a 25-tonne KEP payload which is estimated to destroy a complete airbase, including 'bonus' destruction of support facilities. (TABAS was an early proposal which has since met political and military opposition in Europe. It is not considered a serious candidate for the counter-air mission).

Interdicting Lines of Communication (LOC)

The objective of LOC interdiction is to delay and disrupt Pact follow-on forces which could reinforce the central battle or exploit breakthrough successes. There are about 100 fixed key installations (bridges, railheads and choke points) which, if successfully damaged or destroyed, would result in accumulations of forces for a period of hours to days. These forces could then be attacked in place by aircraft or missiles using large quantities of unguided submunitions. This concept is analogous to suppressing and defeating the IAO above. The mode of attack and the weapon systems are almost identical to those for the counter-IAO operation.

Mobile Targets

FIGHTING THE CENTRAL BATTLE AND ATTACK OF FOLLOW-ON FORCES

The ranges of interest for the central battle involving mobile targets would cover forces in contact and out to thirty kilometres or more. Targets would include tank companies (ten or more main battle tanks or up to 20–30 armoured fighting vehicles, air defence or logistic support vehicles). Interesting ranges for follow-on force attack (FOFA) would be about 30–150 km from the point of contact. Two concepts have been discussed for achieving the delay, disruption and destruction of follow-on forces.

The first, and by far the most traditional, involves, as described above, interdiction of key LOCs and subsequent attacks on the stacked-up ground forces by aircraft (or missiles) delivering bombs or unguided submunitions of a kind now in production in France and the FRG and in development in the US. In this case, what were mobile forces have now become fixed targets.

Table 2: Systems for Acquiring and Attacking Mobile Targets

Range (km)	Target	Target acquisition/fusion	Delivery system	Munitions	Availability
0–30–70	1st-echelon regiments (110–140 + support vehicles) Tank companies (10–13 AFV) Support vehicles Division artillery (70–90)	Netted radar Electro-optical ground-based cameras Emitter locators (CELT) Airborne radar (JSTARS) COMINT/ELINT	Tube artillery Multiple launch system Close-support aircraft	TGW/*Skeet* TGW *Apache*/CWS	Development Development Development
30–150	Tank/mech companies Support vehicles Tactical bridging Tank transporter support	Electro-optical airborne cameras COMINT/ELINT	Conventional missile (T-16, -22) Penetrating aircraft Cruise missiles	TGSM/*Skeet*/TGW MW-1 *Apache*/CWS	Development Production Development
30–600	Tactical missiles (SS-21, -22, -23) Air defences Special support teams	Emitter locators Manned/unmanned reconnaissance COMINT/ELINT	Cruise missiles Penetrating aircraft Advanced-technology aircraft	MW-1 *Apache*/CWS	Production Development Development

The second is the attack on *moving* elements of the ground forces by the use of homing submunitions delivered by indirect-fire delivery systems. The latter is a technical possibility if a reasonable development programme of the components (targeting systems, delivery platforms and guided submunitions) is allowed to move from 'proof-of-principle' demonstrations to a full-scale development.

The key to defeating combat formations either in contact or at a distance is target acquisition of those vehicles that cannot be engaged by direct-fire weapons. For highly effective attack by Advanced Conventional Munitions (ACM), delivery accuracies of several hundreds of meters must be achieved before terminally-guided submunitions (TGSM) are dispensed to allow direct hits. The types of acquisition and attack systems are shown generically in Table 2.

DEALING WITH THE MISSILE THREAT TO WESTERN EUROPE

Surface-to-surface missiles with conventional, chemical or nuclear warheads threaten NATO airfields, nuclear weapon storage and missile sites, command-and-control facilities, ports and other LOC. Defence against this independent missile operation presents a somewhat similar set of requirements to that developed for defence against the Independent Air Operation. It is, however, more difficult, since the missiles are mobile.

Any attacks would come with little warning. This has led some to discuss an anti-tactical missile (ATM) system as the only effective answer to the threat if NATO is barred from striking at the missiles before they are launched. ATM would require the introduction of a new capability. One option is the Improved *Patriot* which has been described by Hubertus Hoffman[6] of the FRG. This would require a portion of the *Patriot* force to be dedicated to this mission, or more missiles to be acquired at significant cost.

However, a number of damage-limiting options should be considered. These include: the location of launchers in storage or staging areas; in hides; in setting-up for launch; and in launch and reloading. The time for NATO to react with air or missile attacks, given ade-

Table 3: Reaction Times for Engagement

Soviet/Pact launchers/missiles	Reaction time
Storage/staging	Days/hours
'Hiding'	Days/hours
Set-up	1–2 hours
Launching/moving	Minutes/hours
Refire	Hour or less
In-flight/intercept	Minutes/tens of seconds

quate surveillance, tracking, targeting and firing sequences, would cover a range as shown in Table 3.

Attacks on the launchers (which are relatively soft) at various stages could be accomplished either by cruise or ballistic missiles or by manned aircraft using wide-area unguided submunitions (MW-1, CWS, *Apache*, etc., see Annex pp. 35–9).

Targeting would require the types of capabilities discussed below. For the future, the targeting problem could be somewhat alleviated if suppressive fire could be brought to bear by advanced-technology aircraft or remotely-piloted vehicles (RPV) which could survive over hostile territory.

SURVEILLANCE/TARGETING AND
  INFORMATION FUSION

Continuous surveillance of enemy activity is a prerequisite for deterrence and warning in the event that deterrence fails. National systems provide strategic surveillance and intelligence gathering, including signals intelligence (SIGINT), communications and electronic intelligence (COMINT/ELINT). This information is crucial to warning and readiness but it is not sufficient for tactical battle needs. A subsidiary level of aircraft surveillance, information fusion and distribution is required in peacetime and for crisis management. In war this information must be transformed into information for targeting and for battle management. A summary of platforms and systems for surveillance and warning (described in Annex A see p. 35) would include airborne electro-optical cameras and radars, electronic emitter locators, airborne and ground-based surveillance and targeting radars, and real-time data links and information fusion centres. All of these systems have been developed and have had numerous field tests. Similar systems exist or are in development in the forces of the European Allies.

EFFECTIVENESS AND COST FOR SYSTEMS TO
  ATTACK MOBILE FORCES

The effectiveness of systems which could be used against ground forces either in the central battle or in the attack of follow-on forces are shown in Tables 4 and 5.[8]

Table 4 shows aircraft sortie effectiveness against armoured companies with available bombs, missiles and area weapons.

Table 5 shows effectiveness and costs for terminally-guided missiles and *Skeet* submunitions delivered by MLRS, artillery and aircraft.

No attempt has been made to provide cost-effectiveness specifics for aircraft systems, because of the difficulties in costing aircraft and because of the attrition question. Suffice it to say that, with the low effectiveness of iron bombs or one-on-one attack systems exemplified by the *Maverick*, repeated attack or the need for high numbers of sorties would undoubtedly result in high attrition of valuable penetrating aircraft.

Table 4: Aircraft Sortie Effectiveness v. Armoured Companies

Weapon	Target[1]	Weapons per sortie	No. destroyed On road[2]	No. destroyed Off road[3]
Present Inventory				
Iron bombs	coy	8	0.8	0.5
Cluster munitions	coy	4	1.6	0.1
Maverick	4 AFV	4	1.6	1.6
Dispenser				
Apache/CWS with:				
KB-44 + MIFF	2 coys	2	5	5
CEB + GATOR	4 coys	2	4	6

[1] Assuming 10–13 armoured fighting vehicles (AFV) per company (coy).
[2] Assuming 15 km/hr in 500 × 500 m area.
[3] Assuming 30 km/hr in 100 × 500 m area.

Source: See N. F. Wikner (cited in note 8).

Table 5: Skeet Systems Effectiveness and Cost v. Armoured Fighting Vehicles

System	Carrier	Skeet delivery vehicles	Skeets	AFV 'kill'*	Cost ($000)	$000 per AFV
MLRS	12 rockets	72	288	13	396	31
Artillery	12 155mm shells	6 per shell	72	4	48	12
Tactical conventional missile 200km	1 missile	22 T-16	88	5–10	450	45
		24 T-22	96			90
Ground-attack aircraft	4 tactical munition dipensers	40	80	10–12	140	14
	1 stand-off attack weapon	48	192	16–30	436	18

*Mobility 'kill'.

Source: See N. F. Wikner (cited in note 8).

Summary Observations and Conclusions
Missions

The defensive missions described here are, in order of priority: the counter-air mission (aimed at defeating the Soviet Independent Air Operations); the interdiction of key lines of communication; destruction of mobile ground forces in the central battle, and delay, disruption or destruction of the follow-on forces. It is emphasized that, if the counter-air operation is not carried out as a matter of urgency, NATO will lose air superiority over its defending forces, and the central battle will be lost. Thus, failure in this mission would rapidly lead to the consideration of the use of nuclear weapons.

The interdiction mission must also be carried out as a matter of urgency. If this is done successfully, it will add to the defeat of the Soviet plan to reinforce with follow-on forces.

It is emphasized that the central battle and the battle against follow-on forces must be carried out concurrently, particularly for those follow-on forces that are within 30–70 km of the FEBA. This would include the OMG forces which would try to exploit any breakdown in NATO defences.

Technology

Available or 'emerged' technology can provide current aircraft with area munitions which could increase force effectiveness (in terms of reduced required sorties) by factors of 5 to 7. The weapons needed are in initial production in the FRG, France and Britain. New stand-off container-dispensed munition systems are in development which could provide smaller aircraft, such as the F-16, *Alpha Jet* and A-10, with significantly greater firepower while providing greater survivability in the vicinity of the target. Accelerating the development of these systems and early production is indicated. The US should consider buying these systems from her European Allies. This would let NATO fill gaps in its conventional capabilities for ground-attack aircraft.

The key to further increases in weapon effectiveness which would help to alleviate the shortfall in NATO force structure is in advanced munitions. Homing submunitions, which could be used against mobile targets, could provide necessary increases in effectiveness by another factor of about 5–10. The key systems for application of these munitions to the central battle would be guns (155mm) and MLRS, and possibly heavy mortars.

Advanced capabilities in surveillance and targeting are a fundamental requirement for the successful introduction of 'emerged' and 'emerging' weapons technology into NATO's force structure. It is also essential for the political-military authorities to have access to prompt information for assessment and decision-making. The technology base for the systems discussed is mature and most of the hardware is available. What is needed is a programme across the Alliance to 'wire' the components together and to develop suitable doctrine and operational concepts.

Accurate guidance systems for ballistic missiles can provide the capability to deliver special effects non-nuclear munitions against a variety of heavily-defended, hard targets. Delivery could be done in all weathers and more reliably and quickly than with manned aircraft. NATO's valuable penetrating aircraft should be used primarily to attack mobile forces (shallow and deep) using available area munitions as described. Future ('emerging technology') stand-off TGSMs should be adapted to these and other aircraft for use in reinforcing the flanks of NATO where aircraft have the flexibility and range to perform these missions. The US has a special interest in developing these systems for 'out-of-area' contingencies and other global commitments.

The technologies described here would be of immense help in redressing the force imbalances today and those projected for the future, when the demographic problems cited are likely to cause even more serious problems. From NATO's standpoint this would favour the defence. The analogy to the exploitation of the benefits of nuclear technology in the 1950s is apparent but it will not be as significant as it was with the nuclear emphasis undertaken thirty years ago. Exploitation of 'emerging technology' by the Soviet Union would add to her offensive capabilities as well. NATO must strive to keep ahead in the non-nuclear qualitative areas to avoid total dependence, in the near future, on the use of nuclear weapons – first use or otherwise.

Interaction of NATO and Pact Forces
The integration of these capabilities into NATO would lead to a raised nuclear threshold on NATO's part. Attaining greater force survivability (through both nuclear and conventional modernization) would lead to greater stability. If recent history is any guide, the USSR's reaction would probably be to reassess her concept of offensive operations and the structure of her forces. Such an effort could take a decade or more.

Indications are that the Soviet Union is proceeding with certain aspects of 'emerged technologies' (anti-airfield capabilities for the SS-23, etc.). A recent statement by Gen. Ogarkov regarded the US 'emerging technology' programme (identified as *Assault Breaker*) as a 'revolutionary turn' in military affairs. Soviet adoption of these technologies would add qualitative advantages to an already overwhelming quantitative advantage.

If NATO can introduce the augmented non-nuclear capabilities described here, the Soviet Union may conclude that her concepts of offensive operations would need significant alteration. Issues the Soviet Union would have to face could include a reassessment of her ability to implement her preferred tactics in the changed circumstances.

Serious questions would arise as to what might happen along her lines of communications in Poland, Czechoslovakia and elsewhere if a 'short' war could not be successfully concluded because NATO succeeded in delaying and disrupting the attack for weeks or months.

The suggested mission capabilities would obviously contribute to credible non-nuclear defence options which are not currently available to NATO. These options would significantly add to deterrence against Soviet/Pact conventional attack.

Political Control
Some high-level political authorities have voiced fears that the pace of new technology is outrunning their ability to understand, influence and maintain political control. To give only one example, 'real-time' surveillance and information processing is viewed as a threat to the political control process rather than as an aid in managing crisis. As Raymond Aron said: 'In the nuclear age, the moment of truth is not in battle but in crisis.' Certainly, 'real-time' capabilities would tend

to force the policy-makers into operating in new modes. They would have to think about some problems in advance; to participate more intimately in the planning and implementation of strategy and defensive concepts; and to make decisions on the appropriate options and balance of forces. Surely an improved thought process could only be beneficial to NATO's deterrent posture.

Conventional Improvements, Deterrence and the Nuclear Threshold

Numerous arguments have been voiced on the effects of conventional force upgrading on deterrence and the nuclear threshold. Some sceptics believe that better conventional weapons would lead to a denuclearization of NATO and a decoupling of US strategic forces from the Alliance. This cannot be a serious concern as long as the US remains in NATO and maintains almost *any* level of ground and air forces in Europe. All the proposals in this Paper emphasize the indispensability of a quality component in the NATO Triad.

Would a strong NATO conventional force posture cause the Soviet Union to pre-empt with nuclear weapons, fearing that she could not succeed in a conventional attack against NATO? Certainly she would realize that nuclear weapons used against Europe could result in a US/NATO nuclear response (and perhaps under some circumstances a response by the independent nuclear forces of France). A selective response by the United States' strategic forces could also be a possibility that the Soviet Union would find it necessary to consider.

The 'Technology Risk' Factor

The critics of using new technology to seek solutions to NATO's shortfall in force structure and firepower have little appreciation for how new technology can be harnessed. They regard the development of 'smart' and lethal terminally-guided submunitions as beyond the grasp of the military-technical communities. They suggest that surveillance and targeting radars cannot possibly work in detecting and targeting the large numbers of Soviet armoured fighting vehicles that must be used if NATO is to be defeated. They criticize the programmes undertaken so far by US (namely, the *Assault Breaker* Programme) as being tested in an 'unrealistic' way, not recognizing that such tests are performed to learn and not to demonstrate. They regard technology as a 'trap' which will result in very costly systems which will not work. They regard the technical 'risks' as not worth the venture to seek non-nuclear alternatives. Most of these critics have had little or no experience in understanding complex weapon system programmes. Some with similar views were around when certain decisions were made on bringing to fruition novel and significant nuclear weapon systems. They were shown to be wrong.

But the President and the Congress wanted this stabilizing deterrent capability. A highly responsible and competent scientific, technical and industrial team was organized by the Navy and told to solve the problems and produce the system we all now know as *Polaris*. It is history that all of these objectives were met and on time.

The technology represented in the *Polaris* programme was far more advanced and 'risky' than the modest technology improvements which have been discussed for the development of surveillance, targeting, accurate missiles and terminally-guided submunitions for the attack of mobile ground forces. The key to minimizing the risks of technology is that of assuring technical competence and focused management. Such a 'special projects' approach must be backed up by urgent demands from serious political leaders of the NATO governments to have complete capabilities by a certain date. They must therefore be willing to make some fundamental changes in the development and acquisition process. One can only despair in even thinking of trying to accomplish this effort through NATO's 240 or so committees, groups, panels, etc., of the Conference of National Armament Directors (CNAD) and with the many fragmented national efforts.

The political and military leadership of NATO must find a way of providing non-nuclear capabilities within the constraints of the economy and force structure. Without convincing elements of a conventional deterrent and defensive posture, danger to NATO grows with every passing day.

Ambassador François de Rose has put the issues very succinctly:

> ... The key task is to create the capabilities that can lift from the Alliance, in the event of a crisis, the incubus of early resort to nuclear weapons in order to avert certain defeat on the conventional battlefield. [NATO must] strive for forces whereby the Soviet leaders could not calculate an early, successful outcome, even on the conventional battlefield ... For the Soviet leaders, premium on swift victory is sharpened by the fact that they cannot be sure of the political or even military loyalty of the satellite countries, where the vast majorities of the populations would hope for the ultimate defeat of the 'Big Brother' who has imposed on them a political, economic and social system that suppresses their national pride, denies human rights and basic freedom and consigns them to a permanently low standard of living ... Heightening NATO's conventional bulwarks would have a pay-off greater than merely raising the nuclear threshold or postponing the West's decision to 'go nuclear' ... The Alliance is at a crucial juncture. The evolution in the relative weights of nuclear and conventional armaments is one of the most important developments to confront NATO since its inception.[9]

NOTES

[1] House Armed Services Committee hearings, testimony of Dr J. V. Braddock, 25 April 1983, p. 1709.
[2] *The Military Balance 1983–1984*, (London: IISS, 1983), pp. 145–149.
[3] For a discussion of this topic see Donald R. Cotter, 'A NATO Nuclear Overwatch Force: Modernized Nuclear and Conventional Capabilities', *Armed Forces Journal*, July 1984, p. 60.
[4] *Armed Forces Journal*, January 1982, pp. 25–39.
[5] Reference ESECS Report, Donald R. Cotter, 'Strengthening Conventional Deterrence in Europe – Proposals for the 1980s'.
[6] Hubertus Hoffman, 'An Anti-Missile Defence For Europe?', *Strategic Review*, Summer 1984.
[7] Dr N. F. Wikner, 'Interdicting Fixed Targets with Conventional Weapons', *Armed Forces Journal*, March 1983.
[8] Dr N. F. Wikner 'Improving NATO's Forward Defence Technological Dimensions For Conventional Forces', (forthcoming).
[9] François de Rose, 'NATO's Perils – and Opportunities', *Strategic Review*, Fall 1983.

ANNEXE A: Weapon Technology

Available Unguided Weapons

Iron Bombs: Standard gravity high-explosive bombs of the 500-lb (MK 82) or 2,000-lb (MK 84) variety. Some have drag devices to allow low-level delivery. These are unguided weapons, sometimes referred to as 'dumb' bombs. They have marginal value, because of delivery inaccuracies.

CEB (US): A *Combined Effects Bomblet*, incorporating blast incendiary and fragmentation effects.

BLU-63: An anti-materiel/personnel submunition carried by aircraft and the *Lance* conventional-warhead missile.

BAD-100 (France): Anti-runway penetrator bomb.

Durandal (France): An anti-runway bomb which uses a rocket booster to achieve runway penetration velocities.

MW-1 (West Germany): A large (10,000-lb) captive dispenser which contains a suite of anti-armour, anti-materiel munitions and anti-personnel mines and runway and shelter penetrators designed specifically for use on the West German *Tornado* aircraft. The munitions carries are:

– STABO: The runway penetrator submunition carried by the MW-1.
– MUSPA: An area denial anti-airfield mine which uses acoustic sensors.
– MIFF: A sensor-activated anti-tank mine.
– KB-44: An anti-armour and anti-aircraft shaped-charge bomblet.
– LASSO: A sensor-aided anti-tank weapon.
– ASW: An anti-shelter (penetrating) weapon.

JP-233 (Britain): An airfield-attack weapon system which combines a cratering munition with mines. These mines are intended to pose a long-term threat to airfild repair crews and vehicles.

Guided Weapons

Maverick (US): A homing anti-armour/hard target air-launched/rocket-boosted missile. Uses TV and imaging infra-red homing sensors.

LLLGB (US): *Low Level Laser-Guided Bomb.* A guidance and control package is adapted to a standard Iron Bomb. Target is designated by a laser, and the bomb homes in on the laser spot. Recent modifications have been made to the guidance package and software to allow extremely low altitude releases. LLLGB can only be used in single engagements; multiple passes are therefore required.

'Emerged' Technology

VAM (US): A runway cratering submunition to be carried by the *Tomahawk* cruise missile.

BKEP (US): *Boosted Kinetic Energy Penetrator.* A slim penetrating submunition which uses a rocket booster to achieve high velocities prior to penetration. The penetration weapon technology is mature. The German 'Roechling Round' was developed in 1938 as an artillery-fired round to defeat the Maginot line. It was used in combat in Russia and tested in 1942 against Belgian forts. The technology was further developed by the US nuclear laboratories for a low-yield Earth Penetrator Weapon (EPW) for the *Pershing* II, and R&D was completed, but the EPW requirement for *Pershing* II was dropped.

KERP (US): A *Kinetic Energy Runway Pentrator* which achieves penetration velocities due to gravity.

ERAM (US): An *Extended-range Anti-armour Munition.* It uses seismic and acoustic sensors to detect armoured or other vehicles.

Apache CWS/CMD (West Germany, France): A family of small dispensers which can carry a variety of submunitions (Those used in the MW-1). The *Container Weapon System* dispenser is a small version of the MW-1 which can be used in captive or free-flight modes. A dispenser with solid rocket motor propulsion system allows greater stand-off. The *Conventional Munition Dispenser* family is tailored for smaller aircraft.

Accurate Missile Delivery Systems

Tomahawk cruise missile: This missile, called *Tomahawk* Airfield Attack Missile (TAAM), can be used to deliver a variety of submunitions. For runway cratering the VAM (see above) would be used. This combination has been tested. The missile is in production.

Conventional Attack Missile (CAM-40): Based on the boosters and terminal guidance system (radar correlator) of the *Pershing* II (in production) this missile, equipped with the 2,500-lb of kinetic energy earth penetrators, could be used for runway destruction and against hard targets, such as bridges and underground facilities.

Ballistic Offensive Suppression System (BOSS): This concept is based on the *Trident* booster (in production) and could deliver a large payload (about 14,000-lb) of kinetic energy runway penetrators. Other large boosters could be used. Consideration has been given under the US 'Counter-Air 90' Concept to the US *Minuteman* first stage, the *Polaris* booster and the French M-4. Basing for BOSS could be in fixed silos or protective hangarettes. A road-mobile version is also feasible.

Tactical Conventional Missile (formerly *Assault Breaker*): There are two contending missile systems under deployment, the T-16 based on the *Patriot* booster (in production) and the T-22 based on an improved *Lance* missile (under development). These missiles can deliver Terminally-guided Submunitions (TGSM), *Skeet* or Terminally-guided Weapons (TGW), described below.

'Emerging' Technology

TGW (US, France, West Germany, Britain): *Terminally-guided Weapon* using millimetre-wave radar guidance system for engaging and homing on armoured fighting vehicles.

Skeet (US): Anti-armour submunition which uses infra-red homing devices to engage armoured fighting vehicles. The infra-red sensor homes on the hot spots from the engines of tanks, AFV or trucks. The US programmes include adaption of these submunitions to 155mm artillery, multiple-launch rocket systems (MLRS) and a new tactical conventional missile. Four *Skeet* submunitions are carried in each *Skeet* Delivery Vehicle (SDV).

TGSM (US): An infra-red *Terminally-Guided SubMunition* with a large shaped-charge anti-armour warhead. 22 TGSM can be carried to a range of 150 km by the T-16; 24 TGSM can be carried to a range of 250 km by the T-22.

Surveillance/Targeting Technology

In addition to current operational surveillance, sensors and intelligence-gathering capabilities, additional new systems are required for real-time surveillance and targeting necessary for the engagement of mobile (or moveable) forces. For example, in the counter-IOA mission against attacking Soviet/Pact aircraft, a combination of Airborne Warning and Control System (AWACS) would be used to identify attack corridors and the egress routes of aircaft returning to MOBs and DOBs. This information would be vital for vectoring NATO aircraft to attack enemy aircraft on the ground. For attacks on mobile forces at some depth the new capabilities would include the following:

'Emerged' Technologies*

JSTARS: An airborne real-time *Joint Surveillance and Targeting Radar System* which can detect, track and provide targeting information to ground- or air-based attack missiles. The radar is capable of detecting armoured concentration.

Netter radars: These are simple ground-based motion detection radars whose output information is netted to provide locations and velocity of targets. The information is processed by commercially available microcomputers to eliminate clutter and to degrade the effects of jamming. Tests conducted in the early 1980s successfully detected personnel or helicopters out to 30 km. The netted system was also able to detect the explosion of artillery shells in the vicinity of the targets, thereby allowing an all-weather/night capability for registering conventional artillery fire.

Electro-optical imaging systems: These cameras convert imagery into a digitized format which can be processed to provide extremely high resolution imagery. The data can be transmitted from ground- or air-based cameras in real time and can then be viewed simultaneously at any ground stations within range. The processing of the information can eliminate smoke, haze and thin cloud. The picture can be magnified 20 to 30 times with little loss of resolution. The imagery can be tape-recorded and printed for use in intelligence assessment or targeting as required.

Emitter locators: A variety of electronic sensors can be used to locate emitters (radar or communications gear) at distances to 100 km plus. Triangulation and processing of the data allows accuracies which can be used for targeting.

Information format: The advent of cheap microprocessors allows processing of a large amount of surveillance and targeting information at all levels of combat forces. One system, the Target Analysis and Planning System (TAP), has been fully tested in Europe. An important aspect of information processing is its distribution to using units.

---

* These technologies are indicated as US developments. There would certainly be similar technologies available in other Allied countries.

Technology and the Future of Arms Control

WALTER B. SLOCOMBE

One great fact of technology – the overwhelming power of nuclear weapons – shapes the strategic situation, and, within that situation, lesser technological facts profoundly affect what policies and strategies are possible. However, despite the immense impact of technology or strategy, technological change and negotiated arms agreements are by no means incompatible, and – for all the very considerable changes in weapons that seem likely in the coming decade or so, and for all the real problems they pose – there exist *important* opportunities for agreement, if the political will exists on both sides to agree.

At the heart of East–West tension lies, not technology, but a variety of far more fundamental, and far more intractable, causes having ultimately to do with the profound differences between the two great alliance systems and the social, political, economic and value structures they exemplify. It is nonetheless true however, that the process of accumulating military forces – particularly nuclear forces, and particularly of novel and more effective types – can be an added source of tension between the two sides. Arms-control agreements, in addition to constraining the level of forces and diverting the competition from the most dangerous areas, may help to permit the parties to forgo complex, expensive or dangerous programmes that would be embarked upon chiefly out of fear of the other side's filling a technological vacuum.

Objectives for an arms-control effort that seek to shape, not stop, technical change would, no doubt, be denounced by some as too modest. For those who believe that the modernization process is itself a key source of tension and misunderstanding, a list of the objectives of arms control would include – and indeed, begin with – seeking to stop altogether or minimize the introduction of new technology. The objectives postulated here, however, implicitly acknowledge that arms-control limits must be integrated with modernization programmes and diplomatic efforts to secure deterrence and stability. Another more ambitious objective, highly relevant to technology, would be to seek to reduce the consequences of a nuclear war if it should occur. This, however, is a goal whose immense theoretical desirability is undermined by the awkward technical fact that even a vast diminution (whether accomplished directly by disarmament or indirectly by defence) of nuclear arsenals compared to present levels would not prevent terrible destruction in an all-out war.

The Record of Technology and Arms Control
Any effort to list the technologies that pose the greatest current problems for strategic stability and for arms control involves a measure of clairvoyance. Before embarking on that effort, it is appropriate to look back at the historical record to test against experience, however limited, some of the more frequently asserted propositions about the relationship between arms control and technology.

The simple proposition that technology has universally, or indeed predominantly, conflicted with the goals of stability and arms control is simply not true. Some developments, like the high-accuracy ICBM have had clearly destabilizing effects. But in other instances the technological advances have been beneficial, even essential, for arms control. The most obvious case is the intelligence technology which has made possible reliance on national technical means for arms-control verification. Photographic intelligence is only the most publicized of a wide range of technically sophisticated, complex and rapidly changing surveillance technologies which serve arms control as well as more specific and traditional military intelligence purposes. The development of these methods in the early 1960s blazed a technological path around the verification barriers that had helped to block progress earlier. Even if future agreements include substantially improved co-operative measures – and in some instances such measures will be necessary – basic reliance will still have to be put on national technical means, because of uncertainty about continued co-operation and about the reliability of data volunteered pursuant to co-operative requirements.

Technology helps verification in another, less obvious, way. One of the key windows open to observation of Soviet forces derives from observing the testing needed for continuing development and improvement of strategic systems. If technology changed more slowly, so that sheer mass and numbers were the main areas of competition, test observations would be far less important as sources of knowledge. Intelligence about the capabilities, as contrasted to the numbers, of military systems is obtained primarily during testing. Effective monitoring of Soviet tests is possible because the development of complex new military devices inherently requires that the capability of the new technologies be demonstrated by repeated tests. Over the years unintended eyes and ears have been able to share in the test results. It is for this reason that the development of encryption devices and other means of concealing test results and patterns is a worrying obstacle to arms-control confidence and progress.

In cataloguing the overall impact of technology on arms control, it is also useful to recall that concern about the risks of unrestrained technical competition can be an incentive to agree on a broad range of issues. In a sense, the great political mystery about US–Soviet arms control is not why two nations who should have a common interest in survival have been able to agree on so little, but why two super-powers with such profound political and strategic differences have been able to agree on so much. The incentives for significant agreements that operate on the Soviet side are little studied and ill-understood, but Soviet concern at what US technical prowess could accomplish, if challenged to a competition without restraint, seems clearly to be a major Soviet incentive to negotiate seriously.

That is by no means to say that it would be in the US interest to mount such a competition. For, if the USSR justly fears American technical prowess, the US justly fears Soviet ability to mass resources and to concentrate technical effort on key military goals unconstrained by democratic society or sovereign allies.

Nor, from a historical point of view, does there seem to be great support for the proposition that technological change has made irrelevant those arms-control agreements that have been reached. First, the idea that technology changes so fast as to render arms control concepts and methods obsolete is at the very least a serious exaggeration. It is, in fact, easy to overstate the rate at which new technologies go from concept to large-scale deployment. A case in point is the development of accuracies sufficient to threaten ICBM survivability, a process that was anticipated when ICBM were first deployed over twenty years ago.

Similarly, the charge that arms-control agreements are inherently incapable of dealing with future technological developments, only dimly perceived at the time an agreement is signed, is not borne out by the experience of arms control. Certainly if both sides are determined to preserve unrestricted all conceivable future technological options, agreement will prove impossible. And uncertainty about what future technology will mean for deterrence and stability may well counsel against efforts to agree on limits long before their subject matter is understood.

However, there is at least one instance of willingness to accept comprehensive limits on systems beyond those immediately understood – namely the 1972 ABM Treaty. That agreement embodies a comprehensive system of limitations on present and future technology, whose base is a general agreement not to deploy defences against strategic ballistic missiles except as permitted by the Treaty. This general ban is implemented at three levels – by complex rules for limiting systems current in 1972, with specific limitations on the expansion of potential radar support capabilities and on the testing of air defence missiles for potential anti-ballistic missile use; by a ban on development and testing of specific sorts of new systems, undeveloped but foreseeable in 1972; and, finally, by a general ban on the deployment of systems based on physical principles different from those so far applied. Most of the technologies now discussed for ballistic missile defence (BMD) fall in one of these last two categories, but they are not for that reason any less limited by the Treaty.

The 1972 Treaty stands as an example of a rather elegant drafting solution to the problem of calibrating limitations to the degree of understanding of the technology at issue. What made the solution in 1972 possible was fundamentally political rather than technological. For, whatever their views about BMD today, the two super-powers were then prepared to agree to the basic proposition that future technological developments of BMD should be presumptively barred, not presumptively permitted. It is changes in political perception, far more than changes in technology, which now threaten to call that agreement into question.

A second broad claim of inconsistency between technology and arms control is the charge that a principal practical effect of the arms-control process has been merely to divert the competition into unrestricted areas and, particularly, to stimulate the development of new technology for those areas. But diversion of effort from newly banned to permitted channels has at times been a conscious part of a treaty scheme. Such was certainly the case for underground testing after the Limited Test Ban Treaty of 1962. Many would argue that an implicit (and partly realized) purpose of the 1972 Interim Agreement on Strategic Offensive Arms was to promote a more even relative balance between sea- and land-based ballistic missiles in the Soviet force.

In other instances, the technological horizon has been clear enough and there has simply been a conscious decision – right or wrong in retrospect – to preserve the maximum number of possible options. This was certainly the case with respect to the development of MIRV at the time of SALT I and of mobile ICBM, cruise missiles and countersilo ICBM at the time of SALT II.

The most serious claim of the baleful effect of technological change on arms control is that it necessarily entails a gradual erosion of the benefits of the agreement as each side applies technology to overcome to effects of the agreed limits. Many argue, for example, that SALT I became irrelevant as each side deployed MIRV and the USSR at least pressed for ICBM yield/accuracy combinations sufficient to threaten the bulk of US ICBM. These are important limits on the benefits that were obtained from the 1972 agreements. Insofar as it is claimed, however, that those effects were unanticipated at the time the agreement was signed, the charge is simply false. Such developments were clearly anticipated at the time, and a conscious decision was made to accept those risks rather than insist on a more far-reaching offensive agreement.

Finally, the claim is sometimes made that technology makes verification too hard by making new systems so plentiful in number and so dual-capable in character as to be hard to count. Here again the evidence is mixed. So far, none of the new systems has, once ready for deployment, actually displayed the virtue of cheapness – and therefore vast numbers at affordable cost – advertized for it initially. Sheer proliferation of numbers has been far less of a problem once weapons are deployed than has been claimed (or feared) at the vugraph stage. In many instances application of high technology to a problem has had essentially no impact on verification. This is, for example, the case with respect to the application of 'stealth' technology to aircraft, of quieting techniques to nuclear-powered ballistic-missile submarines (SSBN) and even, for that matter, of accuracy to ICBM. Even in those areas where the new technology produces greater uncertainty with respect to counts of units, the change may not be an unmitigated disadvantage, particularly where the uncertainty is due to mobility and ease of concealment. For with greater difficulty in counting may well go greater survivability – and hence less sensitivity to precise number counts.

In sum, the charge that technology has been an inherent enemy of arms control and stability is unsupported by the historic record. But what of developments now on the horizon?

Technological Challenges

I turn now to an effort to list some of the impending changes in the technology of nuclear weapons and their support systems that pose the greatest apparent current difficulties for stability and opportunities for arms control.

ICBM Vulnerability

The obsolescence of ICBM as survivable forces is a technologically-produced military and strategic effect of the first order – but not because of an immediate effect on the balance. The continued survivability of other forces (and the difficulties of co-ordinating attacks on all three force elements) mean that the significance of silo-based ICBM vulnerability for crisis stability is, fortunately, relatively limited – and far less than sometimes claimed. Nonetheless, ICBM vulnerability is an event of historic dimensions because a major, previously survivable, part of both sides' strategic forces is being rendered vulnerable to pre-emptive attack.

Efforts to prevent or at least significantly delay this technological development by agreement, notably the Carter 1977 and the Reagan 1982 proposals for deep cuts in Soviet ICBM, have proved fruitless. The task for both strategic planning and arms control is now rather one of ensuring that reactions to this development are more, rather than less, stabilizing and ensuring that those choices do not themselves contain the seeds of new difficulties. In part this is an issue of making sure that arms control which focuses on the important issue of the size and composition of the arsenals does not hinder stabilizing responses to silo vulnerability.

One fruitful approach may be to ensure that future agreements, unlike SALT I and II, are consistent with a move back towards single-warhead ICBM. Similarly, if land-mobile options are to be compatible with agreed limits, methods for their deployment must be taken into account in future arms-control agreements, particularly from the point of view of verification. Future agreements on central strategic systems can fairly be judged, at least in part, by the degree to which they permit, as SALT II did, land-mobile ICBM of various kinds, while addressing (as SALT II did not) the verification problems they entail.

Ballistic Missile Defence

The most publicized recent development in strategic policy debates, and one which is at least in some respects technological, is renewed interest in ballistic missile defences. President Reagan's March 1983 'Star Wars' speech was, quite explicitly, nothing short of a proclamation of a long-term effort to use technology to reverse basic assumptions of the current US–Soviet strategic relationship.

President Reagan's speech, and the resulting substantial increases in US spending on ballistic missile defence work, are by no means the only signs of life on the ballistic missile defence front. The Soviet BMD programme is also vigorous. It includes replacement of the obsolescent *Galosh* BMD interceptors in the ABM complex permitted around Moscow with a far more up-to-date system as the active development of new ballistic missile interceptors. The Soviet programme also embraces substantial work on directed-energy and laser systems of the kind discussed speculatively in the US for ABM as well as other military applications.

The technical feasibility and strategic wisdom of ABM systems form the subject of other Papers in these volumes and will not be reargued here. For present purposes, it is important to be clear that the renewed interest in BMD is far less a response to technological breakthroughs than to a mixture of politics and policy urging that no technological stone should be left unturned in the effort to see if such breakthroughs may perhaps be achived in the future. To put it mildly, the SDI (Strategic Defense Initiative) was not the result of a considered judgment that there are a lot of sound technological solutions just waiting to be applied.

Nonetheless, the renewed interest in BMD – coupled with a serious Soviet violation of the 1972 ABM Treaty – is a challenge to the arms-control regime of the past decade as fundamental as the genuinely technological challenge ICBM vulnerability poses to the strategic assumptions of the two sides.

The Treaty occupies a curiously respected spot in the rationalizations for both sides'

ABM efforts. However, the activities of the two sides represent, in their rather different ways, basic challenges to the agreement's viability. The Soviet explanations for their radar at Krasnoyarsk (Abalakova) and at least some assertions advanced by American spokesmen of how much scope the Treaty affords for hardware experiments suggest a willingness on the part of ABM enthusiasts on both sides to reduce the Treaty to the status of a peculiar historical and legal derelict – something which must be carefully steered around but which scarcely need be formally abrogated, for it need not impact on any carefully planned R&D effort to prepare for large-scale deployments. We face, in short, a real prospect that the ABM Treaty will be modified – not by explicit renegotiation or even explicit abrogation, but by gradually defining it out of meaningful existence.

From the point of view of arms control the basic point to be made is that such decisions should be made explicitly. The renewed discussion of ABM opens an opportunity to secure in the future, rather than to abolish, the current self-denying ordinance on developments that would be expensive and either dangerous or futile (and possibly both) but which either side would find it difficult to refrain from unilaterally.

As argued above, the existing Treaty establishes a comprehensive legal barrier to serious exploitation, and to a considerable degree even to serious exploration, of future BMD possibilities. The specificity and detail of those restraints correspond to some extent to the degree to which the relevant technologies were understood and anticipated in 1972. Nonetheless, the basic principle is clear: not only were familiar BMD concepts to be limited to very low levels, but future developments were to be sharply curtailed.

Certainly the Treaty provides for periodic review and for discussion of limits on new technologies, and, in any event, the viability of the ABM Treaty, like that of any other international compact, depends not on its terms or its legal force but on its continued utility for the two sides. Nonetheless, the Treaty provides a framework for the two sides seeking to reinforce and specify the details of the existing comprehensive constraints. If one judges – as I would – that it is not in the interest of the West for both sides to deploy those forms of BMD that are feasible (as contrasted with wishful), that opportunity should be a high priority.

It is worth observing that, whatever obstacles verification may present in other areas, there are relatively few here. The kinds of advanced technologies which are speculatively proposed for exploitation for BMD are not difficult to verify. All of the systems discussed, especially space-based or ground-based laser or other directed-energy systems, would without exception require very large installations, prolonged construction, and installation and extensive testing over a long period of time.

Satellites
Command and control provide the central nervous system for the immense musculature of modern weapons. A broad spectrum of observers have in recent years expressed concern that the survivability and capability of the nervous system falls far short of that of the weapons themselves. For the most part, communication survivability is a matter of unilateral programmes to reduce the vulnerability of communications networks, both directly and by added redundancy.

The question arises whether there is much potential for arms control in this effort to protect command and control. One area in which US–Soviet agreement can help is suggested by proposals for co-operatively established communication facilities. This whole complex of possible agreements on communication enhancements represents a rather new field for arms control, in that it would seek to provide facilities for crisis control rather than deny or restrict the means of destruction. One widely-discussed idea is the creation of new institutional and technical devices for East–West crisis communication. These would be similar in concept to the existing 'Hot-Line' but of greatly increased capability.

The recent agreement on upgrading the 'Hot-Line' is a first step in this direction. More ambitious proposals call for jointly-manned cross-communication centres and institutionalized periodic exchanges of information. The common thread is to facilitate more rapid, secure and responsive – and credible – communications between the two sides in a crisis.

Such arrangements, even if agreed, would, of course, be useful only so long as both sides wished them to be. Inability to communicate in a crisis is far more likely to result from political decisions, confusion and perennial misunderstanding than from lack of physical facilities. Still, it is hard to see how additional channels could hurt.

The arms-control aspect of the communications survivability problem which has been most discussed has to do with limitations on anti-satellite (ASAT) systems. Both sides have developed, and the Soviet Union has deployed on some scale, interceptors capable of attacking satellites in low orbit. These interceptors are only one, if the most direct, of a vast variety of means of physically attacking or interfering with satellites, ranging from electronic disruption of ground-space links to using ABM battle stations in space against another's satellites. Indeed, a particularly awkward technological fact about the prospect of unrestrained ballistic missile research and development is that many proposed BMD concepts that promise only very modest practical BMD capability could provide a very good ASAT system, even during prototype stages.

No plausible set of arms agreements could bar all these threats. The issue is whether some useful, though less than totally comprehensive, limits are possible.

The technological obstacles to significant limits in this area are obviously formidable. Whereas the task for verification of limitations on strategic forces is simplified by the fact that rather large-scale violations would be necessary to have much strategic significance, proposals for ASAT arms control must deal with the fact that the threshold of 'adequacy' (that is, the ability to detect violations before they become significant) may be quite low. Further, even if ABM technology is sharply limited, a variety of space programmes – even some entirely legitimate civil and scientific work – would offer some potential for attacking satellites.

On the other hand, it is important not to exaggerate the degree to which limitations on ASAT systems must be comprehensive if they are to be useful. It is no doubt true that there is no way by arms control (or anything else) to make it very probable that either side would be able to rely on satellite-based systems in the event of a general nuclear war, and there will always be some means that could be adopted for attempting to attack satellites. Yet that is to state the problem of ASAT weapons too broadly and to pose an unnecessarily difficult task for arms control (or, for that matter, for unilateral defensive and survivability measures).

The reason that less-than-perfect limits would be useful arises from the nature of the threat that ASAT weapons pose to stability. Super-power capacity to threaten each other's space communications and intelligence systems would pose unique threats to stability, but those threats emerge principally at the lower, rather than the higher, end of the range of possible confrontations. In general war, no nation could safely rely on continued use of satellites on anything like the peacetime scale, if only because of the possibility of nuclear or conventional attack on ground stations.

In the twilight situation of crisis or limited war if space-reliant military support systems were vulnerable – not to massive, possibly improvised attack, but to small scale, quick, high-confidence ASAT attack – these satellites would present a very tempting target. The fact that such an attack could be carried out without direct attack on the territory of the other side, or indeed without possibility of loss of life by anybody, might in a crisis make such attacks appear less risky than attacks on other, possibly less important but also less isolated, assets of the other side. The particular threat of the use of ASAT systems in such crisis conditions ranks among the more serious situations conducive to the outbreak of a nuclear war.

Obviously, arms-control efforts to control the ability to mount such attacks is not the only – or even the primary – way of dealing with this problem. A variety of survivability and redundancy measures can be taken to reduce the effective vulnerability of satellites to such attacks. It is also important to reinforce by every possible means – including explicit agreements as to the legal status of satellites – that an attack on the other side's satellites would be a grave aggressive act.

Nonetheless, the threat is sufficiently large and the available unilateral ways of meeting it sufficiently uncertain that it is appropriate to explore whether arms-control limitations on ASAT capabilities are feasible. The utility of such agreements is based not on abstract objections to the militarization of space or the idea of war in space (and the arms-control goal is not to seek to prevent a 'weapons race in space') but on the need to forestall the particular instabilities that ASAT weapons would cause in a crisis.

Any substantive ASAT agreement will be difficult, for it will face not only verification problems but the obstacle of the asymmetry that the USSR already has a deployed system while the more capable US system is still being developed. However, both current systems are still altitude-limited. Even if the verification problems of dismantling the existing Soviet systems and the political problems of a frozen asymmetry block a general ban on interceptors, useful possibilities remain. These include a ban on ASAT tests at higher altitudes and limits on space- or ground-based laser and other directed-energy ASAT devices. As with analogous BMD limits, the size of such systems (and the test programmes they would require) make verification easier.

Even an agreement that went very far along these lines would by no means eliminate all ASAT capability. In particular, failure to maintain effective limits on new-technology BMD would open a fatal loophole in any ASAT controls. However, the possibility that a variety of systems – even including some civil or scientific space devices – could be diverted to ASAT use in an emergency is not a fatal objection to ASAT limits focused on dedicated systems and reinforced by strict limits on tests against space targets.

Grey Area and Dual Capable Forces.
A further area where technological changes pose challenges to arms control is the continuing erosion of the never-very-clear line between strategic and other nuclear systems. Arms-control negotiations have been bedevilled from the very beginning by the impossibility of securing agreement among all interested parties – the United States, her allies and the USSR – on an abstract definition of 'strategic.' Not unreasonably, each has favoured a definition of strategic in terms of threats to targets of strategic importance to the definer rather than of the characteristics of the systems posing the threat.

The problem, however, has continued to deepen. The Soviet medium-range *Backfire* bomber has characteristics which would allow it to be used in certain circumstances for attacks on the United States. The USSR asserts, with at least apparent conviction, that the *Pershing* II is a great source of concern for her because of its potential for attacks on key Soviet command-and-control centres that support forces that are strategic by any definition. On both sides, sea-launched cruise missiles (SLCM) are being developed with potential for deployment on a very wide range of naval platforms. A central part of the Soviet 'counter-measures' to the NATO INF deployments has been to erode further any distinction between theatre and battlefield nuclear weapons by, for the first time, deploying outside Soviet territory missile systems with nuclear weapons with a range sufficient to reach deep into Western Europe from bases in Eastern Europe.

This continued erosion of the distinction between tactical and strategic weapons is echoed in the more obvious technology-driven erosion of the distinction between conventional and nuclear systems. There has been widespread discussion in recent years of the possibility of applying the accuracy and other technology which is making ICBM in silos obsolescent, cruise missiles for long-range attacks feasible, and surface ships more vulnerable, to the development of techniques for attack on strategic nuclear force targets – and even on ICBM silos – without nuclear weapons. (Both sides have for a long time relied heavily on non-nuclear explosives for defence against strategic bomber and submarine forces.)

Here the technical prospects are a good deal less gloomy than for a strong ballistic missile defence. There appears to be a real prospect that over the next few decades accuracy could be greatly improved – albeit at considerable price and with considerable uncertainties about operational effectiveness. Improvements could even reach a point where non-nuclear attacks would be effective against the fixed nuclear forces of both sides, the fixed support bases for mobile assets, and (if surveillance improves as much as is sometimes contended) even the mobile assets now thought immune from all except nuclear attacks and possibly even from them.

The possibility of super-accurate, non-nuclear weapons systems with a principally counter-nuclear, or at least counter-military, mission is but one example of the further erosion of the distinction between nuclear and conventional forces. Another more mundane, and far more immediate, example is the apparent enthusiasm of both sides for moving rapidly to the deployment of nuclear-armed SLCM not physically distinguishable from their conventionally-armed cousins and possibly capable of being fired from literally thousands of torpedo tubes and other launch platforms in the fleets of both sides.

The technical possibility of 'safe' counter-nuclear pre-emption without using nuclear weapons may seem attractive, but the technological and doctrinal achievement of learning how to start a nuclear war with conventional weapons could well prove a dubious one. Moreover, there would be adverse political consequences to 'nuclearizing' what would otherwise be useful and important, but less controversial, conventional capabilities. Both in the arms control and in the military policy context, the sharpest technical and analytical consideration should be given to the prospect of using conventional weapons as vehicles for serious counter-nuclear pre-emption before starting down that path.

The widespread deployment of essentially identical delivery systems for conventional and nuclear munitions also complicates defining the scope of nuclear arms agreements. In part, the importance of this issue is a function of how far arms control is to progress beyond the stages already reached. The agreements so far reached have for the most part constrained only missiles with an exclusively nuclear role and heavy bombers that – despite some conventional missions and, on the Soviet side, the assignment of very similar airframes to support missions like ASW, reconnaissance and tankers – have been sufficiently close to having purely nuclear missions that limits on them had no major impact on conventional capability. As the arms-control agenda – and the pace of Soviet middle-range systems deployments – accelerated, the well-named 'grey area' problem grew more significant in the late 1970s. If longer-range and more capable nuclear delivery systems are introduced without differentiation from conventional platforms, these problems will become still more serious in the future.

It is at a minimum worth considering whether arms control has a role in seeking to promote, particularly for theatre use, the clearest possible distinction between nuclear and conventional forces. An area worth exploring initially is that of nuclear-armed SLCM, either by a ban or a requirement (enforced by counting rules) that conventional SLCM be effectively distinguished from nuclear if they are not to count as nuclear.

Verification and Intelligence
Certainly some new technological developments, particularly in the grey area, will make monitoring more difficult. This is particularly true when, as with current SLCM plans, new systems would severely strain reliance on counting launchers of particular types as a close surrogate for counting nuclear-armed weapons of a particular kind. As the range of systems of potential arms-control interest grows away from the familiar ICBM–SLBM–heavy bomber triad, less direct and less clear-cut intelligence methods will play a greater verification role – which may not be viable politically.

However, it is important to resist the cries of despair that the possibility of effective verification is being fatally eroded by these developments. Even though there are no relevant arms-control agreements to monitor, Western intelligence still has a reasonably good (if far from precise) idea what part of, say, Soviet tactical aircraft have a nuclear capability. Cruise missiles, ground- or sea-launched, while obviously harder to count than ICBM, neatly deployed in silos that take years to build, have been the subject of intelligence monitoring for decades. Current cruise missiles are less capable than their successors, but they are not for that reason any easier to observe, and US intelligence has been able with reasonable confidence to prepare estimates of how many are deployed – and even some sense of how many are nuclear capable. The SS-20s – as well as short-range missile systems deployed for many years – are fully mobile, but US intelligence monitors their numbers quite successfully.

Even in those situations where technological developments probably do reduce confidence in counts of numbers, the significance of verification uncertainties from a military point of view may be decreased to the degree that survivability is increased. This is, broadly, the case for land-mobile ICBM and also for cruise missiles, two systems whose introduction has aroused special concern with respect to the impact on verification. Land-mobile missiles are obviously harder to count with confidence than silo-based systems, but they also seem likely to have somewhat degraded accuracy and lower yield, and in any case their higher degree of survivability, particularly if deployed on each side, reduces the significance of relatively small differences in the size of the force. A broadly similar observation applies with respect to cruise missiles. Their relatively slow flight and their susceptibility to point defences makes them far more likely to be relied on as retaliatory than initiating weapons. Uncertainties in their count are therefore less significant.

Verification of such systems will never have the apparent precision of counting silos or submarines, but – assuming that the sides can agree on substantive limitations – adequate verification measures, employing plausibly negotiable co-operative measures to reinforce existing intelligence methods, should be attainable. Negotiations would, however, take time, and there is always a question whether levels of verification uncertainty that are tolerable from a technical, military or intelligence point of view will be acceptable politically.

Conclusion
This Paper has focused mostly on areas where technology affords opportunities – or does not present quite the barriers sometimes claimed – for arms control. In many critical areas where technology is changing rapidly – including C^3 survivability, accuracy improvements and most conventional force developments – arms control appears to have little potential. Overall, however, analysis suggests that the obstacles to future arms control are not primarily technological. Indeed, technological developments, which are by definition concrete and definite, are inherently more susceptible to management by concrete and definite agreements than are political and strategic differences, which present formidable problems of understanding and confidence even if the political will to agree exists.

In short, arms control is certainly challenged by technology – and especially by the argument that technology can be applied to neutralize the destructive power of nuclear weapons – but it is not technology that is the chief stumbling block. The agenda outlined is both urgent and realistic technologically – managing land-mobile missiles and single-RV options, maintaining and tightening the ABM Treaty, controlling ASAT weapons, strengthening the distinction between conventional and nuclear theatre weapons, constraining nuclear SLCM and holding down overall warhead numbers and power. It may be modest compared to the prospect of nuclear war, but it is very ambitious, given current political realities.

New Technology, Stability and the Arms Control Deadlock: Part II

DR BARRY M. BLECHMAN

The impact of technological change on the stability of the nuclear balance and the risk of war has been long debated by military analysts and practitioners. Recently, however, this fairly arcane and elusive subject has had a major impact on American politics and, prospectively, on the security policies of the United States. Although never stated explicitly, by embracing a negotiated nuclear weapons 'freeze' as its primary goal, the popular arms-control movement (and the Democratic Party in its 1984 platform) has accepted the view that the danger of nuclear war stems primarily from the modernization of weapons.

Only four years ago popular attitudes towards arms control seemed to suggest that nuclear risks were seen to depend most importantly on the size of nuclear arsenals. The SALT agreements, after all, placed greatest emphasis on limiting the *number* of strategic launchers, including only minor curbs on the pace of modernization; even so, the most telling political argument against SALT II was that it did not achieve 'deep cuts' in nuclear forces. These arguments have now gone out of fashion. Indeed, the much higher priority which the arms-control constituency now places on curbing technological change was demonstrated explicitly during the past year by the movement's furious rejection of the 'build-down' concept, a proposal which would permit the introduction of new weapons, but only in exchange for specified reductions in existing forces.

There is of course a third view: that the risk of nuclear war depends on neither force levels nor modernization in the first instance, but on the consequences of both factors (and others) for the stability of the nuclear balance – the incentives provided by the two sides' force postures for one or the other to pre-empt in the event of a crisis. This position, too, is rejected by 'freeze' advocates, who would foreclose *all* modernization, regardless of the likely impact of any proposed new weapon on perceptions of the value of initiating a nuclear exchange.

This new emphasis on limiting technology represents a major reversal for the arms-control movement, which originated as a technical response to the failure of efforts to negotiate 'general and complete disarmament'. Beginning with the Surprise Attack Conference in 1958, arms-control negotiations have been seen as 'a technical method of achieving a practical purpose' – which happens to be one of Webster's definitions of technology. In the case of arms control, the 'practical purpose' is reducing the risk of nuclear war; the 'technical method' is negotiated, mutual limits on weapons. A more satisfactory means of reducing the risk of war would be to reach the political settlements necessary to eliminate the causes of conflict (and of the arms competition). So long as such broad accommodations do not appear feasible, however, limits on armaments offer practical means of at least containing the risk of war. In effect, arms control offers to alleviate the symptoms, leaving treatment of the disease itself to others.

The new emphasis in arms control is quixotic, at best. Technological change can no more be stopped – or 'frozen' – than knowledge of how to design and manufacture nuclear weapons can be banished from the minds of men and women. It is in humanity's nature to seek to understand its universe better and to apply that knowledge to the solution of practical problems. So long as the international political system remains unencumbered by a central political authority with the effective power to enforce a comprehensive system of international law, the defence of national interests and national security from the challenges (real and imagined) posed by other nation-states will be among these practical problems. It is unrealistic and counter-productive to assume that national leaders will often agree to cease applying the products of new technologies for the enhancement of the security (or the power) of their nations. If anything, we should assume that the revolution of weapon technologies will accelerate in the future, in keeping with the general trend in the rate of technological change. In addition, the proliferation of advanced weapon technologies throughout the world provides additional incentives for the leading powers to press for technological innovations to maintain their current advantages.

Even if a 'freeze' on the improvement of nuclear weapon systems were feasible, such an emphasis in efforts to negotiate controls on armaments would be misplaced. In the abstract, technology is neither necessarily 'good' nor necessarily 'bad'; the fruits of scientific exploration can only be applied to purposes which we consider to be either 'good' or 'bad'. The challenge is to channel technological change in the right directions.

It is the case that the application of scientific advances to practical problems has resulted in the development of nuclear explosives and the missiles which can deliver them over great distances in relatively short periods of time. It is also the case that continuing technological advances are greatly improving the capabilities of these weapon systems to destroy opposing strategic forces, raising concerns about the stability of the nuclear balance. But other technological advances have altered nuclear force postures radically in recent decades, greatly enhancing the nuclear powers' ability to avoid war. Objectively viewed – at least as concerns the potential technical determinants of the risk of war – the nuclear balance must be considered far more stable in the 1980s than it was thirty, or even twenty years ago.

At least in the case of the United States, the positive controls on nuclear weapons are *far more secure* than they were in the past and are continuing to improve. Modern command-and-control systems, better electronic locking devices, and such measures as the introduction of inert conventional explosives in the triggering mechanisms of nuclear weapons have greatly reduced the dangers that unauthorized individuals might launch nuclear weapons, that nuclear explosions might result from accidents, or that a nuclear war might begin in response to false warnings of an attack. Incumbent and former officials who have had responsibility for these matters agree that the risk of accidental or inadvertent nuclear war is small. Although efforts should be continued to eliminate whatever dangers may still exist, we can take some comfort in the progress that has been made already.

Secondly, although technological advances have led to the almost certain vulnerability of any fixed, land-based launcher (and perhaps surface ships as well), the capabilities of bomber aircraft, strategic submarines and some types of land-mobile missile launcher have so far managed to stay ahead of the capabilities of the systems that would be used to find and destroy them. While there is no guarantee that this balance of capabilities can be maintained indefinitely, most observers agree that there is virtually no risk to submarines for at least the next ten to twenty years. And even the bombers, perennially threatened with obsolescence, seem to have attained a breathing space in the contest with air defences with the development of air-launched cruise missiles and 'stealth' technologies. Combined with other factors, particularly the 1972 ABM Treaty, these technological advances have permitted each side to maintain survivable nuclear retaliatory capabilities of such magnitude as to deter the initiation of a nuclear exchange in virtually all circumstances – and even to cause both great powers to seek to avoid situations in which such a decision might become plausible. Despite their impassioned rhetoric and deteriorating political relations, the United States and the Soviet Union have not confronted one another militarily in a crisis since 1973. There are many reasons for this relative restraint, but the maintenance of secure retaliatory capabilities through technological innovation is undoubtedly one of them.

Thirdly, the development of photo-reconnaissance satellites and other systems able to monitor events on the territory of foreign states – and, the advanced communications systems which can relay this data back home instantaneously – have led to important changes in the character of inter-state relations.[1] An ability to appraise confidently the size and characteristics of potentially hostile military forces, to observe the development of most major new weapon systems long before they become operational, and (most importantly) to detect variations in the operational patterns of military units which suggest preparations for hostilities – all these have greatly reduced the risk that war might result from misperceptions of the actions of others. We worry, of course, about the precision of our estimates, in view of the closed nature of Soviet society, but these concerns are minor as compared to the uncertainties about national military capabilities which governed international relations before the late 1950s. We must also be concerned that the high levels of military operations which attend crises or global exercises could be used to mask preparations for war. Still, the extent of our knowledge about others is dramatically greater than any historical standard would suggest. As a result, the need to build additional forces or to mobilize existing military capabilities because of unfounded suspicions or fears has been greatly alleviated, providing greater latitude in international relationships.

Advances in the technologies of intelligence systems have also made it possible to consider negotiated restraints on armaments that would have been unthinkable several decades ago. Were it not for the development of national technical means of verification, we would not even be debating the sorts of agreements now contemplated routinely.

Many will find this view of technology 'pollyanna-ish'. But it is not meant to deny that some technological change can have negative consequences – resulting in weapon deployments which create instabilities in the strategic balance and a greater risk of nuclear war. It is to say only that technology, *per se*, is *agnostic*; hence imputing negative (or positive) political implications to its advance – as an inherent and unavoidable quality – can only be misleading. In thinking about how to control the potential impact of technology on arms control and military stability, therefore, one cannot apply a blunt instrument like the nuclear 'freeze' without running undue risks of doing more harm than good. Difficult as it may be, both in terms of negotiations and – at least among the democratic nations – in terms of mustering political support, we must seek more discriminating agreements, arangements that provide incentives for the development of 'good' technologies and disincentives for those which could have negative consequences.

Prospective Technological Developments
A number of new technologies are now in the public view which, if fully developed and deployed, would result in significant alterations of military capabilities. A few of these potential developments can be considered unambiguously positive in their likely impact on the military balance and arms control; several others can be considered unambiguously negative; a couple seem to have an uncertain impact. The following review describes several of these emerging technologies, suggesting their likely effects on both military stability and the prospects for arms control. While the present survey is necessarily rudimentary and incomplete it is only through such case-by-case analyses that the impact of technology can be addressed reasonably and its consequences for arms control and military stability understood and incorporated in relevant policies.

Anti-Satellite Capabilities
There is probably no more serious near-term threat to the stability of the military balance and the consequent risk of war than the prospective deployment of very capable anti-satellite weapons by both the Soviet Union and the United States. In the event of war, the destruction of satellite-based systems intended (among other things) to provide early warning of attack, to monitor events on the battlefield and provide strategic and tactical intelligence to military commanders, and to facilitate communications between commanders in the field and higher level

authorities (particularly the highest civilian authorities) would have adverse effects on both sides' ability to respond to attacks, creating new uncertainties with the potential to aggravate the dangers of the nuclear age appreciably. There would be a risk, for example, that in preparing for the potential loss of satellites, one or both nations might establish procedures that, in certain contingencies, would give greater freedom of action to field commanders, thus reducing the positive controls on military forces.

Alternatively, loss of satellite-based systems might cause the United States to fail to respond effectively to an attack, thus jeopardizing vital national interests. One aspect of this type of negative consequence might have particularly adverse effects. Knowledge that the United States could launch her missiles upon warning of an attack is probably an important element of deterrence, regardless of whether or not a US President actually would take such a step. Deployment of anti-satellite weapons capable of destroying early-warning systems could therefore terminate this deterrent effect.

For these reasons, negotiations to limit anti-satellite weapons should be placed very high on the arms-control agenda. While it is probably too late to ban anti-satellite weapons completely, agreement could be sought on measures with the potential to circumscribe the scope of capabilities available to the two sides. It may still be possible, for example, to prohibit systems capable of destroying satellites in geosynchronous orbits, as well as systems able to destroy many satellites rapidly. It may also be possible to limit the confidence with which each nation perceives those capabilities which had been developed before an agreement went into effect. A mutual ban on field tests of existing systems could, over time, contribute to a reluctance to depend on anti-satellite capabilities in military planning.

Insertable Nuclear Components
This technology is in a relatively early stage of development, but if technical problems are overcome and warheads designed for insertable nuclear components (INC) deployed, it could threaten the viability of any agreement to limit the number or deployment areas of nuclear-armed weapon systems. The technology offers the prospect of an ability to convert specially-configured conventional warheads into nuclear weapons on the battlefield by inserting components containing all the necessary fissile material and other mechanisms. In the absence of the nuclear component, INC warheads would be used like any other conventional weapon. Although virtually any conventional weapon could theoretically be designed for insertable nuclear components, initial discussions have centred on short-range missiles and artillery shells.

If such weapons were deployed, it would mean that agreements, for example, to limit the number of tactical nuclear weapons deployed in Europe, or to preclude such weapons from a corridor along the East–West border in Europe, would be next to useless. Each side would know that the opponent could very quickly nullify any such treaty by airlifting large numbers of the relatively small insertable nuclear components into the demarcated territory and fitting them to previously-deployed, INC-configured warheads. Knowledge of this possibility would probably ensure that no such agreement was reached to begin with, or – if one were concluded – that its positive effects on the stability of the military balance would be minimal, as each side acted to protect itself against this risk of sudden abrogation.

INC technology also has implications for strategic arms-control agreements, since its further development would aggravate existing problems stemming from such dual-capable systems as cruise missiles (see below). Like the examples mentioned previously, any agreement that limited only nuclear-armed cruise missiles and permitted unlimited deployments of conventionally-armed versions would be subject to sudden violation.

What, if anything, might be done through arms-control negotiations to limit INC technology is not clear. This is an important topic for research and analysis.[2]

Improved Communications
Communications technologies could be applied to a much greater extent to facilitate

contacts and the exchange of information between the great powers in the event of crises, and even during hostilities. In July 1984 US and Soviet negotiators agreed to upgrade the 'Hot Line' by supplementing the present teletype system with a facsimile link. This makes possible the exchange of full pages of information virtually instantaneously, whether maps, photographs or pages of message text. The agreement will both speed the rate at which information might be exchanged and expand the quality of that information.

The United States has proposed two additional improvements in communications between the great powers: (a) The installation of a similar facsimile link between the US Department of Defense and the Soviet Defence Ministry, so that technical information might be exchanged between the two sides at times when it was unnecessary, or undesirable, to involve the two Heads of State; and (b) the inauguration of high-speed communications links between each nation and its embassy in the other's capital, thus making possible more rapid communications through normal diplomatic channels. It is to be hoped, now that progress has been made on the 'Hot Line' improvement, that it may prove possible to extend the dialogue to include these additional measures.

In the Autumn of 1983 a bipartisan panel, co-chaired by US Senators Sam Nunn and John Warner, proposed a more elaborate form of improved communications between the two great powers for the control of crises and the risk of nuclear war. They suggested the establishment of national 'Nuclear Risk Reduction Centres' in Moscow and Washington. Each would be manned on a 24-hour basis by military and diplomatic officials of the host nation and liaison officers from the second nation, and would be linked by elaborate communications equipment, possibly including such 'real-time' links as tele-conferencing facilities. The staffs of the Centres would in normal times carry out a variety of tasks designed to prevent nuclear crises from ever developing; the existence of the Centres also would permit an extensive exchange of information should a confrontation develop.[3]

Clearly, in each of these proposals, technology would have positive consequences both for the military balance and for the risk of nuclear war.

Remote Sensors

Several new technologies permit consideration of the use of remote sensors to help build confidence between the US and USSR and also to facilitate the conclusion of several types of arms control agreements. The concept involves four components: (a) unmanned sensors ('black boxes') that would be implanted on the territory of each of the great powers; (b) communications satellites to relay signals from the sensors to the opposing great power; (c) encryption devices to ensure that the signals emitted by the sensor could not be simulated by the host nation; and (d) devices to ensure that the sensors and their encryption devices were not tampered with.

This basic system, which can be elaborated upon in several ways, has several potential applications. In the late 1970s, for example, US, British, and Soviet negotiators discussed the design of such a system that would be the primary means used to verify compliance with a comprehensive nuclear test ban. The concept envisaged emplacing ten unmanned seismic stations on each nation's territory (the number of stations to be placed in Britain had not been agreed upon) that would broadcast encrypted signals via satellite for distribution to the other signatories. The three parties had agreed to the concept in principle and were discussing its details when the negotiations were terminated for other reasons.

More recently, the use of remote sensors to supplement US and Soviet early-warning systems has been studied. The concept here is that the US and USSR would agree to emplace unmanned radars at each other's missile sites. The radars would emit a continuous, tamper-proof, encrypted signal via satellite indicating that no missile had been launched from the site. Launch of a missile would be detected by the radar with an extremely high probability and reported instantaneously. Efforts to tamper with the device would result in a different signal, while the cessation of any signal at all would also suggest tampering with the system. These systems would serve as counterchecks on each side's early-warning satellites, providing a means of avoiding provocative responses to false signals of a launch from one of those satellites. The installation of such devices also might help to build confidence on the two sides of each other's non-hostile intent and have other positive political consequences.[4]

There are additional applications of this concept worth analysing. There are sensors, for example, that can detect the presence of radioactive material at short distances (geiger counters are one primitive application of such sensors). Linked to encryption and non-tamper devices, and to a satellite network, such sensors could conceivably be used to verify the absence of nuclear warheads on ground-based cruise-missile launchers, surface ships, aircraft and even submarines. The use of remote sensors could potentially solve the previously-mentioned problem caused by dual-capable systems, thus facilitating a range of arms-control agreements. The central benefit of these types of systems is that, theoretically at least, they would permit the use of means of verification which can only operate effectively at close range, without compromising the integrity of weapon systems and jeopardizing military security.

Remote sensors could also be used to monitor agreements to establish cease-fire lines, demilitarized zones, and other arrangements to control military conflicts, but these are potential benefits of technology best discussed in other fora.

Emerging Conventional Technologies
These technologies could have a very positive effect on military stability and the risk of war by the end of the century. Essentially military applications of the revolution in electronics, particularly in data-processing capabilities, they promise to increase NATO's ability to defend itself without resorting to nuclear weapons. Emerging conventional technologies include: (a) greatly improved sensors of several types, capable of discriminating faint signals against cluttered backgrounds; (b) vastly improved command, control, communications and intelligence systems that will permit more flexible and tactically effective use of military forces; and (c) extremely accurate weapons, particularly anti-tank systems, capable of locating and tracking their targets autonomously. Eventually, the use of advanced computers and software systems will permit the application of artificial intelligence to military systems; combined in the next century with robotics, these technological developments will greatly reduce manpower requirements per unit of combat effectiveness (or at least that portion of military manpower which must be placed 'in harm's way').

Assuming that they are developed effectively, the emerging conventional technologies offer the prospect of raising the nuclear threshold, making it possible for NATO to rely far less on threats to initiate and escalate nuclear war to deter attacks. Combined with the apparent shift in Soviet military doctrine towards acceptance of the possibility that European conflicts might remain limited to the conventional level, deployments of these weapons should help to stabilize the military balance in Europe, thus reducing the risk of nuclear war. In addition, the deployment of these systems should make it possible for the NATO nations to adopt a more forthcoming attitude towards potential nuclear arms-control arrangements, thus facilitating more rapid progress in negotiations.

Cruise Missiles
These weapons offer an example of how technological advances can sometimes have ambivalent effects on military stability and the prospects for arms control.

The deployment of air-launched cruise missiles has greatly improved the ability of bombers to penetrate advanced air defences, thus making possible continued reliance on these forces for US retaliatory capabilities and, therefore, for deterrence. Advanced generations of cruise missiles will fly somewhat faster and incorporate certain 'stealth' characteristics, thus probably making possible their continued effectiveness despite further advances in air defence systems. The relatively long period of time between the launch of a bomber and the impact of its weapons on target, as well as the ability to recall manned systems, cause most observers to consider bombers to be the most stable of the three components of US strategic forces. By contributing to the bombers' continuing effectiveness, the several technologies which have made modern cruise missiles possible have thus had positive results.

Despite the political furore which has surrounded them, the deployment of ground-launched cruise missiles (GLCM) may also be considered a stabilizing measure. Relatively long time-of-flight is again the key, a fact recognized by the USSR, which has concentrated its propaganda against *Pershing* II ballistic missiles, apparently seeing less danger in cruise missile deployments. An additional point in the favour of GLCM is their lower cost, a fact which (politics aside) would make possible their deployment in larger numbers, thus reducing the value of any single missile and the incentive to launch the weapon pre-emptively because of concerns for its survivability if attacked first.

Cruise missiles do raise serious problems for verifying potential arms-control agreements, however. For one thing, they can be tested to a much greater extent within concealed laboratories than can ballistic missiles, thus raising concerns about possible ways to circumvent negotiated restrictions on their characteristics. More to the point, because cruise missiles are relatively small and can be fired from standard launchers (torpedo tubes and rotary devices in bomb bays, for example), it would probably be difficult to verify restrictions on the number of deployed weapons. This problem is greatly complicated by the ability to equip cruise missiles with either conventional or nuclear warheads. The former, which presumably would not be covered by arms-control agreements, could conceivably be replaced with nuclear versions surreptitiously – or at least there would be concern that such substitutions *might* take place during a time of crisis preceding a war.

As was demonstrated in the provisions of the SALT II Treaty pertaining to air-launched cruise missiles, it is possible to get around these problems through negotiated 'counting rules' and by requiring certain co-operative measures to aid verification. Conceivably, the previously-mentioned remote sensor technologies could be of assistance here as well. This is an area, though, for which the hiatus in nuclear arms-control negotiations is having a considerable effect. Both Soviet and US cruise missile programmes are entering deployment phases and, unless delays are negotiated and the requisite forms of co-operation set in place rapidly, it may soon be too late for the effective control of these weapons.

Technologies for Strategic Defences
This is obviously an increasingly important aspect of the relationship between technology, on the one hand, and stability and arms control, on the other. Theoretically, the deployment of advanced strategic defences could greatly reduce the risk of nuclear war. Two conditions would have to be met, however: first, defensive technologies would have to be shown to be *extremely* effective, particularly taking account of their own potential susceptibility to counter-attack; second, the US and USSR would have to agree to avoid increasing, and even to decrease, offensive force levels as defences were installed.

If the first condition were not met – if defensive systems were installed which worked well, but not extremely well – a situation could develop during a time of tension in which one side or the other convinced itself: (a) that war was almost certain; (b) that it would be much better off if it struck first (particularly if the opposing defences could be overwhelmed or attacked successfully); and (c) that its own defences were sufficient for it to survive the expected retaliation. (In the theoretical literature these are, of course, the classic conditions under which a nuclear war might begin.)

If the second condition were not fulfilled – if defences were deployed without restrictions on offensive force levels – it could be expected that each side would attempt to deploy sufficient forces to be able to overwhelm whatever defensive capabilities the other had deployed. Without limits on offensive forces, while defensive systems might be able to deny each side certain limited options, they would be unlikely to be able to deny all-out attacks. In short, in the absence of controls on offensive force levels, there could be an extremely expensive acceleration of the US–Soviet strategic competition, with adverse effects on political relations and the risk of war, and an uncertain ultimate outcome.

There are several implications of this view of the effect of defensive technologies on stability:

- While it is desirable to explore technological prospects, steps which implied a commitment to deployment – or which would preclude the continued viability of negotiated limits on defences – should be avoided. The possibility of maintaining an arms-control regime that prohibits defences should be retained until it is ascertained that it would indeed be possible to deploy truly effective defences.
- As this exploratory research process is likely to take a considerable amount of time, and as the existing ABM Treaty was designed to deal with a very different set of technologies, it is desirable to talk to the Soviet Union about the possibility of modifying the Treaty. These amendments might deal with difficulties already revealed as concerns the treatment of radars and 'tactical' ABM utilizing older technologies, as well as problems likely to emerge as new technologies enter testing phases.
- Looking towards the future, if the new technologies show promise and deployment looks increasingly likely, it would be desirable to enter into negotiations with the USSR concerning the establishment of a transitional regime in which offensive forces were phased down as defences were deployed. This regime should point towards a situation in the next century in which each great power had very capable defences and only rather small offensive forces. Assuming that any such agreement would also include provisions permitting it to be verified effectively, such a treaty could conceivably serve as a stable basis for the US–Soviet nuclear relationship for many years.

Conclusion
Efforts to limit nuclear weapons can only make progress if they are designed to operate within the realities of contemporary life. The fact that we live in an anarchic international system is an important aspect of that reality, as are the significant roles played by military power in protecting nations' security. For the members of NATO, not the least of these roles are those which pertain to containing the effects of Soviet military power. While some of the tension between East and West results from mutual misperceptions and unwarranted suspicions, there remain fundamental incompatibilities between the interests of the Soviet Union and those of the United States and her Allies. The history of the post-war world provides little empirical reason to believe that the nature of the international political system will change significantly at any time in the near future.

It is also only realistic to recognize that nuclear weapons are a permanent fact of life. They represent a forty-year-old technology, knowledge of which cannot be banished from the minds of men and women. It is unproductive to approach the problem of the risk of nuclear war with an assumption that it might be possible to abolish these weapons. This is a case of the best being the enemy of the good. To seek the total elimination of nuclear weapons is often to reject the far more limited steps which can contain the dangers implied by their continued existence.

Finally, when considering alternative approaches to arms control, it would be unrealistic to presume that it would be either possible or desirable to 'freeze' the technology incorporated in military systems. We live in a world in which the pace of technological change is accelerating, not slowing down. This trend will affect military capabilities at least as much, and probably more, than any other sector. The challenge is to harness technological change for good – to improve the stability of the nuclear balance and to facilitate the conclusion of more far-reaching arms-control arrangements. This can only be accomplished if there is a willingness to examine prospective technologies with a detailed eye and a creative mind.

In the face of the potential horror of the ultimate dangers of nuclear weapons there is an understandable popular impatience with the slow pace of progress in arms negotiations. This sometimes results, as in the past few years, in popular support for simple and sweeping measures intended to alter the situation overnight. It is the responsibility of experts and political leaders to resist these trends, to educate the public about the complexities of the military balance and the deterrence of war, and to exercise the leadership required to gain political support for the necessarily complicated measures that can – in the real world – contain, if not abolish, the risk of nuclear war. These are tasks that require all our support.

NOTES

[1] 'Address by President Carter to the Newspaper Publishers Association', *New York Times*, 26 April 1979, p. 16.

[2] An INC-designed warhead was mentioned as a possibility for the *Harpoon* missile; see *Fiscal Year 1980 Arms Control Impact Statements*, Joint Committee Print, 96th Congress, 1st session (Washington DC: USGPO, 1979), p. 176.

[3] The Report of the Nunn–Warner Working Group on Nuclear Risk Reduction can be found in *Survival*, May/June 1984, vol. XXVI, no. 3, pp. 133–5; and in *Bulletin of the Atomic Scientists*, June/July 1984, pp. 28–9. Also see, John W. Lewis, and Coit D. Blacker (eds), *Next Steps in the Creation of an Accidental Nuclear War Prevention Center* (Stanford Ca: Center for International Security and Arms Control, Stanford University, 1983).

[4] Victor Utgoff, 'Briefing on Unmanned, On-sight, ICBM Launch Monitoring', presented to the Third Annual Seminar of the Center for Law and National Security, University of Virginia (22 June, 1984). A more complete discussion by Dr Utgoff of the potential uses of remote sensors will appear in Barry M. Blechman (ed.), *Reducing the Risk of Nuclear War* (Bloomington: Indiana UP, 1985).

New Technology and Intra-Alliance Relationships: New Strengths, New Strains

HON. DAVID M. ABSHIRE

Introduction

One of the greatest challenges confronting the Atlantic Alliance today is managing the relationship between technological change and the other pieces of the military mosaic embracing leadership, tactics, logistics and strategy. The question is not whether technology can make a difference to NATO and to the Warsaw Pact; it will. It is not whether the nations of the Alliance and the Pact will use new technology; they are sure to. The issue is whether the Alliance will use technology in the most effective way possible. This Paper focuses on the relationship between change and NATO's conventional forces.

NATO's conventional forces are more important today than ever before. The weight and momentum of relentless Soviet force improvements in strategic and tactical nuclear forces as well as in conventional forces, threatens the credibility of NATO's strategy of flexible response. Flexible response remains a good strategy, but it must be made truly flexible, especially at the conventional level. Intensified popular concern over nuclear weapons demands that the nuclear threshold be raised. Both of these concerns can be met by improved conventional forces.

The need to improve NATO's conventional forces is also a transatlantic political imperative. The proposed Nunn–Roth Amendment to the FY 85 Military Authorization Bill focused on the shortfalls in NATO's conventional posture and called upon NATO allies to meet their commitments to force sustainability or face American troop withdrawals. Although the Amendment was ultimately defeated, the congressional debate underlined an issue that is likely to be the source of continuing political friction within the Alliance if nothing is done to remedy the problem.

Fortunately, the Alliance has the opportunity to use new technologies to improve the performance of its conventional forces, enhance deterrence and thereby promote the Alliance's fundamental goal of preserving peace.

New technologies are also creating opportunities for innovative operational concepts, revised doctrines and new tactics that will help NATO make flexible response truly flexible. Military commanders have long desired to do certain things that technology can now make possible.

While NATO can derive great strength from technology, technology can also create strains. An incredibly rapid pace of technological change confronts Alliance decisionmakers with an enormous range of possible options. The stakes and risks associated with their decisions are high. So are the costs – a major difficulty at a time when the Alliance's economic resources are limited. Inevitably that combination produces strains.

These strains are exacerbated by unease within the Alliance that the dream made possible by new technology could become a nightmare in which the opponent exploits the same technologies available to the Alliance while NATO drags its heels in getting helpful technology into the field only to have its conventional forces overwhelmed.

NATO can meet the difficult and complex challenge of managing technological change in the military sphere. Of course, there will be problems along the way. In my judgment, NATO already has mechanisms to put new technology to best use and to reduce some of the inevitable strains. What is needed is an overall strategy to tie its decisions together as well as the leadership, vision and will to implement the strategy and to make that strategy work.

One must be clear about what one means by 'technology' in the NATO context. ET – 'emerging technologies' – has become a buzzword in the Alliance. Unfortunately, the term 'emerging technologies' has not been used precisely but has been used to describe a confusing range of technological developments.

In fact, a three-part distinction can be drawn. *Operational* and *emerged* technology would be used during this decade in weapons projects that incorporate existing or maturing technologies. *Emerging* technology focuses on developing and producing improved conventional weapons for initial fielding throughout the 1990s. *Exploratory* technologies are those that are not yet mature but are potentially useful in projects 15 to 20 years in the future. Emerging technologies emphasize a longer term focus on research and development programmes for weapons that are not yet defined.

A second distinction is also helpful, that is, whether the new technology is introduced as a component to an existing system, or whether it develops as a subsystem or as an entire system on its own.

As an illustration of this point, laser technology exists, having already arrived on the battlefield in fire control ranging for fourth generation Main Battle Tanks. Over the next decade, it may emerge from this passive role to the point where a low power laser is actively used from existing platforms against opposing forces. By the turn of the century, there may be self-contained battlefield laser systems that are as identifiable and common as a main battle tank or tactical aircraft. Thinking about this system, let alone about the force structure, logistics and tactics that might surround it, is still undefined and, thus, it is still in the exploratory phase.

The current debate about technology's contribution to Western deterrence must keep these distinctions clear. In evaluating current NATO thinking and planning, for example, some analysts have exaggerated the exploratory nature of the technology under consideration. In fact, NATO is first focusing on exploiting newly *emerged* technologies. If there is a debate on the utility of such plans it should not be decided on the basis of such distortion but on an understanding of the real situation.

Managing Change And Changing Management

For the NATO alliance the key question is how to manipulate that change so that the conventional balance in Europe can be significantly improved. Over its last 35 years, NATO has shown a great capability to incorporate technological changes into its defence capabilities. Unpredictable, uncontrolled change, however, has caused problems and has made the Allies uncomfortable. It is at those times that Alliance relations suffer most.

As one thinks about NATO's technological potential and how well the Alliance will do in incorporating new technology, three questions must be addressed:

– Can one be satisfied with the way the Alliance has handled technology in the recent past?
– What has the Alliance learned about new technology that will prove useful as it looks to the future? What lessons should not be forgotten?
– Does the nature of new technology suggest the need for new approaches or modification of existing institutions and processes?

A Look at the Recent Past

The extent to which NATO members have been able to develop, share and incorporate technology into their common defence is a cause for justifiable pride. Nevertheless, a review of the recent record shows that NATO must do better if it is effectively to exploit its superior technological resources to strengthen its conventional forces. Several factors give cause for concern.

The Decline of Western Technological Superiority

In the early 1970s there was clear evidence of NATO's technological superiority across the conventional spectrum. A decade later, NATO can no longer make that claim. The Warsaw Pact is closing the technological gap at an alarming rate – to the point that the threat can increasingly be described in qualitative as well as quantitative terms. If this sounds alarmist, consider the following areas in which

117

NATO prided itself for a substantial lead 10 years ago:

- Special 'Chobham'-type armour;
- Second-generation guidance on anti-tank guided missiles;
- Artillery sub-munitions;
- Target acquisition and fire control;
- High energy/manoeuvrability aircraft;
- All aspects of air-to-air missiles and air-to-surface precision guided munitions;
- Multispectrum electronic counter-measures;
- Submarine design.

In each of these areas NATO may still have major advantages in the laboratory. In the last decade, however, the Warsaw Pact has virtually matched NATO in getting these technologies to the field. In short, the Alliance has had problems in translating its technological prowess into operational capability.

A Vicious Production Cycle
There are many reasons to explain the erosion of Western technological superiority in certain key areas. One that must be considered is that NATO asks more of its technology than the Warsaw Pact. NATO requires not only that its weapons keep pace with those of the Pact but that the quality of its weapons be sufficiently high to offset quantitative inferiority. At times this requirement has produced a vicious circle:

- Pushing quality requires taking greater risks with unproven, adolescent technology;
- Trying to capitalize on such technology results in frequent re-design and programmatic delays;
- Changing requirements and slowing programmes generate higher costs;
- Increasing costs produce lower unit buys with stretched and inefficient production rates, adding even higher costs and later delivery;
- Higher costs and later deliveries get fewer systems into the field;
- Fewer systems in the field drive the need to push quality and take even greater technological risks.

This phenomenon has created the danger of what defence analyst Thomas Callaghan has called 'structural disarmament' – fewer and fewer systems for more and more money.[1] The Alliance should recognize that at some point numbers count no matter how good the technology.

Inventory Modernization
In contrast to NATO's earlier performance, the last decade has witnessed a disturbing trend in which each new generation of technology coming to the field represents a declining percentage of the Alliance's total inventory. There has also been a growing differentiation among Alliance members in the technological sophistication of the majority of their forces. If this trend continues, NATO could become a three-part Alliance with respect to technology – the US far outstripping the other Allies in the technological capabilities of her forces; a group of Allies with some 'cutting edge' technology and a large inventory of less capable systems; and all the rest who cannot afford to play a significant role in the high-technology game.

Technology Leakage
If one of the reasons for NATO's diminished technological superiority has been its problems in translating technological prowess into operational capability, another significant factor has been the persistent leakage of the latest advances to the Eastern Bloc. The examples of the Soviet acquisition of Western technology – legally or illegally – are numerous. The Soviet SA-7 heat seeking, shoulder-fired anti-air missile contains many features of the US *Redeye*. More than one-third of all known Soviet integrated circuits have been copied from US designs. Today, Western visitors to Soviet machine tool factories have been surprised if not shocked to see the very latest technologies – three-axis industrial robots, and diamond, boron nitride and ceramic-coded tooling.[2] There is something wrong when the Warsaw Pact gets the West's latest technology faster than the NATO allies.

Avoiding Damaging Fallacies
NATO's last thirty-five years and the historical evolution of technology should not be forgotten by the Atlantic Alliance as it

comes to grips with the exploitation of accelerating technological change. A look into the past might identify four warnings:

Avoid technology as 'the only answer'. Effective defence cannot be achieved by technology alone. Other dimensions are also critical. In the pursuit of technological advantage, one runs the risk of forgetting that technology is only one element of a nation's or an alliance's armed forces. It may not even be the most critical element. The conflict in the Falklands, the military encounters in the Middle East and a series of other examples suggest, in fact, that the human dimension remains paramount in determining the outcome of conflict.[3] No technology has been able to overcome fully the elements of the unexpected, chance or human ineptitude, irrationality, fear and confusion, that make up what Clausewitz so aptly labelled the fog of war. Only human leadership, and tactical and strategic ability, can cope with that.

Avoid the fallacy that technology substitutes for logistic inadequacy. Another set of factors that often gets overshadowed by the fascination with technology relates to readiness and sustainability. It makes little difference how good an army's guns are if there is insufficient ammunition. Similarly, sophisticated aircraft are of little use if they are unable to operate from vulnerable airfields.

The readiness and sustainability of NATO's forces must be improved. Many of the readiness and sustainability measures that NATO should implement are relatively inexpensive. Unfortunately, undefended by powerful legislative constituencies or military and industrial lobbies, these measures tend to be the first areas sacrificed by budget cutters contending with limited resources. The issue is not one of an either/or choice between new technology and readiness and sustainability. Rather it is the question of the balance between the two. A weakness in combat posture undermines NATO's potential to defend early and forward and therefore defeats the purpose of costly efforts to improve sustainability. On the other hand, if the Alliance support posture is weak, combat capabilities will eventually be seriously degraded, eventually to the point where units can no longer operate effectively.

Avoid technology as an 'uninformed answer'. Technology must be exploited in the context of appropriate operational concepts and innovative tactics. The same technology is often available to both sides in a conflict. Yet one side has used that technology effectively and one has not. Why? Winston Churchill provided one answer when he wrote about the early days of World War II: 'I did not comprehend the violence of the revolution effected since the last war by the incursion of a mass of fast-moving armour. I knew about it, but it had not altered my inward convictions as it should have'.[4]

Overcoming the doubts of some of their colleagues, a group of German officers whose inward convictions had been altered became the architects of the successful German *blitzkrieg* assaults of 1939–40. These officers had thought creatively about how to use relatively new technologies and how to integrate them into an overall operational capability. The difference beween the opposing forces, then, was that one side had the force structure, command philosophy, operational concepts and tactics necessary to exploit more fully the capabilities made possible by technology; the other side did not.

Military institutions, like all heavily structured institutions, resist – and at times resent – change, usually with good reasons. The introduction of new technologies on a significant scale demands major upheavals in the training and supply arrangements for the entire force as well as significant alterations in its operational concepts. Moreover, a force can be left vulnerable if the transition to new technology is too rapid or new technologies prove flawed in concept or application – as they sometimes do.

The degree to which technology does and should determine strategy and tactics is always hotly debated. What cannot be disputed, however, is the unbreakable connection between the two and the sterility of analysis that isolates one from the other. Technology should be a tool in the service of strategy. At the same time, that strategy and the implementing operational concepts and tactics should be responsive to the opportunities afforded by technological change.

Bernard Brodie observed about the military commanders prior to World War I that it was their horizons rather than their skill that proved disastrously limited.[5] To ensure that NATO does not repeat that mistake, its military commanders – and political decision-makers – must think creatively. They need to organize their operational concepts into a framework that exploits what new technology has to offer.

Avoid technology as a 'quick and easy answer'. The wide and growing range of technological options imposes difficult choices on defence planners and national policy-makers. What new technology holds out is the promise of making operational skills decisive.[6] Technology contributes to improved conventional performance not only by providing innovative systems that can do things in new ways, but also by enhancing the performance of fielded systems, allowing them to do the same things better.

In a world of rapid transition, high costs and high risks, these possibilities create difficult choices. One choice is between old product improvement and new product acquisition. Some would claim that the latter often degenerates into 'goldplating', making the best the enemy of the good. Despite this criticism, there does exist a legitimate choice about the degree of technological sophistication that is necessary or effective. That choice should be made with a keen recognition of its impact on the speed at which technology can be translated into military hardware and the rate at which hardware can be introduced into the field. It should also be made with a sensitivity to the impact of technological sophistication. Dumb defences can sometimes defeat smart weapons, and there is a limit to what technological sophistication can substitute for the power inherent in numbers.[7]

Another choice exists between the relative emphasis to be placed on (and the allocation of resources to) technology that can be incorporated today versus technology that will have its pay-off in the future. It is the choice between procurement and research and development (R&D), balancing today's threat against tomorrow's. This choice represents the difference between the planner and the commander. The commander's concern is his ability to fight today; the planner's is the ability to fight tomorrow. Both are valid, and it is not always easy to strike the proper balance between them.

A Look to the Future

While one must never forget the relevance of the past when one considers the new, it is equally misleading to ignore the potential uniqueness of the future in stressing the historical continuity of the old. There are several characteristics that seem inherent in much of the new technology that may significantly alter the way NATO needs to think about managing it.

In the past, NATO sought answers about how new technology would affect the military balance (for example, the introduction of battlefield nuclear weapons in the late 1950s or precision-guided munitions in the early 1970s). Today the Alliance seems to have a better understanding of what it wants new technology to do than a knowledge of which systems may be needed to produce the desired result.

New technology will not produce a 'wonder weapon' that is expected to solve all Alliance military shortcomings single-handedly. Rather, current emerging technology encompasses a diffuse range of component technologies which, when netted together and combined with existing weapons, offer the potential to produce a military capability out of all proportion to the increased capability of individual parts.

For example, NATO has long recognized the need for improvement in the amount, availability and accuracy of battlefield information. Such data is necessary to defeat Warsaw Pact operational concepts both by the counter-deployment of NATO's own manoeuvre units and by making its outnumbered fire systems more effective. Here emerging technology offers great promise. Yet, the Alliance is still uncertain about what is the most effective target acquisition sensor technology, what is the most timely and secure method of communicating this information, and how this information is to be processed and shared.

There is a similar degree of uncertainty when one anticipates the use of emerging technology for more effective indirect fire on the enemy: what are the trade-offs in terms of target acquisition, delivery system accuracy, and improvements in the terminal effects of new warheads? If 'smart weapons' have been shown to be inordinately expensive and operationally complex, can 'high IQ' submunitions add increased service life and improved capability to NATO's current inventory of dumb systems?

Uncertainty is both endemic to new technology and indicative of its potential strength. First, the state of the art in the new areas of technology is advancing at an unprecedented rate. For example, the 'weaponization' of microelectronics and composite materials has grown further in the last five years than the technologies of conventional explosives and the internal combustion engine matured over the last fifty. Second, scientific breakthroughs are occurring simultaneously across a broad front of technological application with a high degree of unanticipated overlapping relevance. Third, the component focus of new technologies not only encourages innovation and cross-fertilization, but facilitates its rapid introduction into military systems and their incremental modernization while minimizing costs and block obsolescence.

The very character of the new technology which makes its development so dynamic also challenges NATO's methods of managing it. First, NATO has traditionally focused on new technology in the context of complete weapons systems, the entire design of which was the responsibility of individual governments or a limited consortium. But with new technology the focus will devolve in a direction of nationally-designed and produced components with NATO taking on an increasing role in creating an integrated framework for the netting of subsystems. It will correspondingly have the responsibility of ensuring that the component parts are interoperable.

Second, the component nature of new technology seems to engender, indeed may require, a developmental style of decentralized research, individualized creativity and risk capital. If NATO's technological management approach has been previously dominated by the model of the Manhattan Project and the space programme, perhaps it is time to examine the extraordinary success of the entrepreneurial style associated with the current accelerated advances in information processing. Perhaps it is time to ask whether existing institutional mechanisms inhibit or facilitate the changing nature of technological development.

The third characteristic of the new technology is its changing relationship with the civil sector. In the past, where NATO has focused on major weapons systems (a ship, plane or armoured vehicle), mature technologies associated with these systems have had minimal relationship to civilian R&D. National interests conflicted primarily over who participated in the production of a mass-produced system. However, this is not the case with much of the new technology. With its entrepreneurial emphasis, rapid exploitation of basic research, and component orientation, this technology has a high degree of overlap with the state of the art in non-military applications. If cross-national technology sharing has been difficult in the past, the link between the national competitive edge in global markets and the protection of new technology could make it very difficult indeed. Rather than waging and losing the battle attempting to suppress natural instincts, which may in fact be inducive to healthy competition, it may be important for NATO to explore new management approaches that simultaneously protect emerging technology in the national R&D phase while promoting innovation via competition for the plethora of components which will make up high technology conventional systems of the next decade.

In sum, what appears unique about the nature of emerging technology is the decentralized nature of both its application to the battlefield and its development in the laboratory. If, in fact, the new technology will emerge as a contribution to our collective defence, then NATO's management machinery must be oriented to facilitate this.

On the other hand, given a developmental approach that is oriented towards a component-based emerging technology, this places a premium on existing NATO institutional mechanisms which will be indispensable for providing a mutual, compatible framework for systemic architecture and component integration.

New Technology and Alliance Strengths and Strains

The nature of new technology creates both strengths and strains for the Atlantic Alliance. Those strengths and strains often derive from the same characteristics of that technology.

Operational Concepts

There is no question that new technology can enhance the performance of NATO's conventional forces both by improving the execution of current missions and creating new options. Its impact could be felt across the board. The new operational possibilities created by new technology, however, are also a source of a certain strain within the Alliance. Allies have disagreed about operational applications of new technologies and the relative priority of various roles and missions towards which the new technology should initially be directed.

NATO's experience with the concept of deep attack, an option that new technology is now making available, exemplifies both these strengths and strains. NATO has always considered interdiction an important requirement. What recent deep-attack concepts have attempted to address is how to make this interdiction less risky and more effective.

Deep-attack concepts were designed not to replace forward defence, but to help it succeed. If attacking deep is to make any difference at all, it cannot be pursued in isolation from other developments on the battlefield. It must be closely related to what is happening, for example, on the forward edge of the battle area (FEBA) where first echelons will be engaged.[8]

Those who have criticized deep-attack concepts for being overly offensive have too often confused strategy, operations and tactics. The ideas put forward for deep attack address how specific forces would fight; they are about operations and tactics. There is no inherent contradiction between those ideas and NATO's strategy of forward defence and flexible response. Flexible response can accommodate those ideas and remain a defensive strategy.

On the other hand, while a source of potential strength, it is no secret that there have been considerable differences within NATO over the concept of deep attack. There are several reasons for this. One is a plethora of ideas. Over the last two years the Allies have been exposed to several concepts designed to exploit new technologies – AirLand Battle, Follow-On Forces Attack, Counter Air 90, Army 21 and Emerging Technologies. Quite rightly, the Allies have asked how all of these ideas fit together. A second reason for disagreement has been imprecise language. The 'depth' of a deep attack, for example, was used to mean anything from just beyond direct-fire ranges to distances of hundreds of kilometres. Similarly, it was discovered that West Germany had one definition of the first echelon of Warsaw Pact forces and the US another.

The potential impact of some of the specifics of the deep-attack concept also fostered differences. The question of the delegation of deep-strike authority to lower command levels, for example, created some concern that military operations of such political portent would be insufficiently controlled by political decision-makers. The suggested use of ballistic missiles for runway attack was also criticized because of the possibility that it might lead the opponent to believe that NATO had crossed the nuclear threshold.

Economics

A second set of strengths and strains deriving from the nature of new technology relates to economic considerations. The diffuse nature of the development process of new technology lends itself to the entrepreneurial, free market capitalism of Western economies. The technological base from which NATO can draw is enormous, and it is exploring the entire spectrum of new technologies that could ultimately have an impact on the battlefield. While the United States has 'Silicon Valley', Scotland finds itself the home of 'Silicon Glen', and there is the potential for many other such enterprises throughout Europe. Development of new technology seems to thrive on the 'skunk works' approach characteristic of dynamic, capitalist economies. It is much more difficult for the highly-directed, highly-centralized 'design bureau' approach of the Soviet Union.

A strain emerges, however, when the competition inherent in the Western economic system generates protectionist pressure. Jobs are of greatest concern to most policy-makers in the Alliance, and everyone is keenly aware of the economic and political pressures in Europe's high-technology industries. In several areas Europe lags behind the United States and Japan, sometimes severely. Some Europeans are afraid that the United States is trying to consign Europe to the technological poorhouse. Even if it is only to close that gap, there are those who see no choice for Europe but to protect its technological development as they believe others are doing.

Enthusiasm has also been difficult to generate because of the high costs of new technology in the face of lagging economic recovery. It is always possible to demonstrate that new or improved weapons systems incorporating that technology can be beneficial. It is not always possible to convince people that those benefits are worth the costs. How can NATO manage to introduce new technology in a way that is *affordable*?

Decentralization
A third set of strengths and strains flows from the decentralized, component-oriented nature of new technology. As argued earlier, new weapons systems will increasingly represent the integration of a growing number of sub-systems or components, many of which could come from different countries. Given that there are many pieces on which companies can concentrate, numerous opportunities abound for smaller, creative firms. It is not likely that such firms will be predisposed towards sharing development secrets, yet there can be a significant growth in component sharing. Such sharing would strengthen Alliance efforts to promote defence industrial co-operation.

With a greater number of firms engaged in increased sharing, however, technology is more difficult to protect. The fact that there is such considerable civilian-military overlap in the application of new technology also makes it more difficult to keep it from leaking. Not surprisingly, technology leakage has emerged as a strain in Alliance relations.

One problem has been that some technologies that the US has identified as being critical to national security have not been so identified in Alliance capitals. The United States has been criticized for wanting to control too much. Some argued that by taking a comprehensive approach, the Alliance would be less able to protect effectively those technologies that are truly critical to Alliance security. They argued that the real need is first to determine as precisely as possible which goods are militarily relevant, and, second, to identify which strategic goods cannot reasonably be controlled because they are already widely available on international markets.[9]

Other Americans have responded that to match the Soviet Union's full-scale clandestine acquisition effort, the West needs a full-scale prevention effort. Where there is question about whether an item is militarily critical, it is prudent to consider regulating it until it is determined otherwise. At length a new consensus has emerged from the recent and successful COCOM list review on the militarily critical technologies which must be covered by controls.

Another contentious issue is enforcement of the controls that do exist. Here the Americans criticize the Europeans. There is considerable variation among the Allies in their approaches to enforcement and the penalties they impose on violators. In some NATO countries, for example, illegal transfer of technology is not considered a felony. The legal rules should be harmonized, it is argued, even if it requires legislative action. Only then will the Allies be able to reflect a consistent approach to the problem. While differences remain in national approaches, high-level agreement has been reached on the need to improve embargo administration and enforcement. The COCOM subcommittee concerned has recently achieved a number of specific understandings on improvements and harmonization in enforcement.

In the rapidly evolving arena of technology, where the choices are many, the risks and costs high, and the pay-offs potentially enormous, differences over technology are to be expected among allies. Nevertheless, it should be clear that at a time when we all face limited economic horizons combined with soaring R&D costs, the Alliance cannot afford to subsidize the Warsaw Pact's defence industrial base by continuing to leak hard-won technologies to the East. The cost to our economies and to our overall security is simply too great.

The Need for a Resources Strategy
Confronting new problems and faced with new technologies, the temptation is great for NATO to seek new answers, radically different from those of the past. In this author's opinion, radically new solutions for Alliance management of technology are not necessary. NATO does need a new approach, not in the things that it does, but in the way that it does them. It does not need new committees or new instruments, but a new way of putting together the continuing work and maximizing the synergies of processes already established.

If NATO is to manage technology successfully, it must develop what I call a resources strategy.[10] It is a plan of action which integrates and co-ordinates a range of political, military, and economic assets towards the achievement of objectives. The ultimate goal is to get the most out of the limited resources NATO nations devote to defence, and to encourage them to do more, if it is truly necessary.

This 'strategic' approach with regard to resources has become critical in an Alliance with twice the GNP and the same size population as the Warsaw Pact, yet which is out-produced militarily. One can argue that the prime challenge to NATO in its second thirty-five years is the better management of these superior Alliance resources to secure deterrence. If NATO is not funded adequately, the Alliance ceases to deter. Important action will be impossible and critical objectives unobtainable. A resources strategy, therefore, has two targets: better use of existing resources as a short-term (but continuing) goal; and generation of additional resources for deterrence and defence as a long-term objective. With expensive new technologies, this becomes especially critical. NATO must have a better resources strategy to resolve understandable conflicts of interest and choice, to build on technological strengths, to analyse affordability, to manage timing and change, and to deal with inevitable strains in an Alliance of sixteen sovereign democracies at very different levels of technology with diverse acquisition policies and at different levels of economic recovery.

A successful strategy will capitalize on the very nature of new technology, not run against it. Given the decentralized nature of the development process for new technology, of its impact throughout the spectrum of conventional capabilities and the multiple points of strain and strength, a broad front strategy is required. The elements of a resources strategy should include a better appreciation, a better concept, better planning and co-ordination, better management and co-ordination, better technology protection – and, finally, it requires practical support.

A Better Military Appreciation
A fundamental starting point for the most effective employment of new technology must be a commonly-held appreciation of the military situation that relates the Warsaw Pact threat to NATO's capabilities and puts the change in technology on both sides into proper perspective. 'Bean counts' are a necessary starting point, but one must go beyond them to incorporate the qualitative dimension of the military balance as well. Moreover, there is a need to understand how the situation may be changing. A military appreciation that just takes a snapshot of the current situation and does not present the trends is insufficient for effective policy-making.

NATO today does not prepare a comprehensive and fully-integrated military net assessment that looks at the total balance on each side. The Alliance has suffered as a result, not only from differing perceptions among its members about the threat from the Warsaw Pact but also from lack of agreement about how NATO forces measure up against it.

There is also insufficient common understanding about how technology is affecting the situation. This gives rise to several mistakes. There has been, for example, a tendency to generalize about the overall situation, when the specific situations – between the Central Front and the Southern Flank, for example – are considerably different. Needless to say, the anti-tank balance – and any other technological balance – is not the same for all sectors of the front. There has also been a tendency to equate what NATO has on the drawing boards or in the laboratory with what the Pact has put in the field. The effect has been to skew understanding of how and to what degree Western quality offsets Warsaw Pact quantity.

The Alliance already has many of the elements of a dynamic military appreciation – SACEUR's and SACLANT's annual Combat Effectiveness Report, the military appreciation prepared by the International Military Staff (IMS), and other regular reports. Additional assessments that have been proposed, such as one on the global maritime threat posed by the Soviet Union, present other potential building-blocks.

These studies must be given greater attention by political authorities. Their implications must be better articulated. The findings must be transmitted more effectively back to NATO capitals. These studies must also be more closely co-ordinated and interrelated. Only then will all the Allies have the complete picture, rather than just the pieces of a jigsaw puzzle. They will then be able to locate the appropriately-shaped technology pieces and more clearly understand how technology contributes to the whole.

A Better Conceptual Military Framework
No single doctrinal initiative is a cure-all for NATO. However good, no single improvement – in operating concepts or technology – will provide NATO with a credible conventional deterrent. The challenge is to select the most sensible and practical elements of several approaches and combine them into a coherent effort.

At the December 1983 NATO Defence Ministers meeting, the German Defence Minister, Manfred Wörner, called for the development of a conceptual military framework to integrate the various operational concepts that have been suggested. Picking up Minister Wörner's request, NATO's military authorities have been laying the groundwork for the development of such a framework. The IMS is currently integrating inputs from national capitals and NATO's major military commanders. When it is completed this conceptual military framework should provide a dynamic basis for establishing priorities for NATO's force structure and for providing operational guidelines on how those forces would be used.

Such a framework should clarify much of the confusion that has surrounded the concept of attacking deep by relating it more closely to developments in the forward battle areas where the first echelons are engaged. It should relate military operations to warning indicators and define more precisely the role of tactical intelligence. It should identify how various operational concepts would be tailored to achieve greatest effect in NATO's various geographic sectors where terrain and the local military balance impose different requirements.

An important function of such a conceptual military framework would be to match requirements and technological capabilities. It is here that the lessons learned about the potential for innovative thinking could well be applied.

Better Planning and Co-ordination
NATO does not have a fully co-ordinated process to guide member nations to make decisions in line with Alliance needs. As a consequence there is no agreed basis from which to develop comprehensive priorities, including technological ones.

NATO's force-planning process provides the means by which Alliance planning could be improved. The planning process must also be strengthened by better relating of force planning to that taking place in national capitals. Many of the NATO force goals are heaped on top of national plans. With limited resources devoted to defence, the Allies often cannot pay for the NATO goals. NATO obviously cannot dictate national programmes; but the Alliance can provide better inputs into national planning efforts so that greater harmony among Allied efforts is ensured.

Better planning leads to a better definition of technological needs. Thus it facilitates the decision-making process regarding the difficult technological options confronting NATO policy-makers.

Better Management of NATO's Technological Resources

In addition to these efforts to create a more benign environment for the introduction of new technology, NATO institutions specifically designated to cope with technological change must also be improved.

The major Alliance organization for managing technology is the Conference of National Armaments Directors (CNAD). It was established when the issues became too complex for effective consideration in the old Naval, Air Force and Army Armaments Groups. CNAD was based on each nation's belief that it needed a single national spokesman for the political, economic and technical aspects of armaments research, development and acquisition.

The CNAD organization now consists of nearly 240 groups, panels and special committees, linked through the National Armaments Directors and their resident representatives at NATO Headquarters. There is also a NATO Industrial Advisory Group (NIAG) – 14 national representatives backed by industrialists with the task of advising and assisting the CNAD from the industrial perspective.

Looking back, the CNAD and its ancillary bodies have had significant successes – the F-16 fighter programme, and E3A AWACS (Airborne Warning and Control System) among them. European nations are justly proud of the *Roland* and the *Leopard* II Main Battle Tank. On the horizon are the NATO frigate programme, the NATO helicopter and the Multiple Launch Rocket System (MLRS).

The Emerging Technology (ET) Initiative is a special CNAD effort to deal effectively with the introduction of new technology. The ET Initiative is intended to capitalize on new technology's promise for:

- Better tailoring capabilities to the actual threat, and exploiting Pact vulnerabilities;
- Improving the performance of weapons platforms without making significant and expensive alterations to those platforms or introducing costly new ones;
- Increasing the operational synergism of existing capabilities.

NATO has initially concentrated on trying to exploit newly-available technology. The first step was a series of studies examining the potential impact of those technologies in NATO's various geographic regions. Then, in the Spring of 1984, CNAD agreed on several areas of technology that could usefully be pursued on a co-operative Alliance basis. Those areas were subsequently approved by Defence Ministers. Work is now under way in the various groups under the CNAD umbrella to take those technologies and integrate them into operative military systems. The first step is the resolution of differences over military requirements and the delineation of specific co-operative ventures.

Two further points should be made about the ET Initiative. First, it has been an integrative effort, spurring political, military and industrial managers to work together. They have had to admit to areas of common interest that have traditionally been considered in isolation. Second, the ET effort is not a 'buy America' programme. Rather, it aims to improve the military capabilities of the Alliance in a way that is responsive to the economic and political imperatives of each Alliance member.

The list of opportunities seems endless, but success should not be assumed. Several steps should be taken to move the process of managing Alliance technology forward. One is to strengthen the Independent European Programme Group (IEPG). This group, which includes France, was formed to rationalize the European defence sector and enable it to take part in arms co-operation with the US on a more equal footing. Bolstering the IEPG will allow it to represent more effectively the 'European' perspective on critical technology measures within CNAD. This is now being done under the very able leadership of its Dutch chairman, State Minister van Houwelingen.

Better use can be made of the CNAD representatives in Brussels. The links to industry can be strengthened and the transmission belt from the NIAG to CNAD made more effective. Closer co-operation should also be fostered between military planners and military technologists both at NATO and in national capitals.

The process must also be strengthened above the CNAD level. Policy-makers, not just experts, must devote greater time and attention to technology issues. Those issues should be thoroughly examined by both the Defence and Foreign Minister. More senior levels of the decision-making process at NATO Headquarters, such as the Executive Working Group, must also be brought more into the process.

Improved Armaments Co-operation
Transatlantic arms trade will be an important mechanism for sharing technology throughout the Alliance. Therefore, improved armaments co-operation is a critical component of a resources strategy.

There has been a chorus of complaint in Europe about the unequal traffic on the transatlantic two-way street. The aggregate balance favours the United States by between three to one and seven to one depending on the figures used. It is naïve to believe, however, that the bilateral defence trade of European NATO members with the United States will magically be brought into even a rough balance. The differences in industrial base, markets and other factors are just too great. R&D investment by the United States, for example, is seven times higher than for all her European Allies combined. Nevertheless, a better balance in the transatlantic arms trade must be achieved. Co-operative efforts must be strengthened on both the industrial and the government levels.

Transatlantic armaments co-operation is US policy, and it is NATO policy. But better mechanisms are needed to implement that policy. In the United States, the executive and legislative branches of government must develop an agreement and an action plan in concert with private industry and labour. That process has already begun with both the Department of Defense and the Department of State giving greater attention to armaments co-operation issues. Congress has demonstrated its willingness to play a helpful role with the passage of the Glenn–Roth–Nunn Amendment supporting better arms co-operation by a vote of 87 to 1. Industry has made it clear that it will embrace greater arms co-operation if it is a US government priority.

Europe must also get its house in order. It must increase its investment in R&D and, in fact, the idea of a European Advanced Research Agency has already been floated by the North Atlantic Assembly.[11] European members of the Alliance must also organize their industrial structures and their markets on scale more competitive with those of the United States. An important element in this effort will be the work of the IEPG. If other forces are also successful at promoting greater European co-operation, the United States would welcome that development as long as it is complementary and not competitive with NATO efforts.

Co-operation is not easy. It must overcome tough issues such as offsets, work sharing, third-country sales and competition. Perhaps the most dangerous problem is the growth of technological protectionism. In the long run, a resurgence of protectionism could prove as damaging to the Alliance as neglecting its conventional forces.

No single NATO nation can do the job alone. Just as NATO's approach to operational concepts must be innovative, so creative approaches that make the most of the explosion in technological development can make the West's industrial diversity a major contributor to the common defence.

Technology Protection
Greater sharing of technology must go hand in hand with greater technology protection. It is part of the job of a resources strategy to implement this harmonization. On the one hand, we cannot allow vital technology to aid a Soviet military build-up that in turn forces NATO to take expensive counter-measures.

On the other, good strategy will also promote the rate at which the West incorporates its technology into Alliance weapons systems.

Progress in resolving differences on the protection of critical technologies. The recent agreement in COCOM to update controls on computers and to regulate software exports is an important step. The initiation of a 'Red Side' analysis which looks at the advantages to the Warsaw Pact of the flow of technology is another.

The Alliance must build on these steps in a way that maximizes progress on a multilateral front. Piecemeal, bilateral efforts between Alliance nations could prove so complex as to be ultimately unworkable. An argument can be made, for example, that NATO should have a larger management role in the protection of technology. NATO can contribute a well-developed structure and process for the settlement of disputes as well as a rich military and political context within which to assess the impact of specific technologies.

Unfortunately there has been considerable reluctance to discuss technology protection within NATO councils. COCOM is still considered in many capitals to be the only proper forum for such discussions. COCOM is taking steps better to meet the challenge – strengthening its procedures to identify, track and control militarily significant technology. However, COCOM does not concern itself directly with non-trade aspects of technology protection. A way must also be found to capitalize on the benefits that the NATO process has to offer since greater technology sharing in the Alliance will ultimately be dependent on parallel progress in technology protection.

Political Support
The final element in an effective NATO resources strategy is the political consensus that bonds the military and economic factors together. However sound Alliance military strategy, however well-conceived its arms procurement, however sophisticated its technology, only political consensus and enlightened, resolute Alliance leadership can realize the benefits of new technology for strengthened conventional deterrence.

NATO is not a supranational organization, able to impose measures on member nations. They will only grudgingly give up the prerogatives of their sovereignty, and will most often give precedence to national programmes. While great progress might be made at NATO Headquarters, impediments in NATO capitals can bring to an abrupt halt any momentum that might be generated in Brussels.

Coalitions must be built, and that process must start in Alliance capitals. It must occur not just in Defence and Foreign Ministries but in Finance Ministries and Trade and Industry Ministries as well. It must also extend to national legislatures.

Links between NATO Headquarters and national capitals must be strengthened. Politicians need a proper appreciation and a conceptual military framework as badly as the military authorities, and it is not uncommon for policy-makers in capitals to be unaware of all that is happening at NATO Headquarters and *vice versa*. During the difficult days prior to the initial deployment of *Pershing* II and cruise missiles last autumn, the links between Brussels and the national capitals were exceptionally strong, largely as the result of the work of the Special Consultative Group and the High Level Group. Building on this admirable example, NATO should find a way to improve the transmission belts between Alliance Headquarters and capitals on the whole range of issues associated with improving conventional defence, including the technological choices that are now being made or that must be made in the future.

Conclusion
New technology can be a source of great strength to the Alliance. At its most basic it can improve the military performance of NATO's armed forces. In so doing, technology could make a considerable contribution to enhancing deterrence. Economic spin-offs could be generated, adding to the economic rejuvenation of all Alliance members. Political harmony could be fostered deriving from the co-operation that will be absolutely essential if the process is to be successful.

Technology is a tool, and like any tool it can be helpful only if we know what to do with it and then choose to use it. That knowledge is often hard to come by, and that choice is not often easy. But in the NATO context the needs of deterrence and defence are well defined. The issue is whether the Alliance will be able to manage its resources, including technology, to meet those needs. Ultimately, the issue will be decided by the vision and leadership in NATO capitals and in Brussels.

NOTES

[1] Thomas A. Callaghan, Jr, 'The Structural Disarmament of NATO,' *NATO Review*, June 1984, no. 3.

[2] 'How Far Should US go to Regulate its Technology Exports?' *Christian Science Monitor*, 16 May 1984 and 'Keeping Technology out of Soviet Hands Appears Impossible', *Wall Street Journal*, 15 August 1984.

[3] For a discussion of this point relative to the Falklands War and the Israeli invasion of Lebanon, see Michael Moodie, 'Six Months, Three Wars', *The Washington Quarterly*, Autumn 1982.

[4] Quoted in John J. Mearsheimer, Conventional Deterrence (Ithaca, NY: Cornell UP, 1983), p. 97.

[5] Bernard Brodie, 'Strategy in the Missile Age' (Princeton, NJ: Princeton UP, 1959), p. 59.

[6] Michael Howard, 'The Forgotten Dimensions of Strategy', *Foreign Affairs*, Summer 1979.

[7] Joseph Joffe, 'Is NATO Building an Achilles Heel?' *Wall Street Journal*, 13 June 1984.

[8] For greater elaboration of this point, see Philip A. Karber, 'In Defense of Forward Defense', *Armed Forces International*, May 1984, p. 46.

[9] See, for example, the speech by Mr Norman Tebbitt, Britain's Minister for Trade and Industry, to the North American section of London's Chamber of Commerce, cited in *Science*, 11 May 1984, p. 579.

[10] While the views presented in this Paper are those of the author and address issues on which in some cases NATO and the government of the United States have not as yet taken positions, the need for a 'resources strategy, enlarged here but first articulated in a speech to the Atlantic Treaty Association in November 1983 has since been recognized in the DPC communiqué of May 1984 and is being addressed by NATO's Executive Working Group.

[11] 'Europe Seeks a NATO Research Agency', *Aviation Week and Space Technology*, 4 June 1984.

Defence Research and Development and Western Industrial Policy: Part I

PROF. SIR RONALD MASON

The support of research and development (R&D) in science and technology – its extent, structure, rationale and the way in which criteria for support vary from country to country – are matters of great interest to any student of scientific, industrial and societal policies. In the US, USSR and Western Europe, defence R&D is of especial import in view of the resources allocated and their effect on other possible priorities.

There is a sharp need to distinguish R&D and, even under the research head, the expectations attached to research activities – whether the objectives are 'pure and disinterested', 'strategic' or 'applied'. In the four major industrial countries of the West, little or no defence research has anything but strategic or applied aims; innovative activity is directed to a realization of strategic objectives – perhaps for a quick, far-sighted broadly-based requirement necessitating rather longer term programmes than would be envisaged for applied research. For the latter, one may assume that the main 'barrier' questions have been answered. The science, technology and engineering needed to implement, say, directed-energy weapons in space must be regarded as strategic research, as must important areas of 'stealth' systems; that which is needed to produce cost-effective solutions to the requirement of conventional deep strike against mobile targets must be regarded similarly; that which is needed, say, to further improve the CEP of ballistic missile re-entry bodies borders on straightforward development.

Having said that, however, one recognizes grey areas and the lack of really clear distinctions so that defence R&D policies and their management have far from clear and objective guidelines. They are, quite often, dictated by extrinsic (politico-industrial) factors rather than intrinsic parameters. But it is the case also that the defence budgets of the US, Britain, France and the FRG all bear very similar R&D costs, as proportions of total budgets; three years ago the R&D vote for all of these countries was 14 ± 2% of the respective defence budgets (the Soviet Union was around 21–22%). British spending on *research* was the lowest proportionately – in 1980–81, this amounted to 4% of procurement or about 2% of the defence budget while development accounted for 26% of procurement or 12% of the defence budget (some 42% of the defence budget was spent on equipment, some 20% more than four years earlier and a trend which is now reflected in increasingly well-equipped defence forces).

These bare statistical data deserve two comments which, although relating to Britain in particular, do have some general value. The first is that over one-half of British government R&D funds go to defence (and by some arguments that is too high a proportion of national resources). But the majority of these funds go to development by and in industry. There has been a clear policy decision to maintain a broad-based defence industry to support defence policies which have wider responsibilities and requirements than any other country with a comparable economy. Typically, the equipment budget provides 40% for aircraft and associated equipment/weapons, 30% to ships and maritime equipment and weapons and a little more than 20% to land systems and vehicles (a little less than 10% is dedicated to general support). It is, quite simply, a major change of defence policy – reducing, say, one of our major commitments to NATO – which is necessary to bring defence R&D funds down to a level, measured as a proportion of GNP, to those of France and the FRG. Secondly, Britain has, over nearly a decade, maintained a ratio of R&D expenditures to production expenditure of 1:2.2. By most commercial standards this is a relatively unfavourable ratio but we see here some reflection of the sophistication of defence equipment which in turn is inexorably dictated by the nature of the threat. It could be improved towards, say, the FRG R&D/production ratio by at least three devices: by more off-shore purchases (80% of British equipment expenditure goes on national contracts placed with British industry and 15% to the British share of collaborative projects); by increasing participation in collaborative development programmes and other forms of co-operation; and by seeking greater commonality with civil high-technology programmes and products. These are matters which are looked at in more detail in this Paper.

It follows that the construction of defence R&D policy must be set in the context of defence policy itself and the related operational requirements and in the context of technology and engineering opportunities and their implications for incremental or major changes in investment in different weapon systems. Finally it must be based on judgments of national industrial capabilities, existent or planned.

What might be called the interaction of operational requirements with developments in technologies and weapon systems forms the essential base of a defence research and, more to the point, an advanced development programme. The requirements and the systems' possibilities may not often be in phase and it is often suggested that 'doctrine must lead and technical feasibility follow'. That ignores the real but very subtle synergistic relations between national and international policies, between those programmes which have socio-economic benefits and the often totally independent discoveries in science and their implementation in new technologies. We are certainly at the point where the dynamic of technological change is greater than that which can be associated with politico-social processes; technology is certainly not everything but increasingly it creates opportunities and vulnerabilities which are reacted to rather than planned for in political or social processes. There is certainty in Japan and the United States that 'high technology' must form the base of further economic development; there is increasing agreement in Western Europe also on this strategy although a consensus is under pressure from time to time for a variety of reasons, mostly announced by political fringe groups. The real requirements which an R&D programme must meet for the foreseeable future (assuming that manpower and budgets may at best remain at present levels) are that we will continue to rely on an equipment-manpower mix which is oriented towards equipment; that technology must increasingly be a force multiplier; that we must achieve force multiplication of a number of defence capabilities through the technical improvement of the system or systems contributing to a capability; and associated doctrinal adjustments.

There has been general agreement in NATO on the particular areas of technology which are of increasing importance in the development of conventional forces. They are for the most part related to electronics and materials. The primary and important capabilities to be enhanced are: weapon guidance and control; command, control and information systems; and electronic warfare and related areas relying on advances in electronics technology and devices. There would seem to be general agreement that only secondary advances can be foreseen in platform performance and then only in rather special equipments, such as V/STOL (Vertical/Short Take-Off and Landing) or STOVL (Short Take-Off and Vertical Landing) aircraft and particularly long-endurance aircraft for surveillance and reconnaissance.

These 'emergent technologies' are, of course, forming part of the major debate in the Alliance which, in broad terms, is concerned with raising the nuclear threshold through a significant upgrading of conventional defence and deterrence capabilities. The particular strategic technologies, a number of which are already in place, are those which overlap onto civil programmes in the US, Japan and Western Europe: micro-electronics with emphasis on very high speed integrated circuits (VHSIC); advanced software and high speed algorithm development and machine intelligence; active and passive electronic warfare including signature reduction ('stealth'); new composite materials and advanced warhead designs and materials; particular electronic devices such as high density focal plane arrays; and optoelectronics (lasers).

The uncertainties in a future R&D programme centred around these do not lie with the technologies *per se*; rather it is in the development of the total (weapon) systems with particular characteristics and properties and hence meeting certain operational requirements. The equation of 'emerging technologies' with enhanced capabilities is simplistic, if literally interpreted. System complexity, integration and reliability is being greatly improved by computer-aided design and manufacture; and by the impact of advanced manufacturing technology on batch production processes. But it is here that the prospects for collaboration on equipment begin to look difficult.

There is considerable symmetry between the technical and industrial capabilities of Western Europe and the United States. There are obvious differences of scale but, despite assertions that have come from the United States, the technology gap is not large. There are gaps in systems engineering and in systems implementation which originate in part in the fragmentary national efforts which mark systems development in Western Europe (parenthetically one notes the success of Japan at the total systems approach with the introduction of very successful systems often based on 'yesterday's technology' rather than having a high technical sophistication of components).

Political and economic arguments obviously preclude a future in which the United States uniquely exploits the developments with the rest of the Alliance simply procuring products. The 'two way street' is likely to become more unbalanced unless there is an agreed joint development of weapon systems whose priorities have been recognized by the publication of Memoranda of Understanding (MOU) or staff targets. Industries could then pick up requirements and seek case-by-case arrangements with industries in other countries on a commercial basis. Difficult problems, such as intellectual property rights, can be tackled in a pragmatic way as the development proceeds. Mechanisms such as those used by the infrastructure group for the procurement of air defence radar systems could surely be extended to weapon systems.

The opportunities are present: collaboration should reflect on technical and industrial complementarities and the choice of weapon system(s) on their relative force multiplication value. Thus we understand in Europe, and with little dissent from the United States, that the requirements of surveillance C^3 (communications, command and control) should be amongst the first for enhancement – an agreed set of solutions would have a major impact and would capitalize on the standing of (civil) information technology in the West. Secondly, we have the counter-air requirement – largely through the denial of airfield use. There is little disagreement that long-range (up to 300 km) interdiction against high-value static assets is best achieved using penetrating stand-off weapon systems – which one might speculate to be second generation air-launched cruise missiles (ALCM). Thirdly, the relatively short-range (up to about 30 km beyond the FEBA) anti-armour capability needs to be – and can be – rapidly enhanced using directed munitions or submunitions with relatively straightforward guidance and data processing capabilities available *now*. Lastly, there is a vital need for the Alliance to react coherently to the chemical threat and it needs to be noted that chemical defence technologies are at their most developed in Europe.

Significant opportunities also exist for collaboration on maritime-air weapon systems, but that need not be rehearsed here. The essential point to set down is a simple one: unless there is early agreement on requirements, development policies, and industrial collaboration, Alliance members will be forced into (national) role specialization – and that specialization will be difficult to separate from isolationism. The political challenge is to see that Alliance defence is synonymous with Western security, and that properly constructed R&D programmes can themselves act as deterrents as well as providing the basis for defence capabilities into the next century. But the political parochialisms and industrial suspicions which have marked the past must give way to collaboration based on enlightened self-interest where the overall objective is to further stabilize the West and release resources for meeting the inevitable challenges, the inevitable call for different dependencies and interdependencies, which will emerge in Asia and Africa.

Defence Research and Development and Western Industrial Policy: Part II

HENRI MARTRE

The prime objective of R&D in the area of defence is to ensure the capability of the armed forces for the years ahead. It is characterized both by its extreme importance and the considerable problems inherent in it.

Its importance stems from the fact that its aim is to ensure the continuity of a nation's security, and any error in this field can therefore influence the outcome of a battle, or even a war, and thus affect the destiny of an entire people. The history books are full of examples where qualitative weapons superiority or, even more important, the surprise created by the appearance of new weapons have proved decisive in determining the outcome of a conflict. In this respect one need only mention such innovations as artillery, radar and nuclear weapons. Also of considerable importance is the extent of the financial outlay generated by a military hardware renewal and modernization policy, since this outlay comprises not only the intrinsic cost of R&D, which accounts for 25–30% of the weapons budget for a country producing its own equipment, but also the cost of replacing equipment which, although not at the end of its active life, is considered to be obsolete, plus the cost of training and logistics necessitated by the introduction of this new equipment into the armed forces.

The definition and implementation of such an R&D policy also gives rise to considerable problems, chiefly because of the time needed for these innovations to mature and because of the technical and political changes which can occur in the meanwhile. Indeed, ten to twenty years may be needed from the discovery of a physical phenomenon until its potential military application is fully demonstrated. Similarly, another ten or so years may elapse between the launching of a research programme and the introduction of the relevant equipment into the armed forces. It is thus obvious that it is far from easy to foresee, so far in advance, what will be the actual operational impact of a discovery and even harder to imagine its interaction with other discoveries yet to be made, some of which might supersede it completely and some of which might negate its effects.

Those in charge of directing a defence R&D policy, defining the objectives and making the consequent choices, thus have to bear a burden of responsibility made all the heavier by the weight of uncertainty attached to it. They can afford to neglect nothing which later (too late) could prove to be of major interest. They must nevertheless be thrifty since the resources made available to them will be fiercely disputed by those responsible for the maintenance of existing equipment and the operational readiness of the forces. Efficiency and balance are thus the two main guidelines of their choices. *Efficiency*, since the resources must be reserved for those innovations capable of providing the greatest military benefit in relation to their cost and the best working teams and laboratories. *Balance* must be achieved in various ways. First, to take account of the chronological intermeshing of the various projects. Each has a deadline and they must all be combined in such a way that at all times in the future, both short- and long-term, the military requirements are met. Then, balance must be achieved between the various operational functions to be performed in the context of a given military policy. It is clear that the armed forces can only carry out their missions if they are able to perform a certain number of complementary functions: they must control the situation by means of intelligence and communications, be ready to attack at various ranges, to protect themselves, etc. Finally, one must not lose sight of the fact that for given research activities, changes in military policy could quite possibly occur, thus creating new needs.

Nationalism and Alliance
These are only general principles and each country is obliged to adapt its policies and its projects to meet its financial capacity and scientific, technical and industrial resources. This much is obvious, but it must also adapt them to the rate at which military technology is progressing. This rate is essentially imposed by the competition between the Warsaw Pact countries and those of NATO and by the vast extent of the resources devoted to defence by the two super-powers. This competition is indeed at the root of the main advances made in the weapons field over the last thirty years. Some of these were brought about by derivations and innovations in the civilian sector but which themselves occurred within the framework of this competition. The major Alliances do not, however, hold a monopoly on arms. Other countries are active in this field but, for their products to have any military value and operational competitiveness, they must be brought into line with the characteristics of those created by the major powers. However, the disproportion of financial and technical means obliges those countries who wish to follow a relatively independent arms policy to adopt specific approaches and choose a limited number of market openings of a complexity suited to their capabilities. Experience has shown that this is possible and that, despite the differences in their sizes, many developed (and even developing) nations are setting up arms industries and creating new products.

This phenomenon exists even within NATO itself. For reasons of political equilibrium, but also for industrial and economic reasons, the Allies do not wish to allow the United States a monopoly on arms production, or even development, and they participate in these activities in proportion to the resources they devote to defence. The leading European members of NATO even hope to be essentially self-sufficient in military equipment, by virtue of their own industrial capacity, and they have to a large extent succeeded. How have they managed to do this, when the United States has a military R&D budget five to ten times greater than that of each of the main Western European countries? The reasons are many. The first is that these countries do not develop a product range as wide as that of the United States. Only two of them, Britain and France, produce nuclear weapons and even these two countries, whose product catalogues are the most complete, are not involved in a certain number of programmes. The second reason is that the European countries have appreciably lower development costs than the United States. This is quite simply due to the fact that, having less resources available, they must adopt different methods. In particular, they explore fewer hypothetical avenues, carry out less parallel work and their test programmes have a lower level of redundancy. Similarly, disposing (as they do) fewer work teams, laboratories and industrial plants, government relations with them are less rigid and more continuous. The third reason is that the European countries have benefited from technological transfers from the United States. These transfers have occurred through the granting of licences for the production of certain equipment or components. They have also received information, which, whilst not constituting a technology transfer, has enabled them to orient their work, using public literature or in the context of data exchange agreements. The fourth reason is that the European countries have to a considerable extent co-operated, allowing them to share programme development costs. This has been particularly the case in many aircraft and missile programmes, which are among the most costly. Finally, one must not forget to mention that a certain number of them broadened their military industrial base by exporting equipment within the framework of their foreign policy, and this broadening has enabled them to amortize at least part of their fixed costs.

The combination of these factors has allowed Western Europe to develop and produce the majority of the weapons needed for its defence, weapons of a technical and operational sophistication which are equivalent to the equipment produced by the United States.

Rationalization, Standardization and Interoperability

The question has often been asked whether there is duplication in this area, and therefore wasteful use of resources which is in the long-run prejudicial to the common defence effort. It cannot be denied that, were the United States to produce all the arms for the Alliance, they would be created and produced in better economic conditions thanks to a greater level of amortization of the fixed costs and to the large scale of the production runs. The idea of this degree of concentration is, however, purely hypothetical and comes up against major political and economic objections. The first of these is that the Alliance is formed to combat a common threat, but this does not imply alignment of the foreign and military policies of the Allied countries. These countries retain their independence and responsibility for the defence of their own interests which go much further than the objectives of the Alliance. Their capacity for independent decision-making remains. Another objection is that arms expenditure ties up a substantial part of national resources and no industrialized nation can agree to export this in full, for it would deprive its own economy and industries, in particular at a time when the problems of unemployment are being keenly felt. From a more military point of view, it is quite possible that extensive standardization of arms would entail more problems than gains. The threats are indeed very varied, whether in regard to the weapons of the adversary, the terrain or the circumstances, and the way that they might be used. One must therefore have widely diversified equipment if one is to be in a position to face all possible situations. This is all the more true given the increasing complexity of weapons systems and the development of counter-measures of all descriptions. It is clear that total standardization would make the enemy's task that much easier, enabling him to develop a limited number of defences and counter-measures, whereas diversification obliges him to spread his efforts. This principle is widely applied by the US in her own arms programmes. For a given military mission, the US often simultaneously commissions several weapons systems with characteristics as different as possible. Similarly, from an industrial point of view, she practices a policy of competition between the various arms manufacturers rather than one of rationalization, precisely in order to benefit from the best ideas available. In these conditions, it would be wrong to emasculate the European industrial potential when it is in a position to make a substantial contribution to the defence of the continent.

Diversity must not, however, be confused with dispersal and the abandonment of all attempts at rationalization of the Alliance's resources. On the contrary, it is essential that the armed forces of the Allied countries be capable of operating together under the most effective conditions. This brings up the problem of interoperability, a problem which has been widely examined and one which is of particular importance with regard to telecommunications, ammunition and fuels. Interoperability can however extend to many other important areas of logistic support, including major supply items, methods of transport, etc. Similarly, precautions must be taken and considerable attention must be paid to concentrating all efforts on significant projects and avoiding a pointless and wasteful overlapping and duplication of effort.

Industrial Policy

The problem arises to what extent the development of technologies and weapons will influence the way in which the programmes are implemented and indeed the whole industrial policy of the NATO countries. Much is heard of the new 'emerging technologies' and the important changes to military policy which they could bring about and it could be beneficial to examine their possible industrial impact. One should note first that technological progress was particularly rapid during and after World War II and that the industrial structures then underwent a permanent transformation without any real discontinuity. There is therefore no reason to believe that the present changes will create a rupture and trigger an industrial revolution.

However, among the factors which could accelerate the movement, the two most significant should be underlined. The first is that the complexity of weapons systems would appear to be increasing at a faster rate than in the past, and that the development and acquisition costs are also rising. The second is that the gravity of the international situation following the second oil crisis interrupted the economic growth of the NATO countries and their budgetary resources, and they are now therefore less able to meet an increase in the cost of their military equipment than in the past. A certain number of analysts have shown that the unit cost of arms in constant money terms in the long-term rose once at the same rate as the cost of living in the industrial nations. These nations thus believed that they could bear the cost of the progressive increase in sophistication of their equipment without too much trouble. This is now no longer the case and is a fundamental reason for paying even greater attention to the economy of weapons programmes.

One must first examine the unavoidable nature of the increasing complexity of weapons systems, in particular for the future. All technologies can be seen to be advancing at various rates but the fields in which the most significant progress is being made are electronics and information technologies. The digitalizing of data and the miniaturization of circuits are opening an increasing number of doors to the designer and user, and processing capacity has been multiplied many times in only a few years. This multiplication of the number of computation functions available endows the systems with a much wider performance range, extends their operating modes and protects them from enemy counter-measures, whilst at the same time facilitating and simplifying the task of the operator. These are therefore advantages which can only be neglected at the risk of finding oneself irreversibly outclassed in combat. The same applies to less spectacular innovations but which are still of great military interest, including increasing weapons accuracy and range. One must, however, be wary of falling into excess, and a clear line must be drawn between real operational advantages and those developments which present only a marginal benefit.

Complexity and Cost

If the growth of equipment complexity and costs cannot be avoided, and if the resources available fail to keep pace with this growth, how can one escape marked reduction in the capabilities of the armed forces? Two avenues have already been explored and are worth further investigation. The first consists in pooling resources to develop new equipment. The second aims at optimizing the use of resources by means of closer association between administration and industry.

For the last twenty years, the European NATO countries have co-operated on a fairly wide basis and with a fair measure of success. This meant that development costs were shared by the partners although the overall cost was slightly higher due to the very nature of the co-operation process. Nations have had to compromise on specifications and there has been a certain unwieldiness in the running of the programmes. Co-operation did not, however, permit significant economies to be achieved in production costs because of the need to break up and share the industrial workloads, even if it was possible to organize single-source production of most components. The main, and extremely important, advantage of this process was to bring the European companies to work together, to broaden their mutual understanding and to create efficient organizations.

One can now safely say that the groundwork for increased European co-operation has been successfully laid and it is clear that the awareness of the need for this co-operation is increasingly present in the minds of those concerned. Numerous preliminary consultations between the various countries have thus been held at both governmental and industrial levels to discuss the launching of important new programmes. This spirit of co-operation, which was already common for the major countries, now extends to others and joint projects involving four or five countries are appearing. This development can only be applauded, since it is consistent with the current need to adapt to a changing situation. One must not, however, lose sight of its limitations.

The first of these stems from the fact that sharing development costs results in a significant, although far from massive, saving in the programme cost. Statistics relating to a few operations involving diverse technologies show that a saving of only about 10% of the total cost of the programme can be achieved through co-operation. Another limitation, rather more difficult to evaluate with any accuracy, is that caused by the increase in the number of partners. There is a long history of co-operation between two and sometimes even three partners, but there is some uncertainty as to the efficiency of co-operation involving more numerous associations. Some are highly sceptical on this matter and very pessimistic views have been put forward. One can however hope that realism and the spirit of compromise will prevail over the forces of division.

Other suggestions have been that, in order to make co-operation more profitable, a much closer association between the industrial partners is necessary, even going as far as merging them. Alternatively, the various European countries should specialize and divide up the arms industry between themselves, each country dealing with a particular field of activity on behalf of all the others. These ideas are interesting, but are likely to remain just ideas for as long as the political organization of Europe remains as it is today. It is indeed hard to imagine independent governments, albeit allied and co-operating in many fields, permanently surrendering the independence of their industrial power which is a prerogative of their national sovereignty.

Co-operation in Arms Procurement
The problem of developing co-operation between Europe and the United States also arises when one looks at how to strengthen the effectiveness of the Alliance. One is obliged to recognize, however, that the context is very different from that which has just been examined. The scale is much greater than for the other countries in the Alliance taken individually and the United States' remoteness from the European theatre means that her own ambitions and strategic pre-occupations are not easily integrated into a framework of co-operation. In addition, the US Administration does not favour long-term financial commitments implied by the launching of an international programme and it applies a set of rules which, designed for internal use, are ill-adapted to the complex nature of joint work based on compromise and flexibility. This means that, despite the scope of the American programmes, very few of them are carried out on a basis of true co-operation. This does not mean, however, that this number cannot be increased, but it does mean that it will be a long, hard road and results cannot be expected in the medium term.

Relations between the United States and Europe in the armaments field are nevertheless many and varied and their effectiveness should not be underestimated. At an official level, there is a large-scale exchange of scientific and technical data allowing optimum orientation of programmes and thus avoiding needless and wasteful expenditure of energy. Furthermore, the European countries which cannot develop all the types of equipment they need turn to the United States, either for direct purchases, or for manufacture under licence. It must be admitted that the Americans are aware of the economic problems of their partners and do their best to find ways of compensating on an industrial basis. This is not really the 'two-way street' we had imagined, but the tendency is in this direction and there is hope that the balance of exchanges with Europe will be less unbalanced in the future.

Finally, the industrial relations between both sides of the Atlantic are particularly well-developed and their flexibility imparts a high level of efficiency. There is little doubt that it is towards extending these relations that the most effort should be devoted, since they constitute a basis for later concrete co-operation. This presupposes, however, that the obstacles be not too great and that the US Administration continue a relevant open policy of technological transfer with its allies.

Free Competition versus Rationalization
It remains to be determined to what extent industry can be made more cost-effective, both in design and production. This is a large subject for discussion which tends to oppose the advocates of total competition and those

of excessive rationalization. There is no doubt that competition does stimulate the imagination and provide a strong incentive to reduce costs. It must not, however, be forgotten that arms production involves the incorporation of very high technology over relatively long periods of time and entails considerable intellectual investment and costly equipment which rapidly becomes obsolete. In this field, dynamism is essential, but success can only be obtained through an accumulation of skills and experience maintained only by the strictest continuity. Continuity of this kind is incompatible with the contingencies of competition which involves constant adaptation to meet the changing situation. The acceptable ground therefore lies somewhere between the two and it is the responsibility of the governments to combine stimulation with continuity, a task which is clearly far from easy.

With continuity in mind, it is important to avoid sudden changes of direction in the running of programmes, such as could result from variations in the technical orientation or from financial difficulties. This implies that the programme launch decisions must be very carefully weighed in advance.

As a general rule, the economic running of a programme can only be successful if pragmatic and permanent account is taken of all elements of industrial management, in the same way as economic running of a car demands that the characteristics of the engine be taken into account. This can only be done if there is close co-operation between governmental departments and industry, and provided there is mutual understanding of the difficulties experienced by each.

There would therefore seem to be no miracle cure for the problem of the increasing complexity and cost of arms equipment arising from the constantly accelerating technical advances being made, advances with which the resources available cannot keep pace. Only a pragmatic approach to the questions of international co-operation and industrial politics will allow present trends to be improved and this demands from all those concerned, both government and industry, understanding, a spirit of compromise and a firm will to succeed.

The 'Star Wars' Debate: The Western Alliance and Strategic Defence: Part I

FRED S. HOFFMAN

Twelve years after the Anti-Ballistic Missile (ABM) Treaty emerged from SALT I and seemed to drive a stake through the heart of proposals to build a Ballistic Missile Defence (BMD), they are once more in our midst as an element of the strategic debate. President Reagan's speech of 23 March 1983 revived the issue. What has come to be known as his Strategic Defense Initiative (SDI) has been a major theme of strategic discourse in Western countries since then.

A reconsideration of the basis for the earlier US decision to abandon active defences is an appropriate starting point for evaluating the SDI. The doctrine of Mutual Assured Destruction (MAD) supplied the rationale for that decision and was in turn apotheosized by the ABM Treaty. The assumptions underlying MAD prejudged the key question of how effective defences had to be to be useful. When assessed in a more realistic framework than MAD, defences do not have to be nearly leakproof to be useful in deterring Soviet attack.

Technological advances have also radically changed the outlook on how effective ballistic missile defences can be. 'Emerging technologies' offer the possibility of a BMD that is quite different in important respects from those that were considered and rejected earlier. The new opportunities for BMD may have quite different implications for the long-term future of the arms competition with the Soviet Union from those projected by opponents during the earlier debate. Of special interest to major allies of the US is the prospect of a robust defence against theatre ballistic missiles. In fact this could well turn out to be the earliest application of the SDI technologies.

Much of the comment on the SDI seems to be directed towards a proposal to begin immediately the deployment of BMD. But no such issue is before us; the President's speech dealt instead with the goal of a long-term R&D programme and its implications for Western strategy. Most of the hard and quantitative questions that must be answered for the ultimate systems design and deployment decisions have to await future clarification in the light of the results of the SDI R&D strategic programme. However, we can begin the effort to understand how to assess strategic defences. This requires a clarification of their mission, an analysis of their qualitative aspects and how they might affect the competition between offence and defence, an understanding of Soviet policies on defences, their own as well as ours, and their probable reaction to the SDI. In particular will they refrain from BMD deployments if the US does?

How Effective Must Defences Be? How Should We Judge Them?

Must BMD protect people against Soviet forces and attack plans that have as their highest priority objective the massive destruction of innocent civilians? A positive answer implies that a less-than-leakproof defence is useless; it therefore poses formidable and, according to many critics, insuperable technological difficulties for BMD. The rush to judgment of the critics on this score flies in the face of abundant evidence that predicting technical impossibilities is a risky line of work. But even those who support defences would agree that the SDI would have to be viewed as a very high-risk venture if success in the R&D programme demanded nearly leak-proof effectiveness against a Soviet adversary determined to maintain at all costs the ability to destroy many of our largest cities and to use his forces in that way in the event of war.

The ability to provide a high level of protection against such an adversary was in fact the principal criterion for assessing the utility of BMD in the series of decisions beginning in 1967 and culminating in the ABM Treaty in 1972 – a criterion stemming from the MAD doctrine, that continues to prevail in much of the current discussion. This approach holds that to deter nuclear attack we must threaten deliberately to destroy innocent Soviet civilians; consequently deterrence depends only on the destructiveness of offensive nuclear forces used in retaliation for Soviet attack. A second and entirely distinct objective recognized but rejected in this conceptual framework is the ability to limit damage if the Soviet Union was actually to attack: namely to reduce the destruction of our own civilians by a combination of counterforce attacks, active defences and civil defence. Proponents of MAD viewed defences as irrelevant or unnecessary to deterrence except perhaps for their possible contribution to our ability to inflict 'unacceptable destruction' on Soviet Society by protecting our *Minuteman* missiles. (By and large, however, they opposed such a role for BMD as unnecessary during the debate preceding the signing of the ABM Treaty.) They also largely ignored the incredibility of relying on a suicidal response to deter Soviet attack and especially the incompatibility of such a strategy with Alliance guarantees.

Not least among the problems with accepting MAD as a strategic Commandment enshrined in the ABM Treaty, the Soviet leadership seems to have come from the mountain with a different set of tablets. They give no sign of recognizing MAD as holy writ. They merely note it, in an anthropological spirit, as a Western belief; and in a more manipulative way they exploit it as a doctrine that makes it easier for them to create political problems in the West.

What can replace MAD in Western strategic doctrine? To deter Soviet nuclear attack, we have to understand and work on the motives that might bring Soviet leaders to consider such an act. MAD appears to shortcut that necessity by relying on a response so terrible that it suffices to deter attack, whatever the motive and even if our response is avowedly suicidal and therefore inherently unlikely to be made. The rejection of MAD implies that we must make a closer examination of Soviet motivation for an attack and the contexts within which they might contemplate one.

Soviet leaders are most likely to consider the use of nuclear weapons if they are considering or are involved in serious non-nuclear military operations against the general purpose forces of one or more of the major Western Allies. Their incentives to initiate the use of nuclear weapons will depend on their assessment of their prospects in the conflict if they refrain and the likelihood and nature of Western response if they were to execute a nuclear attack.

Under such circumstances, Soviet doctrine and planning emphasize pre-emptive attacks to deny Western recourse to nuclear weapons. The survival of Western nuclear forces is therefore, as generally recognized, a primary factor in deterrence. But it is unlikely to be the only factor in the Soviet decision unless they confidently believe that they can virtually eliminate Western offensive forces or Western ability and will to use them. A 'bolt out of the blue' attack that leaves thousands of surviving SLBM warheads (not to mention bomber weapons and ICBM that survived an attack) is a very remote possibility.

Soviet doctrine emphasizes the goal of destroying opposing general purpose forces as quickly as possible to preclude the possibility of grave damage to the Soviet Union as a result of escalation. In regionally-confined conflicts, they might thus consider a limited nuclear strike to terminate a local military engagement that might otherwise spread or one that is going badly for them.

The targets of primary concern to the Soviet leaders would be military forces in the US or in theatres of operations – and most probably a combination of nuclear forces and those general purpose forces whose destruction promised to bring the conflict to a decisive and victorious conclusion. A set of particular significance, given the structure of NATO and its strategy, might be the facilities needed to support US reinforcement and resupply of Europe. The Soviet Union might reasonably expect that an early attack making timely reinforcement obviously infeasible would end concerted resistance in Europe.

With respect to damage to civilians, Soviet attitudes might range from indifference to a desire to avoid broadening the destruction while the West retained substantial retaliatory power to inflict widespread damage on the USSR. However, some of the targets that the Soviet leaders might endow with military significance are collocated with urban populations; as a result, an attack on their full target list could cause catastrophic civilian destruction. Widespread defences of the sort considered under SDI could substantially reduce such collateral damage.

If one holds such a view of Soviet motivation, denial of Soviet ability to achieve the specific military objectives of their attack would contribute powerfully to deterring attacks by them. The extent of such 'strategic denial' will depend on the effectiveness of defences.

How Effective Can Defences Be?
The Effects of New Technology

Technological advance since the 1960s offers the possibility of substantially different kinds of BMD systems from those we have considered in the past. While the 'Star Wars' image has focused attention on battle stations in space and directed-energy weapons, the relevant changes are a result of advances in a diverse set of technologies. Miniaturization of components permits mobility. Increasing precision in guidance through devices that home on the target allows us to consider non-nuclear warheads for defence interceptor missiles. Combination sensors and powerful information processing offers the possibility of distinguishing warheads from light-weight decoys outside the atmosphere. Air- or space-based defence platforms together with high performance and long-range surface-based interceptor missiles make it possible to intercept attacking missiles in all phases of their trajectory: boost phase – from launch to booster burn-out; early midcourse – from booster burn-out to completion of deployment of MIRV and exo-atmospheric decoys; late midcourse – from MIRV deployment to re-entry into the atmosphere; and terminal – from re-entry to detonation.

A multi-layer defence incorporating all of these elements would present very difficult problems for an attack planner, beginning in the boost phase when the missile is most vulnerable and a single intercept can destroy large numbers of MIRV. The most effective counter-measures against one layer will not, in general, be effective against others. The random attrition that attacking missiles would experience in early layers makes it much more difficult to concentrate forces on specific targets or to co-ordinate attacks designed to destroy or penetrate later layers.

From the defender's point of view, a multi-layer defence also allows several intercepts, providing the opportunity to compensate for single-shot probabilities (SSP) of successful intercept that are significantly less than unity. A defence that could destroy only half an attacking force in a single intercept, would, on the average, destroy almost 94% of the attack with four intercepts. Four intercepts each with an SSP of 0.7 would destroy more than 99% of the attack. If the later layers can determine which intercepts have been successful, and shoot only against the surviving attackers, the interceptor inventory required to obtain the benefits of multiple intercepts is greatly reduced. With an SSP of 0.5, the ability to 'shoot, look and shoot again' (S-L-S) reduces the inventory requirement, on the average, from four to less than 1.9 per attacker destroyed; with an SSP of 0.7 the requirement falls from four to less than 1.5.

These benefits might also be available to a degree in lesser combinations of layers or even within a single layer. A goal of SDI work on terminal defence is the ability to initiate intercept at high altitude. If such a defence had time to permit two shots at offensive warheads, it would raise the attrition rate to 91% for an SSP of 0.7.

The potential mobility of the terminal defences radically increases the difficulty of attacking the defence directly, a principal weakness of defences considered in the 1960s. Moreover, the radius of protection (the 'footprint') offered by the prospective terminal defence interceptors is far greater than in earlier terminal defence systems. Together, mobility and a large footprint may effectively prevent an attacker from concentrating his forces to exhaust the defence inventory by denying him the ability to assess the number of interceptors that might be assigned to protect any given target.

The ability of the defence to make the 'last move' permits it to allocate its forces to the protection of a specific (and, to the attacker, unknown) subset of a particular class of targets. For target sets where target redundancy forces the attacker to destroy a high proportion of the target set, this permits the defence to engage in a 'preferential' defence, greatly increasing the attacker's force requirements. While such a situation is inapplicable to the protection of civilians against the type of attack assumed in MAD, it is, or can be made relevant to several classes of military targets that would be an important element of a more realistic deterrent strategy. In planning our future forces, we can attempt to exploit the opportunities offered by a widespread territorial defence by 'designing' the military target system we present to a potential attacker.

Within the MAD context, defences must work almost perfectly to limit damage; the burden of uncertainty therefore falls on the defender. But in the context of a more realistic strategy for deterring attack, the burden of uncertainty falls instead on the attack planner. In assessing his ability to achieve the minimum level of attack effectiveness that might motivate a decision to attack, he will have to make assumptions about the effectiveness of defences and allocate his forces accordingly. If he underestimates, the outcome will be doubly disastrous because his attack plan will be poorly designed. He therefore has strong incentives to err on the side of conservatism, which will further increase the costs of overcoming the defences.

Efforts by the attacker to confuse or evade the defences have a long history, the upshot of which is that competition between offensive counter-measures such as decoys and jamming and defensive counter-counter-measures will not be decided early or once-and-for-all. The impact of new technology in this areas seems for the moment to be moving in favour of the defence against ballistic missiles (in contrast to the area of air defence), but the crystal ball is likely to remain changeable if not cloudy. Here again, conservatism is likely to limit the attack planner's confidence in the ability of clever and relatively cheap counter-measures, contributing to the deterrent value of defences.

The preceding discussion has focused on those aspects of technological change that improve the prospects for defences. Clearly, however, a number of problems remain.

The most serious of these is the vulnerability of defences to direct attack. This appears to be a problem particularly for space platforms in predictable and observable low earth orbits that regularly pass over Soviet territory. Though the terminal layer is not dependent on space-based assets, and though its vulnerability to direct attack appears to be much lower than earlier defence designs, it too cannot be assumed to be exempt from attacks on its air-based sensors, either single attacks or attacks spaced over time. The benefits of defences that were discussed above would not accrue to a defence that could be destroyed easily and reliably by the Soviet Union before or during an attack. The vulnerability of defences must therefore remain a major concern during the R&D conducted under the SDI.

In the debate over BMD before the ABM Treaty, opponents listed among the problems for such defences the requirement to release authority to fire defensive weapons within the short warning time available in a ballistic missile attack. Since the defences then under consideration depended on nuclear warheads, such criticisms carried substantial weight in the debate. If the SDI eliminates the need for nuclear weapons, this issue will be far less acute.

Supporters of MAD have also argued that defences are destabilizing in crises for two reasons: first, they assert that protection of people reduces deterrence of nuclear war by reducing its horror; second, the greater effectiveness of defences against an offensive force disrupted by pre-launch attrition allegedly increases the difference in the damage incurred in striking first rather than being struck.

Such arguments ignore the stabilizing effect of defences in reducing the ability of Soviet planners to achieve their attack objectives. Even if the arguments presented were valid, it would be necessary at least to determine the net effect of defences on stability. But they are not valid. The view that any reduction in the vulnerability of US civilians will tempt US decision-makers to attack the Soviet Union has no basis in evidence. History suggests moreover that the Soviet leaders have not shared this view. At times in the past when the US had nuclear capabilities that might have come close to disarming the Soviet Union in a US first strike, the Soviet Union did not view the danger as sufficiently great to deter them from such provocative ventures as the Cuban missile deployment and the building of the Berlin Wall.

With respect to the second argument, it is true that superimposing defences on vulnerable offensive forces might reduce the stability of the nuclear balance. Such an outcome, however, would reflect a perverse approach to the design of a posture including defences. If, instead, we exploited the opportunities afforded by defences to reduce the vulnerability of our military targets, the net result would be stabilizing rather than the reverse.

'Full System Deployment' or 'Intermediate Deployment Options'?

If, as a consequence of the MAD view, all components of all layers in a multi-layer defence must work almost perfectly, the SDI R&D programme must allocate its resources to achieve a fully effective system with all layers operational at the same time. This means assigning highest priority in the R&D programme to the most difficult and technically risky problems, making the entire enterprise a risky technological gamble, on an all or nothing basis.

If, instead, we regard more modest levels of BMD capabilities as useful, options for intermediate deployments are worth having. They might consist of partial deployments or deployments of technically more modest components. They should therefore be available earlier and at far lower technical risk. Because they might be available earlier, they are likely to face a more restricted range of counter-measures during their service lives than the later, more ambitious system.

A decision to emphasize options for intermediate defence deployments is important not only for the defence of US territory, but for major US Allies as well. The primary nuclear threats to their territory are the Soviet theatre ballistic missiles and SLBM. Those weapons may prove to be especially susceptible to defences employing airborne sensors and surface-based interceptor missiles, based on technologies under consideration in the SDI R&D programme. Although the flight time for such missiles is less than for ICBM because the distance they travel is much shorter, their velocities are much lower. On balance, therefore, such a defence may permit multiple intercepts against theatre ballistic missiles even within a single layer. This application might well, on technical grounds, be the earliest available from the SDI R&D programme.

There are also powerful strategic reasons for considering such a deployment. The size and quality of the Soviet theatre ballistic missile threat make it urgent to provide a defence of critical military targets in theatres of military operations. The threat from Soviet theatre ballistic missiles is not restricted to nuclear conflict. Improvements in the accuracy of Soviet ballistic missiles suggest a role in non-nuclear conflict as well. Their speed of attack and current freedom from attrition by defences would make them particularly valuable in the initial Soviet strikes against NATO air facilities and in destroying NATO air defences to clear the way for a subsequent and heavier Soviet air attack. The Soviet emphasis on preventing NATO escalation to the use of nuclear weapons in the theatre also implies that they might attack elements of NATO theatre nuclear capabilities using ballistic missiles with conventional warheads during non-nuclear conflict.

If the Soviet Union can achieve high confidence of destroying NATO theatre nuclear force retaliatory capability, in either a pre-emptive attack or during the course of non-nuclear conflict, the ability of NATO theatre nuclear forces to deter Soviet nuclear attacks will disappear. Unopposed Soviet non-nuclear theatre ballistic missiles therefore threaten the NATO strategy of Flexible

Response in Europe by simultaneously undermining NATO's capability to resist at the conventional level, to escalate to theatre nuclear attacks and even to deter Soviet theatre nuclear attacks.

The possibility of a defence against theatre ballistic missiles has special relevance also to the relation of the SDI to the ABM Treaty. Under the ABM Treaty restrictions, an SDI-type defence could neither be deployed nor carried through full system development if it constituted 'an ABM system'. The Treaty explicitly, if not clearly, defines 'an ABM system' as 'a system to counter strategic ballistic missiles or their elements in flight trajectory . . .'

On the definition of a strategic missile that the Soviet Union has propounded in the course of the INF controversy (one capable of reaching the Soviet Union – or, presumably, the US, but not Europe or Asia), a theatre ballistic missile defence would not constitute an ABM defence and in violation of the Treaty unless it were also given 'capabilities to counter strategic ballistic missiles or their elements in flight trajectory' or it had been tested 'in an ABM mode'. [Article VI(a)]. The differences in the task of defending against theatre ballistic missiles and ICBM or longer-range SLBM means that a defence against the former might be distinguished from one that could be effective against the latter, but it is rather doubtful that such a distinction could in fact be verified by national technical means (NTM).

The issue has arisen with respect to the SA-12, which the Soviet Union has developed and which she is believed to be ready to deploy. An understanding of what the Soviet Union is up to in the area of defence against nuclear attack is essential in assessing the long-term consequences of the Strategic Defense Initiative.

Soviet Defences
The Soviet rejection of MAD in her programme as well as in her doctrine is most clearly visible in the continued priority given to active and passive defences against nuclear attack. The USSR has never abandoned, as the US has, efforts to defend against air attack. Rather Soviet leaders continue to spend large resources on the operation and modernization of air defence. Unlike the US, they have exercised their rights under the ABM Treaty to maintain and modernize a ballistic missile defence around Moscow. Finally, they have made large investments in civil defences apparently to maintain the integrity of the Soviet government and its continued control in the event of large scale nuclear attack.

These large programmes create major ambiguities with regard to Soviet adherence to the ABM Treaty. Soviet modernization of the Moscow ABM system provides a production base for a rapid deployment of a larger and more widespread system, based on components of the Moscow defence, with little warning to the West – the so-called ABM Treaty 'breakout' option. The mobile SA-12 surface-to-air missile system which reportedly has significant capability against tactical ballistic missiles, is also believed to have potential capability against ICBM, if it is coupled with a sufficiently powerful radar.[1] The US government has publicly stated that the large phased-array radar under construction near Krasnoyarsk almost certainly constitutes a violation of the ABM Treaty. This radar takes on a particularly ominous aspect in connection with the other air and missile defence activities. The Soviet Union will undoubtedly describe the SA-12 as an air defence system or one with 'tactical', but not 'strategic' application. Nevertheless, the US assessment, as reported, indicates that it could have both capabilities. If the Soviet Union deploys this system on a large scale in the next few years, 'they will be able to alter US strategic targeting' according to an un-named White House official.[2]

In the light of these activities, there is little reason to believe that the Soviet leaders regard the ABM Treaty as eternal. A more plausible view is that they continually assess adherence to the Treaty in terms of its costs and benefits, political and military, within the framework of a military tradition that has assigned high priority to strategic defence throughout the post-World War II period. Factors that weigh heavily in their assessment probably include the operational capabilities of the systems available to them, the effectiveness of US offensive counter-measures and the readiness of the US to deploy capable BMD systems.

Soviet activities make it clear that there is no justification for the common assumption that the decision to initiate BMD deployment rests with the US alone. If the technology provides militarily useful options, there are strong indications in Soviet history, doctrine and current programmes that the Soviet Union will exercise those options. And, superimposed on the other trends in the military balance, a one-sided Soviet deployment of effective defences could be a disaster for the West.

Defences and Incentives in the Long-Term Military Competition

For the West, the long-term choice is between a strategy that depends entirely on offensive forces and one that includes some degree of reliance on defences. While the ability to defend against Soviet attack might become a useful element of a deterrent strategy, it cannot entirely replace an offensive response. Such a strategy would offer the Soviet Union a 'heads I win; tails I draw' proposition. The issue we will face for a long time is not whether we should rely exclusively on defences for deterrence, but whether we should continue to rely exclusively on offence as we now do, or whether a mixture would be better.

Growing popular reluctance in the West to contemplate increases in nuclear stockpiles has made it increasingly difficult to compete convincingly with the Soviet nuclear buildup. Under these circumstances, the Soviet Union has little incentive to seek agreements which reduce forces on both sides. A mixed force including defence and an effective and more discriminating offence appears to be more compatible with current political trends in the West than sole reliance on offensive forces. It is also better calculated to provide incentives for serious Soviet negotiations on agreements to reduce the nuclear threat.

Initial Soviet responses to the SDI have aimed at deterring the US from active pursuit of the R&D or subsequent deployment of BMD. To this end, they will probably continue to denounce the programme. If Soviet leaders have decided or decide in the near future to themselves deploy a widespread BMD defence in an overt abrogation of the ABM Treaty, they will undoubtedly seek to justify it as a response to the SDI. While SDI might affect such a decision, its effect on their decisions is unclear.

If the Soviet leaders come to believe that they cannot prevent US deployment of BMD, they will consider various force structure responses including possibly far-reaching changes affecting the overall balance of their military forces. The leverage of the defences would play a major role in the specific outcome of the Soviet choice. The defence leverage is generally measured by the ratio, at the margin, of increments to offensive and defensive forces that are mutually offsetting. The net effect of the changes in the characteristics of the defences discussed earlier is to increase radically the defence leverage compared with defensive systems considered in the 1960s, making offensive force expansion increasingly unattractive as a counter.

If SDI defences do in fact provide very great leverage, the Soviet leadership will probably seek other means to achieve the strategic attack goals of their ballistic missile forces, such as manned or unmanned aircraft, or they might undertake a reassessment of the balance between their strategic forces and their general purpose forces.

The uncertainties introduced by BMD will be a major element in determining the long-run response by Soviet force planners. At present, ballistic missile attacks (on the West, at any rate) would, alone among military operations, be entirely unopposed, allowing a Soviet attack planner to adopt similar approaches to those used by a bridge-building engineer for controlling his uncertainties. For such matters as missile accuracy, launch reliability and estimates of the hardness of US protective structures, he can make conservative assumptions based on empirical distributions drawn from test data or engineering estimates. The central element that distinguishes bridge-building from war is absent: an active and unpredictable opponent. If BMD introduces that element into planning for the use of ballistic missiles, the result is likely to be a reduction in their primacy within the Soviet strategic architecture.

The uncertainties created for the Soviet attack planner by defences will, in general, be magnified for the Soviet force-structure planner. He will have to make predictions about as yet unbuilt US defences as he designs the future Soviet offensive forces. These uncertainties will force him to adjust his plans for using those forces in ways that reduce their effectiveness, whether or not the defences actually succeed in destroying the attacking missiles – a form of 'virtual attrition'. Like the attack planner, the force structure will have to adopt a conservative approach, magnifying the virtual attrition an impending defence deployment will inflict on the future offensive forces. This virtual attrition, together with the anticipated attrition inflicted by the defences, will reduce the total contribution to Soviet strategic objectives of resources spent on ballistic missiles and their threat to the West.

The prospects for achieving similarly effective defences against aircraft are less clear. Developments in 'stealth' and greater flexibility to exploit tactical counter-measures may result in lower leverage for air defences than for ballistic missile defences. In any case, the relative effect of introducing ballistic missile defences (given that there are now none in the West, while there are air defences in theatres of operation and vestigial air defences for US territory) appears likely to shift the balance in favour of greater relative emphasis on the use of aircraft as a means of long-range attack.

If there appears to be a role for defences as an element of a long-term viable posture to deter Soviet attack, what can be said of the effect of defences in removing the threat of mass destruction of innocent civilians? In particular, would the Soviet leaders countenance a substantial reduction in their ability to destroy Western civilians? On the one hand there is no persuasive evidence that the Soviet Union prizes the ability to destroy masses of innocent civilians as an element of her wartime strategy, or that her leaders believe that such an ability is needed to deter US initiation of conflict. On the other hand, they might value a retaliatory capability to deter an indiscriminate US response in the event of a Soviet-initiated nuclear conflict.

Also, it is unfortunately quite clear that they currently derive great political advantage from public anxiety in the West over the threat of widespread destruction. They will almost certainly attempt to retain this advantage in the near future if they can.

Defences are therefore unlikely within the foreseeable future to achieve directly the maximal objective of rendering nuclear weapons obsolete and removing the *possibility* of massive destruction of innocent civilians, but they do offer prospects for reducing the military primacy of the most fearsome element of the nuclear threat, ballistic missiles.

The fundamental logic of the SALT process has rested on the proposition that restrictions on defences would make it possible to limit offensive forces, as clearly expressed in the preamble to the ABM Treaty. The present situation, twelve years after the Treaty entered into force, reflects failure in this purpose. Instead of halting 'the nuclear arms race', the period has seen a Soviet growth in this area that far exceeded the upper bound of US intelligence predictions in the 1960s – predictions that did not assume the existence of agreements limiting offensive or defensive arms. The prospects for concluding formal agreements that would achieve substantial, equitable and verifiable reductions in offensive forces appear poor in the light of current Soviet intransigence and her evident intent to exploit any possible ambiguity in agreements. The stated objectives of the ABM Treaty and the SALT process as a whole are not only unrealized so far – they appear to be unrealizable within the current framework of incentives.

Defences could change those incentives substantially. By reducing the relative utility of ballistic missiles, BMD may make it easier for each side to contemplate restrictions on its own forces as a *quid pro quo* for corresponding restrictions on the other.

Defences can also help to resolve the growing conflict between some of the fundamental objectives of national security and the requirements for verifiability of arms agreements. The steady increase in the accuracy of attack systems has provided strong incentives to acquire small, easily hidden or movable missiles. Extreme precision also makes it possible to consider conventional warheads for specialized long-range attack tasks, enhancing deterrence by providing effective, discriminate and credible responses to attacks against which a full nuclear response would be suicidal and hence incredible. From the point of view of verification of arms agreements, however, such systems must be considered as dual-capable. Missiles with the range, payload and accuracy to perform a useful task with a non-nuclear warhead would clearly be effective with a lighter and much more lethal nuclear warhead. These developments will pose insuperable problems for arms agreements unless the parties can tolerate a growing degree of imprecision in their ability to verify the size of the opposing missile force. Ballistic missile defences can help in this respect by reducing the sensitivity of the balance to illegal nuclear missiles.

It is too early to reach definitive conclusions about the effects of ballistic missile defence deployments on the prospects for useful arms agreements. On the whole, however, such deployments appear more likely than not to improve those prospects by comparison with the dismal record to date and the equally dismal current outlook.

NOTES

[1] *Aviation Week*, 16 January 1984, pp. 14–16.
[2] *Ibid.*

The 'Star Wars' Debate: The Western Alliance and Strategic Defence: Part II

PROF. LAWRENCE FREEDMAN

I call upon the scientific community in our country, those who gave us nuclear weapons, to turn their talents now to the cause of mankind and world peace, to give us the means of rendering these nuclear weapons impotent and obsolete.[1]

If these words are to be taken seriously, then 23 March 1983 will be taken as the date when a revolution in contemporary strategic affairs was set in motion. President Reagan committed his government to the overthrow of the entrenched and domineering offence that has reigned supreme in nuclear matters since 1945 and has exercised an overbearing influence on international affairs. The age of the defence is dawning. Mutual Assured Destruction (MAD) must prepare to give way to Assured Survival.

For such a revolutionary declaration, the President's speech was something of a curiosity. It was not the result of any major analytical effort within government nor the subject of consultations with allies. The origins appear to lie with lobbies as exotic as the technologies they promote. When the bureaucracy was tasked to get to work to bring about the new strategic order, they did so in such a slow and confused manner that it was soon robbed of many of its revolutionary credentials.

There was certainly a revolution in method. We have become used to the idea that in the modern world technology leads doctrine. Here strategic requirements were put to the fore which the scientists and engineers were then charged to meet. This was despite the fact that the necessary technology was well beyond the current state of the art and the weight of scientific opinion appeared to be that the President's utopian goal would remain far out of reach. Even if all went according to plan, the new strategic order was unlikely to arrive until well into the next century.

Most successful revolutions are better prepared than this and run more clearly with the tide of history. The full implications of what is now known as the Strategic Defense Initiative (SDI) do not appear to have been particularly well thought out prior to its launch. Given the lack of enthusiasm in Congress and in the bureaucracy, it may well now peter out of its own accord. However, it also has a substantial measure of popular support, a large number of research contracts have been awarded and the effort has now got some central direction from within the Pentagon.

The notion that it would be both more moral and prudent to concentrate on defence rather than on a destructive offence has been around from the earliest days of the nuclear age and can be expected to retain some popularity and influence even if the current initiative lapses. The fact that the concept of strategic defence has managed to reach centre stage – if only for a short time – provides us at the least with an opportunity to discuss its merits and failings.

In what follows I will talk about the SDI rather than 'Star Wars'. SDI is not only the official term but is also more descriptive. The President did not actually mention space-based systems in his speech – they were mentioned in the associated White House briefing. It was inevitable that anything in this area would attract this sort of label – indeed it had already been applied to discussions of anti-satellite (ASAT) weapons and the two are still confused together. In the same way similar projects two decades ago attracted the 'Buck Rogers' label.

It is impossible to discuss this subject without being drawn into a number of technical debates. I will touch on these debates without exploring the various systems being proposed. As I will argue later, the basic question is whether or not there is a shift under way in favour of the defence at the expense of the offence and there seems to be less dispute than one might imagine that there is not. Furthermore, the preoccupation with the efficacy or otherwise of high-technology systems distracts attention from the more basic questions concerning the objectives of strategic defence and their desirability should they prove to be feasible.[2]

Background

In the past the idea that a nation should do its best to protect itself against all forms of attack would not have been considered revolutionary; indeed, to suggest anything to the contrary would have seemed somewhat bizarre, even treacherous.

What has persuaded policy-makers of the limited value of defences against nuclear attack is the high cost of even the smallest failure, and the continuing success of the offence in coming up with new measures to trump any attempts to establish an effective defence.

As the United States began to consider her vulnerability to attack from the Soviet Union, there was a natural inclination to explore the possibilities for defence. In 1952 President Truman created a special subcommittee of the National Security Council (NSC) to consider the Soviet ability to injure the United States. This subcommittee reported in May 1953 to the new Eisenhower Administration with rather gloomy conclusions. The lack of an ability to protect the United States from a nuclear attack was deemed by the NSC to constitute an 'unacceptable risk to our nation's survival'. Complete invulnerability was recognised to be impossible but 'a reasonably effective defense system can and must be obtained'.[3] By 1960 some $20 billion had been spent on the development of an air defence system that was about to be rendered virtually obsolete by ICBM.

This experience did not deter advocates of an anti-ballistic missile defence but it made the US government more wary of committing large sums of money to measures to defend cities from an all-out Soviet attack. At best ABM were seen to be useful in protecting high-value military targets or in acting against small-scale attacks such as might be posed from China. During the 1960s the United States came to the conclusion that the best method of deterring a nuclear attack on the United States was the threat of retaliation in kind. This view appeared to have been accepted by the Soviet Union when she joined the United States in signing the 1972 ABM Treaty. The prevailing view was summed up by Secretary of Defense James Schlesinger in 1974 when arguing in favour of cutting air defences:

> Since we cannot defend our cities against strategic missiles, there is nothing to be gained by trying to defend them against a relatively small force of strategic bombers. I am sure the Soviet leaders understand that an attack on our cities, whether by bombers or missiles, would inevitably result in the destruction of their cities.[4]

There were always objectors in the strategic studies community to this view.[5] During the 1970s the critics grew in strength. Their main target, however, was not the view that nothing could be done to protect populations from nuclear attack but that the only option available to the West in initiating nuclear exchanges would be all-out attacks on cities. If there was criticism of the restrictions on ABM, it was that this denied one option for protecting land-based missiles.[6]

The Reagan Administration came to power less than well disposed towards the 1972 ABM Treaty. There were dark hints that abrogation might be necessary at the time of the 1982 review of the Treaty. In the debate over the basing of the MX (*Peacekeeper*) ICBM, ABM were canvassed as potentially valuable complements to some of the proposed schemes. However, the Administration could not bring itself to threaten to abrogate the Treaty in order to save MX. It is worth noting that, even when announcing the *Densepack* basing mode for MX in November 1982 (which was also the time of the US–Soviet review of the ABM Treaty), the

President clearly disassociated this system from a ballistic missile defence despite the widespread view that such a defence was needed to make it work.

Because ABM technology was discussed largely in the context of the survival of US land-based ICBM, it did not appear central to the Administration's attempts to wrest US strategy away from the grip of assured destruction. This attempt was largely based on changes to targeting plans and developments of more sophisticated offensive systems. This is not the place to review the Administration's efforts in the area of strategic doctrine. Suffice it to say that the efforts to build on the Carter Administration's countervailing strategy and plan for 'prolonged' nuclear wars have failed to convince. The main result was to stimulate adverse reaction at home and abroad, and some substantial critiques by analysts concerned with both the inner logic of the doctrine and the practicality of conducting a nuclear war along the lines envisaged.

Assured destruction was criticized as a strategic doctrine for failing to provide the United States with options other than the mass destruction of civilians in the event of nuclear hostilities (a crime of which it was not actually guilty). To the critics, the failure was compounded by the unwillingness of the Soviet Union to limit its plans in this manner. The resultant debate revolved around what damage the US might need in order to inflict upon the Soviet Union rather than what the Soviet Union might do to the US and the West in general. This was quite reasonable, given that it is the West that is presumed to be the most dependent on a credible nuclear strategy. The difficulty was that, whatever the offensive tactics that might be developed for the West, the problem of the character of any Soviet retaliation and the form taken by later nuclear exchanges – leading to mutual assured destruction – remained.

In the end, if the Administration was serious about its commitment to escape from the grim logic of MAD, then it had to get round its critics' fundamental argument – that MAD was not just a policy choice but was a fact of life in the modern world. If only the Soviet second-strike capability could be undermined, then US strategy would gain a formidable credibility. In this sense the President's speech represented the logical conclusion of the search for a credible nuclear strategy that has occupied US policy-makers since Robert McNamara's days as Secretary of Defense.[7]

Two Steps Forward
There were no hints that a revolution was being prepared in the White House in the first months of 1983. In the discussions within the Scowcroft Commission attempting to forge a bipartisan policy on strategic forces, the potential benefits of BMD were not seen to extend much beyond the protection of land-based missiles. The Commission's Report (released *after* the President's 23 March speech) concluded:

> Applications of current technology offer no real promise of being able to defend the United States against massive nuclear attack in this century . . . At this time . . . the Commission believes that no ABM technologies appear to combine practicality, survivability, low cost, and technical effectiveness sufficiently to justify proceeding beyond the stage of technology development.[8]

A continued research programme was deemed necessary just in case there was a need to respond to a Soviet 'breakout' from the constraints of the ABM Treaty.

This sense that any collapse of the ABM Treaty would be at the instigation of the Soviet Union and not the United States seemed to be in line with Administration thinking. Less and less was heard about the review of the ABM Treaty as it grew closer. Official policy, as outlined in a Presidential Statement of November 1982, stated that the United States did

> not wish to embark on any course of action that could endanger the current ABM Treaty so long as it is observed by the Soviet Union.

There were no plans to deploy any BMD system, even that permitted under the 1972

Treaty, but research would continue on the relevant technology. The objectives of this research effort were:

> stability for our ICBM in the nineties, a hedge against Soviet breakout of the ABM Treaty, and the technical competence to evaluate Soviet ABM developments.[9]

These objectives were broadly similar to those of the Carter Administration.[10] The positive interest was confined to protection of ICBM silos; otherwise the only requirement was to be ready to respond to any initiative taken by the Soviet Union.

The new policy was announced by the President in his speech of 23 March[11] and elaborated further in background briefings and in supporting statements, speeches and interviews by the President and his senior officials, particularly Secretary of Defense Caspar Weinberger and Science Adviser Dr George Keyworth.

The key features of the new policy were as follows:

- It was self-consciously revolutionary and visionary. In his speech the President described an 'ultimate goal' of eliminating the threat posed by nuclear weapons. A few days later he spoke of his initiative as offering an alternative to one in which 'the great nations of the world will sit here like people facing themselves across a table each with a cocked gun, and no one knowing whether someone might tighten the finger on the trigger'.[12]
- Assured destruction would be turned on its head: people and not weapons were to be protected; weapons and not people were to be threatened. The objectives went well beyond guarding against Soviet first strikes or protecting offensive missiles.
- The system would provide total and not just partial protection. As Caspar Weinberger put it: 'The defensive systems the President is talking about are not designed to be partial. What we want to try to get is a system which will develop a defense that is thoroughly reliable and total ... I don't see any reason why that can't be done'.[13]
- It was specifically concerned with 'strategic ballistic missiles' (the only weapons mentioned in the original speech). This aspect appears to rest uneasily with the need for total protection. However the argument was that ballistic missiles posed the most critical test to any defence and, if they could be stopped, then slower-moving forces would pose far less of a challenge.[14]
- The protection would be extended to allies. The President's 'vision' was to 'intercept and destroy strategic ballistic missiles before they reached our own soil or that of our allies'. This statement implies a wider (if not wholly inappropriate) definition of a strategic missile than is normally adopted by the United States. Unfortunately elsewhere in the same speech the President referred to intermediate nuclear force, confirming the impression that the inclusion of allies was something of an after thought.
- At least for the time being, the 1972 ABM Treaty would be respected. The Treaty permitted research, and deployment decisions were years away.
- The objective was 'neither military superiority nor political advantage'. Indeed, in a later press conference, the President suggested that, when the defensive system was developed, one option would be to pass the technology on to the Soviet Union. Secretary Weinberger stated that: 'I would hope and assume that the Soviets with all the work they have done and are doing in this field, would develop a similar defense, which would have the effect of totally and completely removing these missiles from the face of the earth'.[15]

One Step Back

Since the spring of 1983 the policy has been revised substantially and is in a number of respects now reverting back to the sort of rationales adopted prior to March 1983. Instead of the SDI being presented as a self-conscious piece of doctrinal revisionism, it is increasingly being described as a prudent response to an initiative already undertaken by the Soviet Union. Even more significantly, although the objective of a population defence has not been disavowed, the basic objective has now reverted back to the protection of US military capabilities against a Soviet first strike. In May 1984 Secretary Weinberger observed that:

> SDI does not preclude any intermediate deployment that could provide, among other things, defense of the offensive deterrent forces which, of course, we still have to maintain.[16]

As this quotation also illustrates, there is now no pretence that it will prove possible to eliminate offensive weapons as a result of this initiative – at least until the ultimate goal is within reach.

The revisionism may even have moved a stage further. Lt-General James Abrahamson, directing the SDI, told reporters in May 1984 that:

> My specific charge is to ensure that possibility of early deployments in case there is a breakout of the Anti-Ballistic Missile Treaty on the part of the Russians.[17]

Some proponents of strategic defence now find it very hard to imagine that the President ever even considered the idea of defending civilians, although he clearly did.[18]

This more modest tendency has been reflected in the actual development of the SDI. National Security Study Directive (NSSD) 6-83 required an examination of the technology that could eliminate the threat posed by nuclear ballistic missiles to the security of the United States and her allies. A Defensive Technologies Study, headed by Dr James C. Fletcher, and a Future Security Strategy Study, headed by Fred Hoffman, reported in October 1983. These studies were integrated in an interagency group report. The essential conclusion of the Fletcher Panel was that 'a robust, multitiered ballistic missile defense system can eventually be made to work'. The stress, however, was on the 'eventually'. This was a matter for long-term research.[19] This approach angered a number of the more enthusiastic advocates of strategic defence.[20] In his National Security Decision Directive (NSDD) of 6 January 1984 the President sided with the more cautious approach and called for 'initiation of a focused program to demonstrate the technical feasibility of enhancing deterrence and thereby reducing the risk of nuclear war through greater reliance on defensive technology'.[21] To the press, key officials stressed the long-term and speculative nature of the programme.[22] In late March, Lt-General Abrahamson was appointed to direct the SDI. With a certain amount of bureaucratic friction, Abrahamson's office began to pull together a number of disparate BMD-related programmes from around the Department of Defense.

As things stand, the SDI is concerned with long-term research rather than medium-term deployment. The proposals of those in lobbies such as 'High Frontier' for a move to early deployment based on available technology have been rejected on the familiar grounds of overestimated performance and underestimated cost. Known but unfashionable technologies such as nuclear ABM are being discarded and, while a short-term capacity to respond to a Soviet breakout from the ABM Treaty is being maintained, it is not being taken much further. In long-term research the easier technologies are being kept for later while priority is given to the most challenging problems, especially laser technology and the computational capabilities necessary to manage large-scale defences. The assumption is that a layered defence, threatening the offence at the boost, post-boost, midcourse and terminal phases will be necessary to ensure against excessive leakage at any one layer. The effort remains directed at ballistic missiles. While a system capable of dealing with ICBM can also deal with intermediate-range systems (although not necessarily using multiple layers), the problems of dealing with bombers and cruise missiles are quite different.

There appears to be some debate within the Administration as to the need or the desirability of combining an effort to deal with the 'air-breathing threat' with that to deal with strategic ballistic missiles. According to one school of thought, it is by no means clear that in the future (as in the past) bombers and cruise missiles will pose far simpler defensive problems. They do not leave rocket flares at boost stage to allow them to be detected at launch nor do they re-enter the atmosphere. Although their speed is slower than missiles, they are even now difficult to detect by radar and with 'stealth' technology this will be still more difficult in the future. Some proponents of SDI have argued that 'air-breathers' are more stable than missiles because of their slower speed. A Mr William Furniss of the Pentagon has been quoted as suggesting, rather curiously, that if the strategic competition were pushed back towards bombers it 'would get us back to the relatively stable period of the 1950s'. However, it is hard to see how ballistic missile defences could remain credible with an unrestricted bomber and cruise missile threat. To state one obvious problem, ground-based components of the defence would be vulnerable to a pre-emptive cruise missile attack. As Major-General John A. Shard of the USAF put it: 'If you're going to fix the roof, you don't want to leave the doors and windows open'.[23] Current funding for both development and procurement of air defence systems is only a fraction of that on the SDI.

The current plan is for the research phase to be completed early in the 1990s when decisions will have to be taken on whether or not to enter systems development, when prototypes of actual systems are to be designed, built and tested. This will be followed by a transition stage during which there will be 'incremental, sequential deployment of defensive systems' to be followed by a final phase of deployments of high-effective, multiphased defensive systems. It may be another thirty years before this final phase is completed.[24]

The eventual cost remains a matter of conjecture. Current spending is quite modest although it is projected to rise significantly over the coming four years.[25] Richard De Lauer, Under Secretary of Defense for Research and Engineering, has warned that deployment costs will be 'staggering', and suggested that the cost over ten years of deployment would be equivalent to that currently being spent on offensive arms – some 14% of the total budget each year. In current dollars this would amount to a total of some $400–450 bn.[26] This would be after substantial development costs.

More seriously it does not include the costs of introducing parallel defences against bombers and cruise missiles.[27] Furthermore, there can be no expectation of compensating savings in offensive arms. Indeed, it is not inconceivable that there will be increased expenditures on offensive arms to meet the challenges posed by the introduction of Soviet defences. Clearly therefore a substantial amount of new money is going to have to be found if these schemes are to come to fruition. Already there are signs that those responsible for other aspects of US defences are worried that their programmes will be crowded out by SDI.[28]

Ends
The most important development has been the shift away from the protection of civilians as the prime objective of the programme. After the President's speech, Congressional supporters tabled a People Protection Act to:

> implement the call of the President for a national strategy seeking to protect people from nuclear war and to render nuclear weapons obsolete.

They must now feel as if they had succumbed to a life insurance salesman only to discover that the policy only covered the car. We have already noted the move to 'intermediate' objectives involving the defence of high-value military targets. As Lt-General Abrahamson has now explained: 'A perfect astrodome defense is not a realistic thing'.[29] Supporters of this move argue that it is genuinely intermediate in that it will provide opportunities to prove technologies essential to the more ambitious schemes and that it will be possible to move to a complete defence through the addition of extra layers. However, this pushes the President's objective even further into the background.[30] It also means that some of the more difficult policy issues may have to be faced earlier than would have been the case had the SDI concentrated on research in areas critical to population defence.

The intermediate objectives have long been associated with ballistic missile defence:

- *Hard-point defence.* Protection of land-based missiles and command-and-control centres against a Soviet first strike has always been a favoured rationale for ABM.
- *Strategy-denial.* A more sophisticated variant of hard-point defence points to the concentration in Soviet strategy on a variety of forms of counterforce targeting in the conduct of campaigns against Western Europe as well as the United States. By denying the Soviet Union preferred strategic options, it will be deterred from engaging in any nuclear operations.
- *Protection against small attacks.* Even if the system cannot deal with a massive assault it should be able to deal with accidental launches of missiles or smaller nuclear forces.
- *Damage limitation.* By reducing the total number of warheads detonated, the damage to civilian life and property can be reduced though it would still be very high. It has even been suggested that strategic defences offer one way of staving off the 'nuclear winter' by keeping the number of warheads detonated beneath the threshold that might trigger a climatic catastrophe.[31]

The Administration has insisted that the fundamental purpose is to enhance deterrence, and this is particularly clear with regard to the first two objectives listed above. With regard to protection against small attacks, it is only China that could conceivably pose a ballistic missile threat to the United States. It would be somewhat ironic if the anti-China rationale which was deemed to be rather feeble when adopted by Secretary of Defense McNamara in 1967 was resurrected now. For the moment, it is the Soviet Union which will find this rationale most appealing. As for damage limitation, the Administration is sensitive to the suggestion that it is preparing for war and has tended to play this down.[32]

There are, in addition, three subsidiary benefits that might result from continuing with a substantial research effort which did not reach any definite conclusion:

- *Response to breakout.* Maintaining the capability to respond to a Soviet breakout from the constraints imposed by the ABM Treaty tends to be supported even by those who object to the SDI.[33]
- *Bargaining chip.* The prospect of a successful US deployment of an effective defence will encourage the Soviet Union to take arms control more seriously.[34]
- *Diversion of resources.* In order to deal with developing US defensive capabilities, the Soviet Union will be forced to direct resources into improving her offensive counter-measures.

It should be noted with regard to these subsidiary benefits that they still depend on there being a reasonable possibility that the primary objectives can be obtained. For example, the bargaining chip argument is normally taken to suggest that reductions on offensive arms will be easier to obtain as the Soviet Union recognizes the futility of persevering with offensive arms in the face of ever-more-impressive US defences. However, if US defences fail to impress then no negotiating leverage is provided at all, except possibly in encouraging further restrictions on the defence.

Nor would there be much point in responding to a breakout from Treaty constraints with a comparable defensive build-up if the resultant defences were likely to be ineffective. The Soviet Union has been more energetic in the past with both air defences and ABM: the US response has been to strengthen the offence.

In its original form the President's initiative was vulnerable to the standard criticisms made against similar proposals in the past. The first side to achieve an effective defence would put the other at a considerable disadvantage. The other would have advance notice of this shift in the strategic balance and might be tempted to pre-empt before the shift had become absolute. So the transition period would be one of immense strain, and indeed the problem of transition will be stressful if any serious change in the existing strategic order is contemplated. Once the new defences were in place then the favoured side might be tempted to exploit its advantage during a crisis by launching a nuclear strike in the expectation (which might turn out to have been disastrously misguided) that it would receive nothing in return.

These rather grand strategic problems are now somewhat pushed into the background, along with the objective of 'people protection'. The SDI will achieve less than originally envisaged and so, by the same token, is less potentially destabilizing than its detractors have suggested. Most important of all, the 'intermediate' objectives do not take us out of the condition of mutually assured destruction. An opponent determined to inflict unacceptable damage could still do so. In principle these objectives are perfectly consistent with 1960s-vintage strategic doctrine.

Indeed their most likely effect is to reinforce a concentration on city-targeting. As any defence would have some damage-limiting capacity, the Soviet Union might feel obliged to compensate by improving her area-attack capabilities to guard against any diminution in the 'ultimate' threat. Furthermore, to the extent that the United States succeeded in denying to Soviet planners lucrative military targets, the planners would have little choice but to stress 'soft' targets such as cities. There seems to be some attempt by supporters of SDI to suggest that this does not matter because of a lack of Soviet interest in counter-city targeting. This argument is hard to take seriously. It is particularly difficult to imagine any President taking it seriously during a crisis or in the early stages of war.[35]

It is certainly the case that Soviet doctrine puts a lot of stress on counterforce targeting, but the conviction with which this is done can easily be exaggerated. Furthermore, this approach is most relevant to the European theatre where the problems of protecting military assets are much more severe. It is important to deny the Soviet Union a first-strike capability, but they are nowhere near achieving such a capability at the moment. The problems of land-based missile survivability are acute but that is not the case with sea-based systems and strategic defence is irrelevant to the problems of anti-submarine warfare. It has to be asked how much expense and bother the 'intermediate' objectives are worth. As strategic problems they may not be as urgent as suggested by those proposing the SDI as a solution. Any major deployment of strategic defences will add to Soviet uncertainties about what she can get away with and so to some extent reinforce deterrence. However, it is doubtful that the increment of deterrence will have been worth the price, especially if other elements of the force structure have declined as a result of the diversion of resources to SDI.

A definition of the objectives of SDI which might be considered neutral might be: 'the progressive elimination of offensive nuclear options through the application of defensive technologies'. This definition raises the question of which side is likely to benefit most from the denial of targeting options. In the past it has been the West rather than the East that is believed to have been most in need of a credible nuclear strategy. Unless the advocates presume that the Soviet Union will not be able to follow a US breakout, which would require a considerable act of faith and contradict their own statements on the advanced stage of Soviet research and development, then it must be expected that Western options will also be reduced. Contrary to the received wisdom, the presumption behind much of the advocacy of the SDI appears to be that the Soviet Union is in the greatest need of nuclear options. We find George Keyworth suggesting that the great advantage of SDI in the long-term will be 'to enforce retaliation as the sole rationale for nuclear delivery systems.'[36]

This is by no means an unreasonable objective, but it contradicts NATO's current position that it is most in need of a threat of nuclear escalation to deter aggression. The response by the US Administration, and other Western governments, to proposals to remove nuclear weapons from strategic calculations in Europe through 'no-first-use' declarations has been that this would make Europe 'safe for conventional warfare'. Presumably this objection applies to the same effect being achieved through the neutralization of both sides' offensive nuclear weapons. The introduction of effective defences therefore could reduce the risks surrounding conventional operations – the very area where the Warsaw Pact is believed to enjoy its most significant advantages. Even if the result of both sides protecting vital military assets was to reduce the opportunities for sophisticated nuclear operations, according to the conventional wisdom in NATO the Alliance has most to lose from such a development. It may well be that we would be better off if neither side had the ability to mount such operations at any nuclear level. The point is that the SDI only appears to be improving the position if it presumes that NATO's fundamental problem – the incredibility of the threat to use nuclear weapons first – has already been dealt with by other measures. To stabilize strategic relations on this new basis, the SDI would have to be accompanied by a major improvement in conventional defences.

Allies
This brings us to the whole question of the impact of all of this on the Alliance. The Allies were not consulted about the 23 March speech and their response has been muted to say the least. The initial reaction was simply to hope that the speech was an aberration and that there would be no significant follow-through. This is still the hope but no longer the expectation. In addition to briefing teams sent round to NATO capitals, Defense Secretary Caspar Weinberger gave a briefing to Ministers at the Nuclear Planning Group meeting in Turkey in early April. This seems to have had a negative reception and was followed by the West Germans expressing their doubts publicly. The French, after initially toying with the idea of developing their own defensive systems (in line with the established practice of asserting that France can follow any new technological line should she so desire), have now become quite hostile and have even tabled a proposal at the Geneva Committee on Disarmament that would prohibit space-based defences. With the British they are particularly concerned about the impact on their national nuclear deterrent. Alliance concern reportedly led to consultations in Washington in July 1984.[37]

In addition to the special concerns of the British and French, there have been more general concerns expressed about the effect of the SDI on arms control and strategic stability. While supporters of the Initiative argue that an effective defence would render the US nuclear guarantee to Europe much more credible, the European concern has been that the overall effect would be 'de-coupling'. Either Europe would remain extremely vulnerable and so be kept hostage by the Soviet Union, or else the United States, now safe and sound behind her protective shield, would withdraw from her international commitments.

The Administration has sought to ease these concerns largely by insisting that the protective shield would indeed extend to Western Europe. Having already promised to do one impossible thing why not promise another? There is every indication that the promise was made lightly. There has been no discussion of how, if at all, the Allies would contribute to either the construction or the costs of such a system. While it is the case that the ability to intercept during the boost phase would provide some defence against medium- and intermediate-range missiles, the shorter flight time is certain to limit what might be achieved by multiple layers and the sheer diversity of threats faced by Western Europe (especially those Allies bordering the Warsaw Pact) would threaten to overwhelm all defences.

Again, of course, more modest objectives for the SDI change the debate. The problems faced by the British and French remain and one can expect their anxiety levels to grow the more it looks like the ABM Treaty is close to collapse. But otherwise, the fact that there is unlikely to be real invulnerability for the United States means that there is less need to worry about 'Fortress America'. This does not of course mean that that the Europeans will stop worrying along these lines.[38] The most significant result of the shift to the more limited objectives (and one that does not seem to be fully appreciated in Europe) is that it puts the promise of extending strategic defence to Europe in a completely different light.

There are a large number of military targets of interest to the Soviet Union in Europe. Protection against air attack is already considered necessary for many, so protection against missile attack could be seen as a natural complement. Furthermore, tactical anti-ballistic missiles (TABM) are not directly prohibited by the ABM Treaty, and their deployment would therefore have fewer international repercussions than strategic defences. Furthermore, there is already a candidate for a TABM in the *Patriot* missile which is near deployment in an air defence role.[39] It would be ironic if an initiative that began stressing the defence of the American people against strategic ballistic missiles ended up proving extra protection for military installations in Europe!

Patriot reveals more about the problems than the possibilities of strategic defence. The current bill to introduce it to perform its primary air defence role is $11 bn. Testing has been disappointing and the current expectation is that deployment may not be complete until the 1990s.[40] Furthermore, as one proponent of TABM has warned:

> I don't think we can afford the numbers required. . . . One response by the Soviet Union would be to MIRV the front-end of their heavy tactical missile systems, which would stress any TABM system.[41]

Means

We come next to the whole question of the feasibility of the attempt to introduce effective defences. The SDI controversy has been a gift to disputatious scientists and therefore rather forbidding to the non-scientist. But it is also the case that the scientific debate is highly speculative since no specific systems have as yet been adopted. Lt-General Abrahamson has complained that many of the critics of SDI are 'creating an Edsel and then going back and shooting it down'.[42] They have, of course, nothing else to aim at for the moment. It may also be the case that the critics are still attacking the President's original concept rather than the one that is now guiding the bureaucracy.

The President's original speech was not made on the basis of any new technological assessments,[43] and we have noted the lack of enthusiasm in the initial reactions of the responsible figures in the Pentagon. The Fletcher Report's endorsement of the Initiative was cautious, certainly too cautious for many of the SDI's more enthusiastic proponents.[44]

It is generally agreed that the fundamental question behind the technical arguments is whether or not a trend is under way to shift the advantage from the offence to the defence in the long-standing duel between the two. It is also generally agreed that there is no firm evidence as yet that such a shift is under way. However, one proponent of the SDI, Robert Jastrow, has argued that the shift has already been developed as far as point defence goes. It will, he argues, cost twice as much to counter the defence as to build it.[45]

It is necessary to examine this argument very carefully. The equation for the offence–defence duel does not just involve weighing the cost of protecting an individual target against the cost of penetrating that defence. It is also necessary to put into the equation the value of the target being protected. As point defence is designed to protect high-value military assets, then its failure might be decisive – in which case this is what is going to matter much more to the enemy than the cost of the offence or the defence.

Second, the defence costs include protecting assets that may be important but which the enemy has no intention of attacking. The more complete the defence the more there is going to be wasted effort. If it is desired, on the other hand, to protect only a few critical installations then the offence–defence duel may only be a small part of the total battle and so the relative costs will be relatively unimportant and outweighed by the value of the installations themselves.

Third, because of the problems of lead times, the defence has to anticipate possible changes in the offence which might be different from those that the offence chooses to make. It is being suggested that this time the penalty may be the other way round in that the offence will need to prepare countermeasures before it can be sure that any particular defensive problem will actually materialize. By following a number of defensive possibilities in research, the USSR will be forced to hedge against a wide range of possible developments. The Pentagon has argued:

If, for example, the Soviets persisted in attempts to expand their massive offensive forces, a flexible research and development program would force Soviet planners to adopt counter-measures, increasing the costs of their offensive buildup and reducing their flexibility in designing new forces in a manner that they would prefer.[46]

So, in addition to arguing that the past cost advantage favouring the defence is to be relinquished, it is also argued that the lead-time advantage is also to pass to the defence. It does not as yet seem evident why this should be so. It would be surprising if the Soviet Union was already doing much more than tentative research herself in response to the SDI and, given the enormous amount of time needed to even deploy the sort of systems envisaged, there seems no reason for the Russians not to bide their time until American plans become clear.

This relates to a more general proposition that only holds if things can be truly shown to be moving the way of the defence. It has been asserted that the development of an impressive defence will force the Soviet Union to stop investing in offensive missiles and thus serve the cause of stability. In the 'transition phase', as outlined by Lt-General Abrahamson in May 1984, it is envisaged that:

> as the US and Soviet Union deploy defenses against ballistic missiles that progressively reduce the value of such missiles, significant reductions in nuclear ballistic missiles would be negotiated and implemented.[47]

Elsewhere, he has made it clear that he envisages a downgrading of Soviet offences as a natural response to the progress of the SDI.[48] But if in practice it is nuclear ballistic missiles that are still reducing the value of strategic defences, and there has yet to be anything other than an assertion that the reverse is likely to be true, what does that mean for the new initiative?

There seems no reason to believe that the Soviet Union will not continue to invest in offensive arms. She has shown herself in the past, perhaps foolishly, willing to resist technological trends. When the offence was clearly in the ascendant, she still invested heavily in defences. It would be surprising if in the face of the SDI she meekly bowed to US technological supremacy and provided the US with a strategic walkover.[49]

The SDI only looks promising so long as the offensive problem is not allowed to get out of hand.[50] Two judgments are worth quoting on this issue. The first is that of James Thomson of the Rand Corporation on the basis of an extensive project conducted on strategic defences with full access to classified information. In testimony to Congress he considered whether the offence or the defence would have the economic advantage in an arms race:

> We concluded that the offense would have the advantage. This advantage became overwhelming if we were attempting to protect populations to a very high level of effectiveness, or what might be called near leak-proof defenses. At lower levels of protection, the offense still had an advantage, but not so pronounced.[51]

The second is that of James Fletcher himself:

> The ultimate utility, effectiveness, cost, complexity and degree of technical risk in this system will depend not only on the technology itself, but also on the extent to which the Soviet Union either agrees to mutual defense arrangements or offensive limitations.[52]

Arms Control
The SDI may well be dependent on a prior agreement limiting offensive arms. The continued lack of progress in START poses the problem of an unconstrained offence. But if the SDI succeed without the sort of arms control that we currently lack, it cannot prosper with the sort of arms control that we currently have.

It cannot move beyond the research stage without abrogation of the 1972 Treaty. Those wishing to stop the SDI need take no exceptional arms-control measures. Their task is only to ensure compliance with the current provisions. This, of course, is easier said than done, given that it is difficult to draw the line between research and development and between ABM and the related anti-aircraft and anti-satellite technologies.[53] If both sides step up their strategic defence activities then the Treaty is going to be put under severe strain, even if there is no formal abrogation. Furthermore, the question of unambiguous violation may arise sooner rather than later as a result of the need to test critical components. A 'demonstration test' would be a highly risky venture if it could only be undertaken after rejection of the Treaty but without any confidence that it would lead to a successful system. The only possible area where deployment might be permitted would be with TABM and here there would be problems if it were designed to deal with systems of any significant range, because it would also be able to deal with SLBM. It may also be the case that the development of anti-satellite technology (ASAT) provides opportunities to develop components of ABM without doing so directly, although these tests may be sufficiently direct to lead to charges that the ABM Treaty is being violated.[54] Equally, recent developments in mid-course interception systems are of value in the development of ASAT. It is therefore likely that an ASAT treaty would impede the SDI.

This to some extent would depend on the nature of the systems banned under an ASAT treaty. Current thinking in the Administration appears to be that low altitude systems cannot be verified and therefore should be excluded. If only high-altitude systems were banned, while this might interfere with development in the short- and medium-term, in the long-term it might help the SDI because it would alleviate a critical vulnerability of any system dependent on space-based components.

For the same reasons that the Administration might prefer an arms-control regime that allowed unconstrained defensive deployments and a highly restricted offence, the Soviet Union is unlikely to provide them with such a regime. The linkage between offensive and defensive arms control is well established, and has always been stressed by the United States. At the time of the 1972 Treaty, the US issued a unilateral statement to the effect that she would reconsider her support for the Treaty without a later Treaty on offensive arms, and this position was apparently reiterated in the run-up to the 1982 Review Conference (although it was hardly the Soviet Union that was responsible then for the lack of a Treaty on Offensive Arms).[55] The linkage is now likely to be played back at the United States. Any treaty on offensive arms will depend on continued adherence to the ABM Treaty. The same is likely with an ASAT treaty. Soviet, and for that matter French, proposals against the 'militarization' of space are clearly designed to get at both the SDI and ASAT. While it has been the American attempt to link discussion of ASAT with offensive weapons that has gained most of the publicity in the squabbling over the agenda for the proposed September 1984 Vienna talks, there was also an American desire to separate ASAT from SDI. Those promoting SDI are clearly anxious that any early agreement in this area could abort the initiative before it had a chance to prove itself.[56]

Without limitations on offensive arms this Administration may be reduced to arguing, as the Nixon Administration was forced to when promoting the *Safeguard* ABM system fifteen years ago, that the Soviet Union will maintain sufficient offensive forces to warrant making the effort but would not build them up to a level that would overwhelm the defence.

The offence–defence duel is not about to swing in favour of the defence, and the effectiveness of strategic defences in the future will depend as much on offensive constraints as on technological innovations. This leads to the proposition that the primary objectives informing the SDI might be more readily achieved by negotiated offensive limitations. Disarmament is certainly cheaper than strategic defence, it could begin right away, and the margins of error with regard to verification might well be far less than the potential leakage in a high-technology defensive system. It would also be under human control and not depend on a highly complex system to perform exactly to specification at its first serious test in the moments after a Soviet missile launch (or what might be suspected to be a Soviet missile launch) – and while the President is still being alerted to the fact that something may be happening.

Consider the consequences of a failure of a multilayered defence to perform as advertized. If, as a result of the deployment of this defence, the enemy had increased its offensive capabilities in order to deal with expected performance levels which were *not* reached at the critical moment, the result would be that far more warheads than would otherwise be the case would land on the homeland. The system would have been utterly counterproductive.

If the President really wants to eliminate offensive nuclear weapons from the face of the earth, why not propose just that to the Soviet Union? If it is desired to reduce the target sets available to the nuclear offensive, then reduce the flexibility by cutting its numbers. If it is desired to limit the damage to the United States should deterrence fail and reduce the risk of the nuclear winter, then at the very least propose reductions to small stockpiles.

There are of course objections to all these proposals but the issues of principle raised are no different from those connected with the SDI, and the practical difficulties, while significant, are nothing as compared with the introduction of effective strategic defences.

Conclusion
One major difference between disarmament and the Strategic Defense Initiative is that, whereas the former requires early and active co-operation between the United States and the Soviet Union, with the latter there is only a presumption that the two will follow a similar path because of similar calculations as to their security interests. This may lead some to hope that if only the United States can identify her interests more clearly, inherent economic and technical strengths will see her through to a decisive strategic breakthrough.

There is an ambiguity running through the whole SDI. Is this designed to restructure the super-power relationship on a quite different but still essentially equal basis? Or is it a unilateral strategic move by the United States to achieve an advantage over the Soviet Union?

In the more recent promotion of the SDI, considerable stress has been put on the risk of the USSR winning this new strategic race. Thus Lt-General Abrahamson has stated:

Were they [the Russians] to deploy the fruits of their programs unilaterally, the consequences to our national security would be grave.[57]

Why would it be grave? Possibly for the same reasons that the Soviet Union might believe it to be grave if the United States got there first. Whatever the protestations of peaceful intent and in the absence of negotiated constraints, a strategic defence is only likely to be most effective if the other side's offence has already been depleted through a first strike – the logical first layer of a multilayered defence.

In his original speech the President remarked:

I clearly recognise that defensive systems have limitations and raise certain problems and ambiguities. If paired with offensive systems, they can be viewed as fostering an aggressive policy and no one wants that.

It is now clear that, with the revision of the SDI away from the President's original utopianism, defensive and offensive systems are likely to be paired. What seems at times to be envisaged is not so much a tidy substitution of the defence for the offence but a continuing competition across the board in offensive and defensive systems, with strategists on both sides exploring areas of comparative advantage. It appears to be part of the continuing effort to develop plans for a nuclear strategy that is similar to conventional strategy in its flexibility and control.

The problems that have already been identified in conducting a controlled nuclear war in today's relatively straightforward strategic environment would be as nothing compared with the more confused environment now envisaged. A President is even less likely to be confronted with a credible war plan in this environment. Meanwhile the problems of crisis management would intensify. There would be doubts as to whether one's own defences were functioning properly combined with fears that the other's were completely reliable, and uncertainties over what sort of interference with the other side's defences would be sufficiently provocative to trigger war. And still there, at the back of everybody's minds, would be the sure knowledge that if things got out of hand, and who could say that they would not, the end result could be mutual destruction.

President Reagan's speech of March 1983 may have launched a thousand research projects but it did not launch a strategic revolution. He was offering a false prospect of invulnerability, an illusion that he had some bold escape plan from the harsh realities of the nuclear age. This would have quickly been dismissed as the ramblings of a sentimental idealist had he not been President of the United States and had he not backed up his vision with the promise of a technical solution that was soon found to be wanting.

As dreams go, this one did not last long – about six months. But as the dream was forgotten the initiative that it had inspired rolled slowly into motion, imbued with a contrived sense of scientific adventure and still masquerading as a strategic revolution. So far the resources devoted to this enterprise have not been large but they could become substantial. Other costs will still be incurred. This episode has done little for the President's reputation as a responsible leader, has put additional strain on arms control and inserted another controversy into the Alliance. Most seriously of all it has served as yet another distraction for those unwilling to face up to real dilemmas that confront us in the strategic environment of the mid-1980s.

NOTES

[1] President Ronald Reagan, Speech on 'Defense Spending and Defensive Technology', 23 March 1983.

[2] My method in this Paper has been to rely throughout on statements from Administration sources. Using no more than these sources it is possible to establish a vigorous debate on the objectives, scope and prospects of the SDI.

[3] David Alan Rosenberg, 'The Origins of Overkill: Nuclear Weapons and American Strategy, 1945–1960', International Security, Spring 1983, p. 32.

[4] Secretary of Defense James Schlesinger, *Annual Defense Department Report FY 1975*, 4 March 1974, p. 67.

[5] One of the most effective who also put great stress on the potential of ABM technology was Don Brennan. See, for example, his 'The Case for Population Defense', in Johan Holst and William Schneider (eds), *Why ABM? Policy Issues in the Missile Defense Controversy* (New York: Pergamon Press, 1969).

[6] For a representative sample of views on the ABM issue in the early 1980s see 'ABM Revisited: Promise or Peril?', *Washington Quarterly*, Fall 1981.

[7] Strategic defence as a necessary alternative to assured destruction has been a constant theme of the Administration's case since March 1983, despite the fact that previous policies which had not involved BMD (and which did not require 25 years to yield fruit) were already supposed to have brought the 'MAD era' to a close. For an early presentation of the policy along these lines, see Fred Ikle 'The Vision vs The Nightmare', *Washington Post*, 27 March 1983.

[8] *Report of the President's Commission on Strategic Forces* (Washington DC: USGPO April 1983), pp. 9, 12.

[9] *President's Statement, 22 November 1982, Current Policy, No. 435* (Washington DC: Department of State, November 1982). This was the statement that announced the MX *Densepack* basing mode.

[10] 'We continue treaty-permitted R&D on Ballistic Missile Defense as a hedge against Soviet breakthroughs or breakouts that could threaten our retaliatory capability, and as a possible point defense option to enhance the survivability of our ICBM force', Secretary of Defense Harold Brown, *Department of Defense Annual Report, Fiscal Year 1982* (Washington DC: USGPO, 19 January 1981), p. 116.

[11] According to *Time*, 4 April 1983, the President discussed the issue with Keyworth in 1981. Keyworth set up an advisory group including Edward Teller, Consultant Edward Frieman and Former Deputy Secretary of Defense David Packard to study ABM and they reported early in 1983 that the idea seemed technically feasible. It was brought up briefly at a National Security Council meeting on 11 February 1983 after which nothing happened until the President himself raised the issue with National Security Adviser William Clark. The Pentagon and the State Department were to study the problem further (but not ACDA). However, the President decided that he would prefer to announce the plan with some fanfare rather than let it be studied quietly.

[12] Press Conference, quoted in *New York Times*, 26 March 1983.

[13] *NBC*, 'Meet the Press', 27 March 1983 (Quoted in *Baltimore Sun*, 28 March 1983). See also the report of the news conference of 24 March (*New York Times*, 25 March 1983). However, it is of note that Keyworth was more relaxed on this score. 'The objective is to have a system that would convince an adversary that an offensive attack will not be successful. It has to be a very effec-

tive system, but it would not have to be perfect to convince an adversary that his attack would fail'. Interview, *US News & World Report*, 11 April 1983.

[14] The briefing accompanying the President's speech confirmed that he was not talking about bombers or cruise missiles, *Aerospace Daily*, 29 March 1983. On the rationale see Weinberger quoted in *Government Executive*, July/August 1983.

[15] Reagan Press Conference, 29 March 1983; Weinberger 'Meet the Press', 27 March 1983.

[16] Speech to National Press Club, Washington DC, quoted in *Baltimore Sun*, 2 May 1984. The shift is clearly illustrated by two quotations from George Keyworth, a year apart. In June 1983 he told an interviewer that: 'It may be a worthwhile technological development to defend your offensive missile capability, but it is only marginal to the President's overall strategic objective, which is to move from a dependence on offense to a dependence on defense', *C&EN*, 20 June 1983. In June 1984 he told an audience in Dallas that the President had a near-term as well as a long-term goal. The initial goal was to protect only the US strategic missiles through a primitive capability to intercept ICBM during the boost phase, *Washington Post*, 17 June 1984. However, Keyworth remains true to the ultimate objective. See, for example, his 'A Sense of Obligation: The Strategic Defense Initiative', *Aerospace America*, April 1984. See also *National Journal*, 17 March 1984.

[17] *New York Times*, 10 May 1984.

[18] For example Robert Jastrow: 'Reagan vs the Scientists: Why the President is Right about Missile Defense', *Commentary*, January 1984. 'Critics of President Reagan's plan spoke as if he were proposing a defense of entire cities and their populations, but he made no such suggestion of that kind in his speech'.

[19] *Aviation Week & Space Technology*, 24 October 1984. Summaries of all three reports can be found in *Senate Foreign Relations Committee, Strategic Defense and Anti-Satellite Weapons* (25 April 1984).

[20] The Republican Platform for the 1984 elections stated that in order to 'begin to eliminate' the nuclear missile threat, 'we will use superior American technology to achieve space-based and ground-based defensive systems as soon as possible'. A White House aide was reported to have complained that this statement was 'a little more futuristic than we would have wanted it', but claimed that it had been toned down by substituting 'achieve' for 'build', *Baltimore Sun*, 23 August 1984.

[21] *Washington Post*, 26 January 1984.

[22] For example Charles Mohr in *New York Times*, 23 March 1984, quotes Richard De Lauer, Under Secretary of Defense for Research and Engineering, informing Congress that 'Our state of knowledge of the relevant technologies is inadequate' and that an 'informed decision on whether to go ahead with a system could not be taken until the early 1990s', and Robert S. Cooper, Director of the Defense Advance Research Projects Agency, admitted that the researchers had no 'gold, silver or platinum bullet' in sight against missiles. See also *Washington Post*, 24 March 1984.

[23] *Washington Post*, 25 August 1984. George Keyworth has specifically linked the SDI with 'capabilities to defend more effectively against the air-breathing threat of air-planes and cruise missiles'. Lt-General Abrahamson, however, has stated that: 'At this time in the program there is clearly no (such) mandate', *Science*, 10 August 1984.

[24] Lt-General James Abrahamson, *Testimony to the Defense Subcommittee of the House Appropriations Committee* (11 May 1984). Richard Cooper, Director of DARPA told the Senate Foreign Relations Committee (26 April 1984): 'If we decided say in 1995 or the year 2000 to do this it would take us 10–20 years to put it in place'.

[25] Prior to the President's speech some $1 bn was being spent on strategic defence. This was expected to grow by about $500 m in FY 1984 without the new initiative, which in fact added only some $250 m of new funding. After Congressional cuts the level of funding was not far off its previous target (although the balance of spending has been substantially altered, with a shift away from the preparation of a system capable of early development to the investigation of the more exotic technologies. According to a Congressional Budget Office study, prior to the new initiative less than 30% went on new technologies; that proportion has now jumped to 55%, *Washington Times*, 24 May 1984.) For FY 1985 some $3.8 bn is being requested, and during FY 1986–9 some $25 bn is required. It has been reported that two-thirds of this amount ($15–18 bn) might have been spent even without the new initiative, *Baltimore Sun*, 13 May 1984.

[26] *Hearings before the Research and Development and Investigations Subcommittees of the House Committee on Armed Services, HR 3073 People Protection Act* (10 November 1983), p. 26. In 1981 the cost of a damage denial system was put by Administration witnesses to a subcommittee of the Senate Armed Services at a figure of $500 bn, with a limited defence costing some $100 bn, *New York Times*, 31 March 1983.

[27] On the difficulties of getting the Pentagon and Congress interested in a $7.5 bn plan to improve US air defences see *Wall Street Journal*, 28 March 1984.

[28] See, for example, General T. R. Milton USAF (Ret.), 'Talking Real Money', *Air Force Magazine*, July 1984.

[29] *Science*, 10 August 1984.

[30] The intermediate rationale is developed in Fred S. Hoffman, *Ballistic Missile Defense and US National Security, Summary Report*, prepared for Future Security Strategy Study (October 1983) and in Keith Payne and Colin Gray, 'Nuclear Policy and the Defensive Transition', *Foreign Affairs*, Spring 1984.

[31] Payne and Gray, *ibid.*, p. 840.

[32] Defense Department General Counsel William H. Taft IV challenged the 'Congressional Findings' section of the proposed People Protection Act which stated that that 'The President has called for changes in United States strategic policy that seek to save lives in time of war', on the grounds that the objective was to reduce the 'likelihood of war'. Quoted in Ashton Carter, *Directed Energy Missile Defense in Space* (Washington DC: Congress of the United States, Office of Technology Assessment, April 1984), p. 65.

[33] A 'national campaign to save the ABM Treaty' is reported to favour research on advanced ABM systems as a hedge against a Soviet break-out, *Washington Post*, 20 June 1984.

[34] The late 1983 interagency report following up the President's speech is believed to have stated that: 'Even prior to deployment, the demonstration of US technology would strengthen military and negotiating stances'. Quoted in William Arkin, 'SDI – Pie in the Sky?', *Bulletin of Atomic Scientists*, April 1984.

[35] Thus we find the following in the interagency report: 'By constructing or eliminating the effectiveness of both limited and major attack options against key US military targets and thus leaving only options for attacking urban areas – which would be of highly questionable credibility – defences could significantly reduce the utility of strategic and theater nuclear forces and raise the threshold of nuclear conflict'. *Defense Against Ballistic Missiles: An Assessment of Technologies and Policy Implications* (Washington DC: DOD, March 1984). For those who suspect the opposite there is a precedent for this. In the early 1960s when the US adopted a 'cities-avoidance' strategy and backed this up with a surge in missile production the Soviet Union lacked a comparable capability and so was forced to stress the more terroristic aspects of her nuclear arsenal (for example by exploding a 56 megaton nuclear device).

[36] Speech delivered at University of Virginia, reproduced in *Science and Government Report*, 15 July 1984.

[37] *Baltimore Sun*, 24 April 1984; *Boston Globe*, 30 July 1984. On his return from Turkey, West German Defence Minister Manfred Wörner expressed his concern that the US programme should not 'open up a new dimension in the arms race', *International Herald Tribune*, 12 April 1984. More recently he has toned down his criticisms on the basis of assurances that the US is only seeking parity in research and development to the Soviet Union and that any eventual defensive protection would be extended to Europe, *Baltimore Sun*, 13 July 1984. Although in private the British have expressed worries, they have refrained from doing so publicly taking a 'wait and see' view. See, for example, the testimony of Defence Secretary Michael Heseltine to the House of Commons Select Committee on Defence, *Statement on the Defence Estimates 1984 First Report, Session 1983–84* (22 May 1984). For a discussion of the stakes of the British and French in the ABM Treaty, see Lawrence Freedman, 'The Small Nuclear Powers', in Ashton Carter and David Schwarz (eds), *Ballistic Missile Defense* (Washington DC: Brookings Institution, 1984).

[38] See Lawrence Freedman, 'Europe and the ABM Revival' in Ian Bellany and Coit Blacker (eds), *Antiballistic Missile Defence in the 1980s* (London: Frank Cass, 1983).

[39] Richard De Lauer told a Congressional Committee that: 'Included in the program are technologies for defense against the shorter range nuclear ballistic missiles . . . which may not have trajectories high enough to permit their attack with exoatmospheric systems, and which have short times-of-flight. Such technologies are important for defense of our allies'. *Statement before the Subcommittee on Research and Development of the Committee on Armed Services, House of Representatives* (1 March 1984). On *Patriot* as a TABM see *Aviation Week & Space Technology*, 9 April 1984; *International Herald Tribune*, 5 April 1984. The *Hawk* SAM is being considered as an anti-cruise missile weapon.

[40] *New York Times*, 18 July 1984.

[41] *Aerospace Daily*, 18 November 1983.

[42] Quoted in the *Washington Times*, 19 June 1984. The two most substantial critical studies are the report prepared by the Union of Concerned Scientists, *Space-based Missile Defense* (Cambridge, Mass.: March 1983) and Ashton B. Carter, *Directed Energy Missile Defense in Space* (Washington DC: Congress of the United States, Office of Technology Assessment, April 1984).

[43] In his speech the President acknowledged that the technology might not be ready for decades but said that 'current technology has now reached the point where it is reasonable for us to begin the effort'. A few hours earlier, Major-General Donald Lamberson, an assistant to Richard De Lauer, had been asked by a Senate subcommittee whether he could recommend 'an acceleration of the space-based laser technology program on technical grounds'. He answered 'Senator, no, I cannot at this point in time', quoted in *Washington Post*, 1 April 1984. Richard De Lauer himself was quoted as saying with regard to exotic ballistic missiles defenses that their difficulty has been 'understated', *New York Times*, 1 April 1984.

[44] For a report suggesting that many members of the Fletcher Commission are unhappy at the way that their report has been used to confirm the feasibility of SDI (rather than just to suggest that it deserved to be researched), see *National Journal*, 7 July 1984.

[45] Jastrow, *op. cit.* in note 18, p. 29.

[46] DOD Report (Washington DC: USGPO, March 1964). See note 36.

[47] See note 24.

[48] 'When they see that we have embarked on a long-term effort to achieve an extremely effective defense, supported by a strong national will, they will give up on the development of more offensive missiles and move in the same direction'. *Science*, 10 August 1984. One of his principal scientific assistants, Gerold Vonas, has suggested that this effect will appear as soon as real technological achievements have been demonstrated: 'As the Soviets see these technology achievements they will begin to question the validity of their previous investment in strategic weapons'. *Aviation Week & Space Technology*, 8 October 1984.

[49] According to Soviet scientist E. P. Velikhov: 'Our country – relying on its powerful scientific, technological and economic potential – is quite capable of responding as appropriate. But we will take our own road', *Washington Post*, 24 June 1984. For an extremely useful discussion of the Soviet response, see Sidney D. Drell, Philip J. Farley and David Holloway, *The Reagan Strategic Defense Initiative: A Technical, Political, and Arms Control Assessment*, A Special report of the Center for International Security and Arms Control (Stanford Ca: Stanford UP, July 1984).

[50] According to Richard De Lauer, 'There's no way an enemy can't overwhelm your defenses if he wants to badly enough. It makes a lot of difference in what we do if we have to defend against 1000 RVs or 10,000', quoted in *Government Executive*, July/August 1983.

[51] James A. Thomson, *Strategic Defense and Deterrence, Statement before the Defense Appropriations Subcommittee of the House Appropriations Committee* (9 May 1984).

[52] Dr James Fletcher, *Statement before the Subcommittee on Research and Development of the Committee on Armed Services, House of Representatives* (1 March 1984).

[53] The Administration has charged that a Soviet radar under construction at Krasnoyarsk in Central Siberia, is 'almost certainly' a violation of Article VI, paragraph B of the ABM Treaty which states that 'future radars for early warning of strategic ballistic missile attack' should not be constructed 'except at locations along the periphery of its national territory oriented outward'. This radar is 500 miles back from the border and oriented towards the Siberian landmass. The Soviet Union has responded that this radar is for space tracking which is allowed under the Treaty. *The President's Report to the Congress on Soviet Noncompliance with Arms Control Agreements* (23 January 1984). The June 1984 HOE test using a *Minuteman*–I booster could be in contravention of Article VI(a) which, *inter alia*, precludes giving missiles other than ABM interceptor missiles capabilities to counter strategic ballistic missiles in their flight trajectory and testing them in an ABM mode. Testing of technologies suitable for ABM in an ASAT mode could also be considered to be in violation (see note 54).

[54] George Keyworth is quoted as saying that: 'It may not necessarily be the best way for the ASAT mission but a geosynchronous anti-satellite capability is important to test the technology to destroy missiles', *Aviation Week & Space Technology*, 18 July 1983. The *Talon–Gold* spotting and tracking system which is relevant to both ASAT and SDI is another example of this link.

[55] Strobe Talbot, *Deadly Gambits: The Reagan Administration and the Stalemate in Nuclear Arms Control* (New York: Alfred A. Knopf, 1984), p. 320.

[56] 'Most of the people in this Administration feel that you build the system before you do arms control. A completer ban on weapons in space would tend to foreclose most of your most effective strategic defense options'. Major Peter Worden, quoted in *Science*, 10 August 1984.

[57] *Aviation Week & Space Technology*, 21 May 1984. There is little doubt that the Soviet Union has been engaged in active research in the relevant areas. According to Richard De Lauer, the two sides are equal in laser technology, the Soviet Union is ahead in large rockets able to lift heavy loads in space and the United States is ahead in data processing. What is interesting is that heavy boosters is one of those areas where the Fletcher Commission recommended putting off research because it would be relatively easy to catch up if progress was made in the more difficult areas. On the other hand, data processing has been acknowledged to be the most critical area for the success of any SDI.

Conclusions

DR ROBERT O'NEILL

Our opening plenary Papers, in setting the stage for the committee discussions, led our thoughts through closely interconnected issues. Although they did not trespass greatly on each other's vital ground, each author showed that the future of his field would be influenced by developments in the others. The credibility and stability of deterrence rests on both nuclear and conventional forces, as well as on arms-control measures. It rests also, as the French Foreign Minister Cheysson (in his opening remarks) and Ambassador Abshire reminded us, on the interplay of national and international politics. M. Cheysson gave us timely advice that we need to address all of these factors if we are to produce something useful to national and Alliance leaders.

Each of the authors of these opening plenary Papers judged technology to be at least neutral, although Henri Conze warned us particularly to beware of deluding ourselves that it can, in the short term, change the East–West balance, or that new conventional technologies can greatly reduce our dependence on nuclear weapons. In other words we should put ourselves, and our leaders, in the dock rather than technology itself or those who foster it.

Technology and Strategic Systems

Clearly, technological developments pose many problems for the continued viability of strategic systems, old and new. Brent Scowcroft drew our attention to several of them: increasing missile accuracy; decreasing ICBM survivability; increasing vulnerability of C^3 systems; decreasing survivability and penetration powers of bombers; possible breakthroughs in strategic ASW; the double-edged nature of the sea-launched cruise missile; and the problems of ballistic missile defences.

Many of these concerns were reflected in the discussion of Committees 1 and 2 (on the Strategic Defense Initiative (SDI) debate and land-based systems). The debate in Committee 1 was characterized as 'surprisingly rational', leading some to feel, probably wrongly, that significant consensus emerged. Others noted that it concealed deep passions deriving from differing perceptions of the world and Alliance policies, passions which for the most part were kept in check but on occasion burst forth to remind us that this was a debate of no mean or transient significance.

The technical feasibility of the whole concept came under strong challenge but Fred Hoffman offered a stout defence of the decision to carry out more research in this area. There was wide agreement with Lawrence Freedman that the technical problems to be overcome were daunting although David Schwartz, in accord with a theme which was common to most committee discussions, cautioned that it is difficult to judge a project so enveloped in uncertainty regarding cost and its effect on Soviet–American relations, arms control and extended deterrence.

Debate moved to the question of whether Mutual Assured Destruction (MAD) could or should be set aside by ballistic missile defence (BMD). Some, in support of the SDI, contended that the Soviet Union did not accept MAD and that MAD in any event neutralized the possibility of limited Western nuclear responses to Soviet aggression. Others, opposed to the SDI, pointed out that whether or not the Soviet Union accepted MAD as a doctrine, it was a fact and they had to take it into account in calculating consequences of any move against the West. Similarly the West had to accept it, unless a highly leak-proof system of defence could be developed which took care not only of ballistic missiles but also aircraft, cruise missiles and all other means of nuclear delivery against cities.

Proponents of BMD responded that it did not have to be leak-proof to be useful, particularly through its capacity to complicate Soviet planning for attack on military targets. Defences would improve deterrence, frustrating both limited and full-scale attacks. Opponents stressed that any system that was not leak-proof left cities vulnerable and popular support for it would be difficult to win. What would be the worth of such a huge and costly effort? What would be the opportunity costs?

Soviet responses to the SDI in terms of offensive force structure were also disputed, some arguing that it would impel them to negotiate lower agreed limits but many more contending that offensive force increases, together with more re-entry vehicles and penetration aids, would be the result. The likely Soviet defensive response was not as contested an issue, although opinions varied on how seriously the Soviet Union was already committed to a BMD programme of her own. A significant Soviet BMD capability would inhibit Western nuclear options, particularly important for extended deterrence. The West stands in greater need of such options than the Soviet Union.

At the end of the debate, there was general agreement on the desirability of pursuit of some BMD research as a prudent hedge against Soviet breakout, although Richard Garwin declared that a more effective option would be to counter Soviet BMD with better US penetration aids. This view was contested by Albert Wohlstetter. But many, particularly Europeans, saw the full SDI programme as very divisive within the Alliance, placing a strain where it was not needed, and risking the undoing of many years of promoting a sense of solidarity of shared risks. Albert Carnesale summed up the European argument thus: 'Western Europe objects to any change in a security system that seems to be working well enough as it is; therefore the burden of proof is on those who propose change'.

In terms of the effect of the SDI on arms control, those supporting the proposal argued that it could provide leverage to bring the Soviet Union back to strategic negotiations and, conversely, that arms-control agreements to limit offensive forces would strengthen the effectiveness of BMD. Opponents argued that BMD would work in the opposite direction, leading to offensive force increases and, most particularly, abrogation of the ABM Treaty which would open the door to the development of high altitude anti-satellite (ASAT) devices and cause widespread popular dissent in the West, notably Europe. Clearly the Reagan Administration has a long way to go in terms of convincing informed Westerners that the SDI is a wise move, and efforts to do so will once again cause severe Alliance strains.

Committee 2, in reviewing the future of land-based strategic systems, agreed that some such weapons would be essential to the West for a long time to come, despite their increasing vulnerability. They could be replaced in part by other systems such as the D-5 SLBM but for reasons of command and control, battle management and maintaining secrecy of SSBN deployments, ICBM should be retained. Some participants, particularly from the host country (France), pointed to the difference between having missiles on one's own soil and having them at sea, in terms of the greater psychological and political impact of an enemy strike on home territory compared with loss of a submarine at sea.

Survivability was clearly the major problem to be solved and, in view of the increasing accuracy of Soviet missiles, mobility seemed to offer more hope than superhardening of silos. It also had to be remembered that all strategic systems were vulnerable, albeit to differing degrees, and the true art of force structure was to build, out of individually vulnerable elements, a total deterrent whose viability as an entire force could not be questioned in any remotely probable circumstances. Nonetheless, severe political and fiscal problems currently block the way towards deployment of a new US ICBM system and the operational doubts already raised about proposed new systems and basing modes are formidable.

The Soviet Union could be expected to continue to place great reliance on land-based systems. Her geographic situation and political structure greatly eased the difficulties of their deployments. Her new missiles under development were impressive and there was seen to be no likelihood that the US would wish to follow suit to that degree. The future for ICBM is thus somewhat unbalanced between East and West and there is little prospect of it changing. French participants emphasized the continuing important role that their land-based strategic missiles would play. Some Americans argued that fewer and more vulnerable ICBM still represented a wise investment, provided that there was approximate equivalence with the USSR in all three legs of the Triad.

Nonetheless, such matters were held by others to be purely academic because of the political difficulties in the way of any mooted US deployment. The debate on this whole question was thus strongly political rather than narrowly strategic.

Conventional Technologies
As if the problems of strategic systems were not bad enough, Henri Conze threw some iced water on those who hope for a drastic improvement in the conventional balance through a technological revolution. It is salutary for us to note, given his professional experience, his scepticism about the importance of new technologies. This attitude undercuts to some extent his concern that the debate on this topic might postpone the taking of real action, but it does not remove it. The urgency of improving the conventional defences of the West gives us little choice but to act, but we must do so carefully and selectively. What Conze, between the lines, and other participants not so indirectly, have told us is that improvement must come through progress on many fronts: manpower; individual training and motivation; tactical proficiency; and organization. Where technology can help most, Conze advises us, is in target acquisition and recognition, electronic warfare, C^3, and new materials for missiles, engines, armour and enhanced computing power.

In assessing the impact of new technology on the NATO–Warsaw Pact balance, the committee discussions focused on several topics, but perhaps most interestingly on the relationship between technology and operational concepts. These discussions were predicated on awareness that great uncertainties attend any assessment of the impact of new technologies. We have little idea as to how rapidly they are likely to be deployed on either side. Cost estimates may be wildly wrong. The money required may bite into other areas of defence preparedness in ways that are difficult to anticipate. The systems are of such complexity that their operational use may be restricted, requiring the maintenance of existing systems to close the gaps in coverage.

Despite these uncertainties, nobody disputed that new technologies would come into wide use and impact strongly on operational capabilities and doctrines. But there was hot debate on whether or not the Soviet Union would adapt her own doctrines to reduce significantly the vulnerability of her forces to such new Western capabilities. This discussion revealed significant divergence of view as to what Soviet doctrines actually are, with some believing that Operational Manoeuvre Groups (OMG) have a more modest probing function while others contended that their role is more strategic and extensive. In any event, a growing Western capability to strike targets, fixed or mobile, at considerably greater range than today, would induce Soviet leaders to avoid major force concentrations until the very last moment, thereby complicating their planning. We need to do further work on the implications of this vulnerability for the OMG concept as a whole before we can conclude the arguments as to whether the costs of new technology equipment programmes are justified. The intensity of this debate and the fundamental nature of the topic suggest that we should increase our efforts to probe these doctrinal questions.

Until these doubts are resolved it is very difficult to assess the worth of the Follow-On Forces Attack (FOFA) concept to the point that trade-off evaluations can be made with any accuracy. Hence the development of new-technology forces to implement FOFA operations may be misdirected or considerably delayed. Critics also pointed to the dangers inherent in the FOFA concept of reliance on a wide array of real-time command, control and data processing facilities. Such responsiveness may well prove unattainable under operational conditions, thereby nullifying the worth of major investments which will have depleted alternate means of operating.

These doubts were countered by 'emerging technologies' (ET) advocates who argued that the debate should not be only about FOFA because there were many other missions that new technologies would facilitate. They also challenged their opponents to produce better proposals and pointed to the importance of ET in raising the nuclear threshold. Of course it can be argued that what in fact raises the nuclear threshold is NATO's reluctance to be the first to use nuclear weapons because of the Soviet attainment of nuclear parity, rather than enhanced Western conventional capability. Nonetheless there seemed to be wide agreement, particularly amongst Europeans, that new technologies had a vital role to play in closing the conventional gap and that public opinion would support new investments, particularly in developing capabilities that strengthen defence on and around the Central Front itself rather than against forces coming from a long way behind it.

Thus, while public controversy builds up on the 'deep strike' issues, there is a good prospect that public confidence in Western defence concepts may be regenerated by judicious procurement of equipment designed to increase greatly the losses of enemy forces within 40 kilometres of the front line, to quote one of the participants who seemed to be the least common denominator of the group. Others thought that public opinion would support considerable deepening of the target area.

Concern was expressed also about the difficulties of maintaining political control of operations in the new technology environment. Some argued that the speed of operations would inhibit political leaders from using their real-time C^3I capabilities to the full, giving the military freer rein than before. Sir Harry Tuzo pointed to the way in which use of new technology systems could border on pre-emption, requiring extremely strict political controls in time of tension before any outbreak of hostilities.

Out of these discussions came awareness of a need for more analysis of criteria for determining the mix of nuclear and conventional forces, investigation of the above-mentioned uncertainties involved in new-technology force development, and study of the likely Soviet responses to various NATO policies.

In the light of all these uncertainties, the difficulties inherent in the task of Committee 4, on implications for force structure and rationalization, are not difficult to comprehend. Yet it moved in a thorough and workmanlike way to investigate the constraints on such developments and ways of overcoming them. The constraints identified included: the conservative effect of existing force structures; differences in interpretation of what Flexible Response actually means (and hence how to fashion forces for that strategy); general economic pressures; unwillingness of European governments to yield up any of their sovereignty; and the political dilemmas created by new technology concepts, particularly for the Federal Republic of Germany, in attempting to improve relations with the East while at the same time reinforcing capabilities to retaliate in depth against Warsaw Pact forces.

Although lengthy discussion of a transatlantic division of labour failed to produce coherent results, other than to reject Senator Nunn's hope that Europeans might provide their own defence against a first echelon attack while the United States would reinforce against a second, the need for such a division of labour was clear.

As a general mechanism the United States should encourage the formation of European consortia to produce the new equipment that will be required, turning what has been described as 'a one way autobahn and thirteen footpaths' into something more like a two-way street.

Economic constraints dictated the assertion of a strict order of procurement priorities for the major new equipment and stock-building that is needed. Such priorities had to be agreed on an Alliance-wide basis and the task was seen as urgent.

Little, if any, progress seems to have been made in the area of rationalization scouted in Ingemar Dörfer's paper. His emphasis on the utility of spending more on reserve forces is worth noting, although the means of payment, namely funds currently earmarked for European air force modernization to be released by the stationing of six more US air wings in Europe, are unlikely to be realised. Nevertheless, rationalization in less spectacular areas may prove possible and is certainly desirable if Europe is to achieve a defence strength fully comparable with its economic and demographic resources.

Implications for Arms Control

In introducing our discussion on the implications of new technologies for arms control, Walt Slocombe argued against the mood of despair which so often accompanies such debate. While appreciating the way in which technological change *can* undermine the utility of existing agreements, he pointed out in his treatment of BMD that it *need* not, and indeed could serve as a reinforcement for the ABM Treaty. However, given the Soviet proclivity to press to the limits of compliance and beyond, as in the case of the Pushkino phased-array radar, a little technological leverage may well prove essential for the US. The implications of the SDI in this regard may not be so helpful, however, particularly if the Soviet Union interprets the planned research programme as an indication that the US intends to break the ABM Treaty.

In accepting the desirability of land mobility as the best solution to the problem of ICBM vulnerability, Slocombe warns that methods for deployment must be part of future arms-control agreements. Hence this factor must be taken into account now in designing deployment options. On satellite vulnerability he draws our attention to the possibilities of a ban on high-altitude ASAT tests and limits on space- or ground-based laser and other directed-energy ASAT devices. He recognizes the dual-capability problem as serious but gives us hope that technology can help effective verification rather than frustrate it.

In the prevailing political climate it is difficult to see much, if any, of this agenda being carried into practice. Indeed one cannot help but be struck by a general atmosphere of hopelessness regarding the short-term future of arms control, both within this conference and amongst the wider professional community. One hopes that some will respond by generating new approaches but we are forced to recognize that until there is a change in the climate of East–West relations, the incentives to do so are few.

Pierre Lellouche highlighted the close linkages which this situation encourages between technology, strategic doctrine and arms control. Technological change or uncertainty raises questions both for our doctrines and our arms-control policies. At a time when the potential for change in doctrines is high, we must also expect change in our arms-control policies. Until we have settled our doctrines, we will not be able to settle our arms-control policies.

In view of the difficulties encountered by the committees in discussing doctrines, it is not surprising therefore that the arms-control committee found it hard to propose new steps which had any prospect of achievement. Much of its discussion focused on the causes of the current deadlock, which were perceived as being essentially political, with particular reference made to underdeveloped awareness of security interdependence by both sides. The committee supported Walt Slocombe's view that, although technology caused complications for arms control, it was not responsible for the current impasse. The idea that technology, once discovered, somehow pushed its way into weapons deployments while nobody was watching was rejected. The outlook, not surprisingly, is pessimistic: the causes of the deadlock were agreed as long-lasting. Even should the political climate moderate in 1985, years would be required for it to find expression in new arms-control agreements. These East–West tensions are bound to feed West–West strains, although the Soviet Union seems reliable in terms of saving us from total disarray by her own ill-calculated behaviour. Should she ever become adroit in long-term diplomacy we will really be in trouble.

Despite this chilly prospect, the committee discussions evinced considerable enthusiasm for at least attempting a new round of negotiations emphasizing ASAT controls. Other means believed to be worth further investigation were a chemical warfare (CW) treaty and, unilaterally, ways of controlling testing and improving verification techniques. The notion of preventive or pre-emptive arms control did not attract much support. Some agreed that problems such as BMD would provide an incentive for both sides to return to negotiations to limit offensive weapons. Many others countered that the logic is more likely to run in the reverse direction.

The inter-relationship between technology, doctrine and arms control was seen as an important topic, but clearly it is insufficiently understood and stands before us as a challenge for future investigation. The conflictual relationship of deterrence does not sit easily alongside the co-operative relationship of arms control, yet indisputably there is an interaction between them which is intensified by technological change. Whether the quest to intensify changes which might assist both relationships together proves to be a search for the philosopher's stone remains to be seen. At least we can come to grips with the questions of trade-offs regarding those changes which either assist the one and impede other, or simply complicate both.

Technology Management in the Alliance
Problems of research and development policy were an even more important part of the work of Committee 5. In its discussion, heed was taken of the formidable political, economic, social and even, although somewhat ambiguously, military pressures which exist to maintain independent national R&D and production capabilities. Despite the acknowledged advantages of international specialization, most countries, particularly the larger states of Western Europe, remain understandably very reluctant to surrender capabilities before grim necessity forces them to do so. Increasing dependence on the US causes a wide array of problems in Europe, but willingness to pool resources effectively while good markets still exist for national European industries is low.

A comprehensive research and development effort could clearly influence beneficially industrial policies and industrial development, and there was recognition that shared R&D was highly desirable. History over the past decades has demonstrated, however, that national or competitive elements intrude and make progress in this area difficult or impossible to achieve. Progress was relatively easier at the research, rather than the development stage. Shared research could be achieved as the recent efforts by Admiral Inman in America attest. One concrete suggestion to surmount some of the technical obstacles would be to concentrate Alliance research on some single technical production problem, such as production of higher-capacity microchips, since the proprietary aspects of such chips came not with the chips themselves but through the programmes, i.e., the 'software', applied to them. Techniques such as that might permit more across-the-board collaboration in later development.

Ambassador Abshire offers a prescription for a resources strategy designed to maximize gains from the limited capabilities of individual Alliance members. He points rightly to NATO's superior resources *vis-à-vis* the Warsaw Pact and its inferior record in military production. One does not need to go all the way with his analysis that the prime challenge to NATO in its second thirty-five years is resource management to acknowledge that this challenge is indeed in the first four or five. Alliance resource management needs to be founded on a better common military appreciation of the threat and a fuller conceptual or doctrinal framework. There is room for more co-ordinated guidance for national defence decisions which relate to Alliance needs, although it may not always be heeded. Special bodies for managing technological change such as the Conference of National Armaments Directors (CNAD) and the Independent European Programme Group (IEPG) should be strengthened and, to foster the growth of research and development investment in Europe, the notion of a European Advanced Research Agency is worth support. As Ambassador Abshire indicates, creation of organizations is not enough: political support is vital and it must rest on firm domestic and external foundations. As Committee 5's discussions suggest, much remains to be done to consolidate these foundations before any major new structure can be built.

Conclusion

Finally let me make a few general observations based on the experience of sitting in the plenaries and the committees, de-briefing the rapporteurs and thinking about their reports. New technology is coming, as surely as day follows night; and coming on a wide front. Individual developments may not be as revolutionary as were nuclear weapons, but major changes are coming in many, many areas and their management and absorption pose major challenges. There will be delays and bottlenecks. It will happen by gradual increments, like a slowly breaking wave, whose overall impact is nonetheless tremendous. Behind this wave are more. Some we will catch; some we will miss. It is no use complaining: if we want to live in our present style and standard, we have to learn to manage change.

The waves seem likely to continue to be slow, but if they are too slow we will be becalmed. We need to maintain and stimulate their creative energy. The new technology will be expensive. It can easily prove too expensive if not properly managed. Yet, given the political, social and demographic differences between the Soviet Union and the West, we need it to be sure of our security. Furthermore, we are not blind to the advances in military technology made by the Soviet Union, although we are also aware that they are not moving so fast and so effectively that their policies cannot be affected by our own pace of development.

In all this haste, we must not sacrifice military effectiveness and stability simply in order to take on new devices. The Soviet leaders, as tough-minded, practical people are most unlikely to fall into this trap. We, with our greater pressures to accommodate to change, must remember that we face risks as well as gains and must learn to distinguish folly from enterprise.

Most of the committee discussions were, as their participants recognized, founded on uncertainty. It is hardly to be wondered at that they had difficulty in reaching specific conclusions. They bring home to us the awareness that in this environment of extensive technological change, uncertainty is pervasive – in technological capability, in strategic doctrine, in arms control, in political relations within the Alliance as well as with the Soviet Union. It is not going to fade, particularly in an age when major wars are not available as a laboratory for testing equipment, men and concepts. We must learn to live with it better than the Soviet Union. We ought to be able to, unless of course we are creating much more uncertainty in our own national houses than they are in theirs.

These remarks are written as a conclusion to the conference already held. In many ways they are also an introduction to the conference the Institute is planning for 1985. The IISS is not going to give up the search for a deeper understanding of the doctrines of East and West; and of how they relate to each other and to arms control under the influence of technological change. We will not repeat ourselves: we will go forward from this basis, however uncertain it might be. We will grapple with some of the bigger questions which this conference has opened up but, for good reasons, has been unable to close.

Nobody is flattered to be compared with Czar Nicholas II, of whose Hague Peace Conference of 1899 Michael Howard has written in the most recent issue of *International Security*, that it 'was no more than a ripple in the current of international politics'. Yet, if this conference in Avignon should achieve that status, we may feel well pleased.

Index

ABM systems 4, 101
ABM Treaty (1972) 4, 7, 17, 99–100, 101–2, 108, 114, 140, 141, 145, 146, 147, 153, 158, 160, 167
   Reagan administration's views of 150–2
Abrahamson, J. 153, 154, 158, 159, 161, 163n24
Agnelli, G. 45
air warfare 2, 29, 63, 88–9
   and emerging technology 72
   importance of counter-air operation 92
   with non-nuclear forces 89
airforces, restructuring of 44
Airland Battle Doctrine 53, 80n2
air-launched cruise missiles (ALCM) 7
ALCM *see* air-launched cruise missiles
Alison, G. 23n4
anti-satellite systems (ASAT) 9, 103–4, 109–10, 160, 167, 170
anti-submarine warfare (ASW) 8, 54, 55
anti-tactical missile system (ATM) 90
Arkin, W. 164n34
armaments co-operation 127, 138
arms control 98–114
   and balance between strategic forces 32
   and communications technology 105–6, 110–11
   and cruise missiles 112–13
   and dual-capable forces 104–5
   and ICBMs 101–2
   objectives of 98
   preventive arms control 56–7, 58
   and satellites 102–3, 109–10
   and SDI 159–61, 167
   and strategic defence technology 113–14
   and threat of barrage attacks 30–1
Aron, R. 93
ASAT *see* anti-satellite systems
Aspin, Congressman Leslie 32
Assault Breaker programme 38, 43, 75, 93, 94
assured destruction doctrine 3–4, 5, 140, 141, 143, 149, 166
   criticized 151
   and deterrence 26–8, 33
   requirements for 3–4
ASW *see* anti-submarine warfare
ATM *see* anti-tactical missile system
Augustine, N. R. 45

Backfire bomber 104
ballistic missile defence (BMD) 4–5, 55–6, 101–2, 166–7
   and anti-satellite systems 103
   and barrage attack threats 31
   emerging technology and 140
   and ICBM survivability 7
   problems of 143
   Reagan administration's view of 151
   and SDI 155
   Soviet response to 146
barrage attacks 30–1, 33
Bartlett, D. F. 52n3
basing
   close to populations 18–19
   'deep underground basing' 16
   diversity of 22, 23
   and 'flushing' on strategic warning 20–2
   future policies for 22–3
   modes of 12–13
   multiple protective shelter basing 22
   and 'responsiveness' 19–20
   silo-basing 5, 6, 12, 17, 24, 26
   and survivability 13–17
Bertram, C. 52n13
BMD *see* ballistic missile defence
bomber forces 7–8
   Backfire bomber 104
   EMT of 28
Boss/Axe 89
Bowen, A. M. 37
Boyd, A. M. 81n33
Braddock, D. V. 95n1
Brennan, D. 162n5
Brodie, B. 120, 129n5
Brown, H. 19, 23n3, 44, 162n10
Brussels Double Track Decision 57
budgetary constraints 42–3, 48–50, 169
   see also costs
Burt, R. 52n3

C^3 (command, control and communications) 9, 102
   and European military budget 42
   and new technology 55, 60
C^3I 41, 62–3
Callaghan, T. 118, 129n1
CAM-40 89
Cameron, Lord 52n9
Canby, S. L. 39, 45, 76n3, n6, n9, 81n31
Carter, A. 163n32
Carter administration 17, 101, 152

chaff 76–7
city-targeting 156
CNAD *see* Conference of National Armaments Directors
COCOM 123, 124, 128
Collins, J. M. 37
command, control and communications *see* C^3
communications technology 110–11
 and arms control 102–3
conventional forces 60–5, 168–70
 in air and on land 53–4, 88–9
 for attacking FOFA 89–90
 for defence 48
 defined 62–3
 emerging technology for 112
 importance of new technology for 94–5
 for interdicting LOC 89
 for missile attacks 90–1
 within NATO 85, 116, 131
 and NATO-Warsaw Pact balance 66–79, 84–95
Cooper, R. S. 163n22, n24
costs 82–3
 of defence research 130–1, 137–8
 of equipment and operating 72–3
 of new technology 118, 123
 see also budgetary constraints
Cotter, D. 42, 45, 48, 70, 72, 75, 80n10, n19, 81n23–9, n36, 82n44, n47, 82–3, 95n3, n5
counter-force strategy
 counter-air problem 64–5
 for military targets 28
 and munitions limitations 75–9
 requirements for 3
 against small warheads 78–9
 against VISTA and terminal guidance 76–7
crisis stability 40–1
cruise missiles 112–13
Cuba Missile Crisis 20
Currie, M. 42, 46

D-5 missiles 6, 15
DARPA 43
decentralization 123–4
deep strike 39, 41, 169
 budget for 42, 49
 cost-effectiveness estimates 82–3
 effectiveness of 66
 forces within Europe 42
 ineffectiveness of deep strike munitions 75–9
 NATO concept of 122, 125
 problems of technologies of 72–4
 and selective ET 43
 through land and air forces 54
'deep underground basing' 16
defence
 ascendancy over offence 1–2
 forward defence 47–8, 66

German White Book on 38
heavy and light defence 10–11
history of defence policy 150–4
multi-layer defence 142
for NATO 40, 124
point defence 11
population defence 154
shield defence 10
see also ballistic missile defence, strategic defence
defence research 130–9
 and armaments co-operation 127, 138
 areas for 154–7
 budgets for 130–1
 collaboration between US and W. Europe 132
 costs of 137–8
 and industrial policy 136–7
 and nationalism 135
 policy for 131–5
 rationalization in 136
Deitchman, S. J. 49, 52n23
De Lauer, R. 42, 45, 51, 154, 163n22, 164n39, n43, n50, 165n57
detente 40–1
deterrence
 and assured destruction 26–8
 concepts of 5–6
 by denial 13–14
 emerging technology and 40
 extended deterrence 16
 in NATO 85, 124
 survivability and 13–15
 by threat of retaliation 13–14
 and vulnerable missiles 16
disarmament 160–1
dispersal for survival 30
Dispersed Operating Bases (DOBs) 88, 89
division of labour 38–52
DOBs *see* Dispersed Operating Bases
doctrinal templates 74
Donnelly, C. N. 45, 70, 80n7, n9, n14, n16
Dorfer, I. 45, 50
Douhet, G. 1–2, 3
Drell, S. D. 164n49
dual-capable forces 104–5

early-warning systems 111–12
economic constraints *see* budgetary constraints
Eisenhower, President Dwight D. 150
electronic warfare 62, 66, 67
emerged technologies 117
emerging technologies (ET) 38–43, 117, 136, 140
 for conventional weapons 112
 and defence budgeting 42–3
 R & D programmes for 131–2
 see also new technology
Emerging Technologies Initiative 126
Enthoven, A. C. 27, 34n2

ET see emerging technologies
event templates 74
exploratory technology 117

Farley, P. J. 164n49
Finch, L. C. 37
Fletcher, J. C. 153, 159, 165n52
Fletcher Report 153, 158
'flexible response' strategy 19, 40, 47, 63, 122, 169
flush-on strategic warning 20–2
follow-on forces attack (FOFA) 43, 66–7, 69, 71, 84, 168
    automation of command and control of 75
    conventional weapons and 89–90
    deep attack on 79
forward defence 47–8, 66
France
    deep strike and NT in 40
    defence priority 65
    modernization of nuclear forces 42
    and problems of NT 63–4
Freedman, L. 164n37, n38
'freeze' 107, 114
Fry, J. 52n33
full system deployment 144–5
Furniss, W. 154

Gabriel, C. 88
Garber, V. 45
German White Book on defence 38
Germany see West Germany
Glakas, T. P. 37
Gordon, M. 81n30
Gore, A. 32, 34n10
Gray, C. 163n30
Greenwood, D. 39, 45
ground-launched cruise missiles (GLCM) 113

Halloran, R. 45
Heseltine, M. 164n37
heat-seeking IRs 77–8
Hines, J. G. 70, 80n12
Hoffman, F. 153, 163n30
Hoffman, H. 90, 95n6
Holloway, D. 164n49
Holst, J. J. 45, 52n3, 162n5
'Hot Line' 102–3, 111
Howard, M. 52n17, 67, 80n4, 128n6

IAO see Independent Air Operation(s)
ICBM 55, 104, 167–8
    accuracy 6
    alternatives to 28–9
    alternative targets 29–30
    and balance between strategic forces 32
    and extended deterrence policy 16
    survivability 6–7, 8, 98
    vulnerability 24, 26–8, 33–4, 101
IEPG see Independent European Programme Group
Ikle, F. 162n7
INC see insertable nuclear components
Independent Air Operation (IAO) 88
Independent European Programme Group (IEPG) 126, 171
INF see Intermediate Nuclear Forces
insertable nuclear components (INC) 110
intelligence technology 98–9, 105–6, 109
interdiction 72, 89, 92, 122
Interim Agreement on Offensive Weapons 4
Intermediate Nuclear Forces (INF) 40
interoperability 136

Jastrow, R. 163n18
Jervis, R. 47, 52n12
Joffe, J. 47, 48, 52n10, n14, n16, 129n7

Kantner, H. 52n33
Karber, P. A. 48, 52n7, n8, n15, n28, n31, 129n8
Kent, G. A. 34n3
Keyworth, G. 152, 162n11, n13, 163n16, n23, 165n54
Knopf, A. A. 165n55
Komer, R. 43, 44, 45

Lamberson, D. 164n43
Lanchester's formula 68
land-based strategic weapons 12–37
    basing of 12–13, 18–19
    composition of 24–5
    and deterrence 25–33
    diversity of 22
    'responsiveness' of 19–20
    and strategic warning 20–2
    survivability 13–16
laser technology 117
Limited Test Ban Treaty (LTBT) (1962) 100
lines of communication (LOC) 89
Luttwak, E. 80n9

McNamara, R. 47, 151, 155
MAD see Mutual Assured Destruction
Main Operating Bases (MOB) 43, 88–9
Mangold, E. 81n33
Mason, R. 41, 45
massed forces 69
massive retaliation 2–3
Mearsheimer, J. J. 129n4
Midgetman 18, 20
Milton, T. R. 163n28
Minuteman 17, 18
MIRV 4–5, 100, 142
missile silos see silo-basing
MOB see Main Operating Bases

175

mobile targets 89–90, 91
modernization 86
Mohr, C. 163n22
Moodie, M. 129n3
Moran, T. H. 30, 34n5, n6, 37
multiple protective shelter basing (MPS) 22
munitions 72, 75–9
Mutual Assured Destruction (MAD) 140, 141, 143, 149, 166
MW-1 submunition 43
MX missile 6, 12, 15, 16

National Security Study Directive (NSSD) 153
nationalism, and defence research 135
NATO 19, 23
   and concept of deep attack 122, 125
   and decentralization 123–4
   decline in technological superiority 117–20
   defence research 135–9
   defensive missions 84–5
   economic considerations 122–3
   environment in 85–6
   new technology in 38, 42–3, 46–50, 53, 66, 122–4, 171: future for 120–2
   non-nuclear defence within 46
   nuclear and conventional weapons 85–6, 116
   resources strategy for 124–8
   restructuring in 43–4
   and SDI 157–8
   and Warsaw Pact competition 135
NATO Industrial Advisory Group (NIAG) 126
NATO/Warsaw Pact balance 168
   new technology and 66–79, 84–95
naval forces 44, 54–5
Nerlich, U. 52n3
new technology (NT)
   and arms control 98–106
   changing nature of 120–2
   competition in 99
   constraints on 48–50, 51, 60–1, 107
   in conventional systems 66–79, 84–95
   decentralization of 122–3
   developments in 109–14
   and division of labour 50–1
   effects of total reliance on 116–20
   failure of 67–79
   and flexible response strategy 47
   and forward defence 47
   in NATO 38, 42–3, 46–50, 53, 66, 120–2, 171
   and NATO resources strategy 124–8
   neutrality of 58, 66, 108
   and strategic system development 1–10, 13
NIAG *see* NATO Industrial Advisory Group
Nixon, R. 160
NSSD *see* National Security Study Directive
'Nuclear Risk Reduction Centres' 112
nuclear weapons 14

and concept of deterrence 5
effect on nature of conflict 1, 2
within NATO 85–6
Nunn S. 49, 50, 52n3, n30, 111

Ogarkov, Gen. 93
Operational Manoeuvre Groups (OMGs) 39, 68–71, 84, 168
operational technology 117

Patriot 90, 158
Pattie, G. 52n35
Payne, K. 163n30
peace movement 40
Peacekeeper 12, 15, 16
People Protection Act 154
Perry, W. J. 11
Pershing 46, 48, 53, 104, 113
Petersen, P. A. 70, 80n12
PGM *see* precision-guided missiles
photographic intelligence 98
Pincus, W. 34n11
point defence 11
Polaris programme 94
population defence 154
precision-guided missiles (PGM) 53–4
preventive arms control 56–7, 58

R & D *see* defence research
Ralph, J. E. 81n21
rationalization 38–52, 169–70
   in defence research 136
   and free competition 138–9
reaction times 91
Reagan, President Ronald 9, 101, 140, 149, 155, 158, 161, 162
   defence policy 150–4
'real time' technology 62
reassurance 40
Regan, D. 49
reliability 73
remote sensors 111–12, 113
reserve forces *see* follow-on forces attack
Resnick, J. 34n1
resources, NATO strategy for 124–8
'responsiveness' 19–20
Rogers, B. W. 39, 42, 46, 48, 49, 52n4, 68–9, 70, 80n8, 83
Rogers Plan 53, 70–1
Rose, F. de 95
Rosenberg, D. A. 162n3

SA-12 145
Safeguard ABM system 4, 160
Sagan, C. 30
SALT I agreements 4, 5, 100, 101
SALT II agreements 100, 101, 107, 113

satellites 102–4
Schelling, T. 16, 23n1
Schlesinger, J. 150, 162n4
Schneider, W. 162n5
Schultze, F. J. 45
Scowcroft Commission 24, 151
SDI   *see* Strategic Defence Initiative
sea-based tactical systems 58
sea-launched ballistic missiles (SLBM) 7, 8, 28
sea-launched cruise missiles (SLCM) 8, 9, 54, 55, 104, 105
Sentinel 4
service compatibility 41–2
Shabecoff, P. 34n4
Shard, J. A. 154
shell game 17, 18
shield defence 10
silo-basing 5, 6, 12, 17
   vulnerability of 24, 26
Simpkin, R. E. 81n36
SLBM   *see* sea-launched ballistic missiles
SLCM   *see* sea-launched cruise missiles
SLGM 24
Smith, W. K. 27, 34n2
Soviet Pact 93
   erosion of airpower 88–9
Soviet Union 2, 3, 4, 9
   ABMs in 4, 5
   concept of deterrence in 5–6
   counterforce targeting in 156
   counter-measures to BMD system 56
   defence systems in 145–6
   emerged technology in 93
   ICBMs in 6, 29, 31
   Operational Manoeuvre Groups (OMG) 39, 68–71, 84, 168
   weapons systems development programmes 31
SSBN 8
stability 98
   and arms control 53–8
   and defensive technology 113–14
'Star Wars' debate 9, 101, 140–62
Starry, D. A. 80n15, 81n32
Steinhoff, J. 89
strategic defence 9–11
   desirable effectiveness of 140–2
   effectiveness of 142–4
   and full-system deployment 144–5
   in the long term 146–8
   and the USSR 145–6
   see also defence
Strategic Defence Initiative (SDI) 55, 101, 140, 144, 149, 150–2, 161–2, 166
   and ABM Treaty 145
   aims of 154–6
   and arms control 159–61, 167
   feasibility of 158–9

   impact on NATO 157–8
   revision of 152–4
strategic forces, balance between 31–3
strategic systems 104, 119
   concept of deterrence and 5
   development of 1–5
   future policies for 6–11
   and technology 166–8
Stützle, W. 50, 52n29
submarines 7, 8, 19
Surprise Attack Conference (1958) 107
surveillance/targeting technology 91, 93, 97, 98
   see also VISTA
survivability 6–7, 8, 13–17, 23, 98

TABAS   *see* Total Air Base Attack System
tactical anti-ballistic missiles (TABM) 158
Taft, W. H. 163n32
tank 1, 78
Tebbitt, N. 129n9
technology trap 67–8, 94–5
terminally-guided anti-armour submunitions (TGSM) 72
testing 99
TGSM   *see* terminally-guided anti-armour submunitions
Thompson, J. 159, 164n51
Total Air Base Attack System (TABAS) 89
Triad 3, 24
   as deterrent 25–6
   future of 8–9
   new Triad 22
Trident II 6, 15, 28, 31

Ulsamer, E. 34n13
United States 2, 3, 6, 7, 8, 9–10, 23, 24
   armaments co-operation 127, 138
   arms control 107
   attitudes to strategic systems 9–10
   bomber force 7
   control of new technology in 123
   defence policy 4–5, 42, 47, 51, 150–4
   defence research 132, 135
   and 'extended deterrence' 16
   land-based systems 167–8
USSR   *see* Soviet Union

Van Creveld, M. 80n1, 81n33
Velikhov, E. P. 164n49
verification and new technology 100, 105
Very High Speed Integrated Circuits (VHSIC) 61
Very Intelligent Surveillance and Target Acquisition (VISTA)
   countering VISTA and terminal guidance 76–7
   weaknesses of 72–5
Very Large Scale Integration (VLSI) 62
Voigt, K. 48, 52n11

vulnerability 73
  desirability of 15–16
  of ICBMs 24, 26–8, 33–4, 101
  and stability 15, 16

warheads 78–9
Warner, J. 111
Warsaw Pact 84
  air defence systems 43
  conventional supremacy 54, 64
  doctrine of 68
  and NATO 84–5, 135
  technological advances in 117, 118
Washington, G. 5
weapons
  deliverable on continental US 36
  deliverable on USSR 35
  developments in 1–5
Webster 107
Weinberger, C. W. 38, 45, 46, 51, 52n34, 152, 153, 157, 163n14
Western Europe
  armaments co-operation 127, 138–9

concerns over SDI 157–8
and defence 51, 132, 135
emerging technology in 42–4
and flexible defence strategy 47
forward defence of 39
missile threat to 90–1
selective detente and 41
strategic forces 24–6
West Germany
  and concept of deep strike 40
  defence budgeting 42
  forces in 44
  and forward defence 39
  selective detente policy 41
Wikner, F. 42, 45, 95n7, n8
Wilson, P. A. 30, 34n5, n6, 37
Wohlstetter, R. 21, 23n5
Worden P. 165n58
World War II, German strategy in 70, 119
Wörner, M. 45, 125, 164n37

Yonas, G. 164n48